Benevolent Repression

BENEVOLENT REPRESSION

Social Control and the American
Reformatory-Prison Movement

Alexander W. Pisciotta

NEW YORK UNIVERSITY PRESS
New York and London

NEW YORK UNIVERSITY PRESS
New York and London

Copyright © 1994 by New York University

Library of Congress Cataloging-in-Publication Data
Pisciotta, Alexander W.
Benevolent repression : social control and the American
reformatory-prison movement / Alexander W. Pisciotta.
    p.   cm.
Includes bibliographical references and index.

1. Criminals—Rehabilitation—United States—History.
2. Corrections—United States—History. 3. Prisons—United States—
History. I. Title.
HV9304.P57 1994
365'.7'0973—dc20   93-41515
                                    CIP

New York University Press books are printed on acid-free paper,
and their binding materials are chosen for strength and durability.

Manufactured in the United States of America

10 9 8 7 6 5 4 3 2 1

To My Parents

Contents

List of Illustrations

Acknowledgments

One of the greatest pleasures of completing this book is finally having the opportunity to thank colleagues, institutions, and friends who helped me travel into the past and sort out the history of the American reformatory-prison movement.

First, I would like to thank Nicky Rafter and Beverly Smith for reading every page of every draft of the manuscript. Their insightful criticisms and suggestions greatly enhanced the quality of this work. More importantly, their encouragement and cheerful prodding kept me on task when I felt, on many occasions, that the project was too big and should be abandoned. *Benevolent Repression* would not have been completed without their efforts.

John Conley helped me conceptualize the project and encouraged me to move from a narrow case study of the Elmira Reformatory to a history of the entire reformatory-prison movement. John Meyer and Marc Renzema served as a sounding board for ideas and provided constructive criticisms of the manuscript. Okan Akcay guided me through the literature on public relations, marketing, and diffusion of innovations theory. John Steber introduced me to general semantics and helped me apply it to the field of criminal justice. Jack Treadway and Sam Walker provided valuable suggestions on the publication process. Bea Iceman's editing greatly improved the quality of *Benevolent Repression*.

A New York State Archives Research Residency Fellowship and grants from the Kutztown University Research Committee were absolutely indispensable. Librarians at Kutztown University, Rutgers University, Princeton University, the Library of Congress, the New York Public Library, New York State Library, Massachusetts State Library, and the Center for Research Libraries in Chicago helped me gather hundreds of books, articles, annual reports, and laws. Archivists in Minnesota, Massachusetts, Ohio, Pennsylvania, Michigan, and Illinois guided me through their extensive collections. Special thanks are reserved for the many staff members at the New York State Archives who have, over the years, helped me with this as well as a number of other historical projects. Barb Kegerreis, the Interlibrary Loan Technician at Kutztown University, made my work far easier by securing distant books and data sources. Sage Publications graciously granted me permission to use material from my article "Scientific Reform: The 'New Penology' at Elmira, 1876–1900," *Crime and Delinquency* 29 (October 1983): 613–30.

Superintendents of the Elmira, Ohio, Connecticut, New Jersey (Rahway), and Massachusetts reformatories allowed me to tour their institutions. I would like to thank my mentors, Freda Adler at Rutgers University and Tom Blomberg at Florida State University, for encouraging my interest in the rather peripheral field of criminal justice history.

Finally, I would like to express my enormous debt to my family. My wife, Kathy, and my sons, Al, Chris, and Matt, invested thousands of hours of family time into this project. Without their understanding, support, and extraordinary patience, the story of America's third penal system would remain untold.

Benevolent Repression

Introduction

This book is the product of an accidental discovery. In the fall of 1978 I was doing research in the New York State Archives for a history of the American juvenile reformatory movement. While reading the correspondence of one of the turn-of-the-century parole officers at the Western House of Refuge, Rochester, New York, I came across a puzzling entry. Parole officer Lewis Haas made notes on a conversation he had with Zebulon Brockway, superintendent of the highly acclaimed Elmira Reformatory.

> Brockway ... never let an opportunity pass to speak slightingly of this institution [Western House of Refuge], its methods and leniency and expressing our great mistake in dealing so kindly with these boys [noted Haas. Brockway would] sneer most contemptuously at our Sunday-school training and ask me if I brought some more of my good little Sundaschhol-boys [sic] down to him to train. "Do you know" said he, "what I do with them? Put them in red suits and lock them up and let them stay there until their time is out."[1]

The tone and substance of Brockway's comments seemed odd. I knew that Brockway had been the first superintendent of the Elmira Reformatory—completed in Elmira, New York, in 1876—probably the most important penal institution ever opened in the United States. Elmira was the world's first reformatory-prison for "youthful offenders": first-time male offenders between

1. Records of the New York State Agricultural and Industrial School, *Chaplain and Parole Officer Correspondence*, Lewis Haas to Superintendent F.H. Briggs, 21 January 1903.

the ages of sixteen and thirty. Brockway was and still is widely regarded as the father of the "new penology" and the "rehabilitative ideal." The Elmira system introduced "prison science" and the "medical model" into American corrections. Historians have credited him with developing some of America's most significant and long-lasting penal innovations, including indeterminate sentencing and parole.

Brockway's new penology served as the ideological foundation of the American correctional system for over a century. Punishment-oriented conservatives did not make headway in undermining the rehabilitative ideal until the 1970s. Why, I thought, did the "Father of Rehabilitation" speak so harshly? Why was the most important penal reformer in American history, the architect of many contemporary treatment programs, advocating punishment for juvenile offenders? Did Haas misinterpret, misquote, or perhaps misunderstand Brockway?

I could not pursue these questions. Although my interest was piqued, my topic was a history of juvenile—not adult—reformatories. Moreover, New York's archivists informed me that even though they had found inmate case histories and conduct ledgers from Elmira's early years, these records were housed in a cold, unlit, and abandoned building on the institution's grounds. These fascinating records were totally disorganized, impossible to work with, and not to be transferred to the archives for at least another year. Given the lack of primary data sources, I decided to stick to the task at hand. The story of Elmira had waited for more than a century. Would several additional years matter?

However, as I reviewed the literature on the history of corrections and social control, I tried to learn more about the new penology.[2] To my amazement, I discovered that historians had little to say about Brockway, Elmira, the adult reformatory movement, or the birth of American prison science. For instance, David J. Rothman's seminal works on the history of American corrections from colonial times to the 1940s, *The Discovery of the Asylum* (1971) and *Conscience and Convenience* (1980), discuss the Elmira Reformatory and adult reformatory movement only in passing or in footnotes. Outstanding works on juvenile justice history, most notably Robert M. Mennel's *Thorns and Thistles*

2. Reviews and critiques of American correctional historiography include: Takagi, "Revising Liberal Conceptions"; Conley, "Criminal Justice History"; Hindus, "The History of Crime"; Pisciotta, "Corrections, Society and Social Control"; idem, "Theoretical Perspectives"; Ignatieff, "State, Civil Society, and Total Institutions"; Mennel, "Attitudes and Policies"; see generally pieces in Cohen and Scull, eds., *Social Control and the State*; Bellingham, "Institution and Family"; Weiss, "Humanitarianism, Labor Exploitation, or Social Control."

(1973) and Steven L. Schlossman's *Love and the American Delinquent* (1977), examine the care of delinquent and dependent children and, accordingly, provide little analysis of the treatment of young adults.[3] Historians have focused their research efforts on either adult prisons or juvenile reformatories, not on the "in-between institutions" which comprised the adult reformatory movement. The evolution of the new penology and the birth of America's "third penal system"[4] have been ignored.[5]

The few studies that have been made of Elmira, the adult reformatory movement, and Brockway are descriptive chronologies and hagiographies which promote, with a few isolated exceptions, an uncritical march-of-progress theme.[6] Blake McKelvey's *American Prisons: A History of Good Intentions* (1977), for example, concludes that Elmira was "the model for other reformatories, demanding imitation rather than originality," and that Brockway "stands

3. In defense of Schlossman and Mennel, their purpose was to examine juvenile institutions, not adult reformatories. I do not mean to imply that their analyses are in any way flawed. Rothman's *Conscience and Convenience*, in contrast, purports to provide an analysis of key late nineteenth- and early twentieth-century penal movements. Excluding adult reformatories within this context is a serious oversight.

4. Criminal justice historians commonly refer to the adult prison movement as America's "first" penal system, the juvenile reformatory movement as the "second" system, and the adult reformatory movement as the "third" system. These terms are chronologically, ideologically, and programmatically based. Historians generally cite the Walnut Street Prison, which opened in Philadelphia in 1790, as the nation's first prison and the foundation of the "first system." The New York House of Refuge, which opened in New York City in 1825, introduced the juvenile reformatory movement and the "second system." The opening of the Elmira Reformatory in 1876 introduced the "third system."

5. I was, to be sure, perplexed by this gap in the literature. Why have leading criminal justice historians not examined America's most important penal institution and penal reform movement? Two explanations seem plausible. First, criminal justice historians generally study the development of social control institutions chronologically. Adult prisons and juvenile reformatories opened in the late eighteenth and early nineteenth centuries; hence, they received priority attention. Second, state archives also gave priority attention to the records of longer-established adult prisons and juvenile reformatories. In New York, for example, the records of the Auburn and Sing Sing Prisons and New York and Western Houses of Refuge were on deposit before the records of Elmira. The paucity of records on adult reformatories, coupled with a lack of discussion in prior literature, has contributed to this historical blind spot.

6. Histories of the Elmira Reformatory, the adult reformatory movement, or the new penology are: Nalder, "The American State Reformatory"; Robinson, *Penology in the United States*, 120–52; Gillin, *Criminology and Penology*, 621–44; Barnes and Teeters, *New Horizons in Criminology*, 547–68; Putney and Putney, "Origins of the Reformatory"; Hawes, *Children in Urban Society*, 146–57; Eriksson, *The Reformers*, 98–106; McKelvey, *American Prisons*, 64–115, 161–69, 234–66; Gill, "State Prisons in America"; Jenkins, "The Radicals and the Rehabilitative Ideal"; idem, "Temperance and the Origins of the New Penology"; Pisciotta, "Scientific Reform"; B. Smith, "Military Training"; Waite, "Penitentiary to Reformatory"; Currie, "Managing the Minds of Men."

without rival as the greatest warden America has produced." Torsten Eriksson's *The Reformers: An Historical Survey of Pioneer Experiments in the Treatment of Criminals* (1976) describes Brockway as a "creative genius" and a "gifted man of action." Herbert Johnson's *History of Criminal Justice* (1988)—a recent text that will serve as a primer for many students of American correctional history—praises Brockway and concludes that Elmira was "a sterling example of successful application of rehabilitative techniques."[7]

The failure of historians to examine critically the adult reformatory movement leaves a significant gap in our understanding of the history of American corrections and social control. More important, it distorts our understanding of the historical roots of current criminal justice system policies, practices, and debates. I have tried to remedy this failure by providing a history of the American adult reformatory movement from Elmira's opening in 1876 to the close of the Progressive Era (1900–1920).

This book addresses the following questions: When, where, and why did the American adult reformatory movement start? How did the opening of Elmira and the diffusion of reformatory-prisons transform America's approach to thinking about crime and treating criminals? Did adult reformatories fulfill their stated goals and objectives by providing kindly treatment and reform? How has this movement and its underlying ideological foundation—rehabilitation—shaped current criminal justice policies, practices, and debates?

My arguments are grounded on two concepts: benevolent reform and benevolent repression. The twenty adult reformatories opened in the United States between 1876 and 1920 promised benevolent reform: humane, constructive, and charitable treatment. In fact, they delivered benevolent repression. So-called "prison science" attempted to instill youthful offenders with the Protestant ethic and American values: the habits of order, discipline, self-control, cheerful submission to authority, as well as respect for God, law, country, and the principles of capitalism and democracy. These institutions were designed to transform the "dangerous criminal classes" into Christian gentlemen and prepare them to assume their "proper place" in the social, economic, and political order: hard-working, law-abiding lower-class citizens. America's new reformatory-prisons were, quite simply, aimed at taming and training criminal elements of the working class.

However, I will demonstrate that adult reformatories did not achieve their overt goal of benevolent reform or their covert aim of benevolent repression.

7. McKelvey, *American Prisons*, 138, 169; Eriksson, *The Reformers*, 98; Johnson, *History of Criminal Justice*, 225.

Most of these highly acclaimed institutions were, in fact, ineffective and brutal prisons which did not provide kindly reform or "Christian treatment." But the state's failure to reform did not, ipso facto, translate into effective coercion. Nineteenth- and early twentieth-century reformatory-prisons did not, as Michel Foucault has argued in *Discipline and Punish* (1975), succeed in their attempts to manage the minds, bodies, and souls of men; despite their grand aims, these institutions did not effectively discipline the dangerous classes.

However, the reformatory movement had an enormous impact on Americans' approach to thinking about crime and treating criminals. These institutions invented a new criminal class: the dangerous youthful offender. The opening of reformatory-prisons added a new layer to the nation's network of social control. Indeterminate sentences lengthened prison terms; parole extended the new penology and the coercive arm of the state into the community. The diffusion of prison science contributed to the professionalization of penology and the creation of "scientific criminology." Perhaps most important, the founding of America's third penal system enhanced the status of the nation's correctional system and legitimized the repression of the dangerous, criminal classes.

The adult reformatory movement is not merely a historical curiosity. Modern correctional institutions continue to serve as dumping grounds for society's human refuse—now unskilled, uneducated, lower-class blacks and Hispanics. Contemporary reformatories and prisons still try to instill offenders with the Protestant ethic and transform them into "Christian gentlemen." Even today, core treatment programs (academic and vocational education, religion, mark and classification systems, military drill, indeterminate sentencing, parole), the most vexing problems (overcrowding, underfunding, escapes, riots, violence, drugs, suicide, arson, predatory homosexuality), as well as explanations for failure (lack of money, inadequate staffing, uncooperative inmates), disturbingly reflect the past. Like our nineteenth-century predecessors, we continue to balance the conflicting aims of benevolent reform and benevolent repression— with as little success.

This book is structured to provide a systematic overview of the adult reformatory movement and to develop these themes. The first three chapters focus on the Elmira Reformatory from its 1876 opening to 1899. Chapter 1 identifies factors which led to the founding of this path-breaking institution. I analyze the Elmira system in detail and demonstrate how the new penology transformed the entire American criminal justice system and was widely hailed as an international model. Chapter 2 provides a detailed look at Elmira's internal operation. I demonstrate that this "model institution" was one of the most, if not the most, ineffective and brutal correctional institutions in the United States. Chapter 3 explores the human dimension of incarceration; seven case histories provide the inmates' perspectives on the Elmira system and highlight the problems that Brockway encountered in attempting to implement prison science and the new penology.

Chapter 4 traces the diffusion of the adult reformatory movement to the close of the nineteenth century. I examine the origin, aims, structure, population, programs, and problems of ten reformatory-prisons opened between 1877 and 1899. These institutions adopted Elmira's central aim: to instill their charges with the Protestant ethic and transform them into productive citizens. However, they did not blindly copy the Elmira system. Other reformatory-prisons developed unique organizational personalities which reflected state-specific penal cultures. However, there was a wide disparity between the theory and practice of these institutions; like Elmira, they promised reform, delivered repression, but generally failed to socialize their charges.

Chapters 5 and 6 examine Progressive Era penal reforms. In chapter 5, I return to Elmira and demonstrate how and why scandals forced Brockway to resign in 1900. Elmira's new keepers went on to discover a new class of criminal, the mentally defective offender, and to introduce a new approach to reform, eugenic prison science. Chapter 6 examines the operation of the adult reformatory movement from 1900 to 1920; by the latter date, twenty reformatory-prisons were operating in the United States. Drawing on systems and organizational theory, I explain how this movement fractured, splintered, and eventually self-destructed. By 1920, the adult reformatory movement was no longer the central focus of the American penal system. Incapacitation and social defense had become the new aims of the American criminal justice system. Finally, chapter 7 summarizes my major findings and themes, compares and contrasts past and present correctional practices, and presents some unsettling predictions for the future of American corrections and social control.

My purpose in writing this book is to call attention to the new penology, outline the contours of the adult reformatory movement, and ponder linkages between past and present social control systems. I demonstrate, with much regret, that America's search for "reform" has been a long and painful experience. Why do we continue to repackage programs and ideologies which have been tried and failed? Why do we continue to promise benevolent reform but deliver benevolent repression?

Chapter One

Making Christian Gentlemen:
The Promise of Elmira, 1876–1899

The Elmira Reformatory led America's search for methods of reform in the late-nineteenth century. This chapter provides an overview of the origin, development, and operation of this institution during its "golden age of reform." The first section examines forces that led to the founding of the Elmira Reformatory in 1876, explains how the Elmira system evolved, and describes how the new penology was, in theory, supposed to rehabilitate inmates. The second demonstrates how the opening of Elmira and the introduction of prison science sparked a paradigmatic revolution which transformed America's approach to thinking about crime and treating criminals. Finally, there is the career of America's most important penologist—the father of the new penology, the Elmira system, and the adult reformatory movement—Zebulon Reed Brockway. Brockway was, in the eyes of many, the arm of the state, the hand of God, and a penological genius.

The kindly rhetoric of Elmira's highly successful public relations and marketing campaign masked a repressive class control agenda. These findings support many of the central themes presented by Michel Foucault in *Discipline and Punish* and by David Garland in *Punishment and Welfare*. The Elmira Reformatory, much like the adult prisons and juvenile reformatories which preceded it, attempted to build "docile bodies" and "manage the souls of men." The Elmira system was designed to instill youthful offenders with the habits of order, discipline, and self-control and to mold obedient citizen-workers. The "socialization" and "normalization" of offenders was aimed at controlling the lower classes and, on a practical and symbolic level, contributing to the development of an orderly society. America's new medical model legitimized the social control of the dangerous classes and attempted to fit the lumpenproletariat into their "proper place" in the social, economic, and political order: namely, law-abiding and hard-working proletarians.

Origins of Elmira: Crime, Criminal Justice, and the Crisis in Corrections

The post–Civil War era was one of the most dynamic periods in American history. Unparalleled demographic, social, economic, and political changes shook the nation. The relative decline of agriculture and the rise of industrialization were the primary catalysts of change. The influx of millions of immigrants contributed to the growth of America's industrial complex by supplying inexpensive labor. New production, distribution, consumption, and exchange networks formed, and the United States rapidly emerged as a world economic, political, and military power. But industrialization and urbanization resulted in increases, or at least perceived increases, in a variety of "city-related" problems: crime, delinquency, poverty, moral decay. America became, as historian Robert Wiebe puts it, a disorganized and distended society. Traditional American values—the rural, Protestant village-farmer lifestyle—crumbled. "America in the late nineteenth century," concludes Wiebe, "was a society without a core."[1]

Post–Civil War New Yorkers were firmly convinced that crime, deviance, and social disorder were skyrocketing and that New York City was rapidly degenerating into a moral cesspool and den of iniquity. Edward Crapsey, a police reporter, expressed the sentiments of many fearful observers in his analysis of "the nether side of New York." The city was rife with crime and delinquency. Seven thousand grog shops, five thousand prostitutes, three thousand profes-

---

1. Wiebe, *The Search for Order,* 12. More radically oriented historical works focus on class, racial, ethnic, or religious conflict and the economic exploitation of the lower classes during this period. Some of the standard works in this tradition include Williams, *Contours of American History*; Baran and Sweezy, *Monopoly Capital*; Dowd, *The Twisted Dream*; Braverman, *Labor and Monopoly Capital*; Boyer, *Urban Masses and Moral Order.* I will not attempt to critique Wiebe's thesis or consider alternate interpretations of the Progressive Era. Link and McCormick review the literature in *Progressivism.* Irrespective of the historical accuracy of Wiebe's thesis, one point is clear: many Americans were convinced that social disorder was increasing; they launched a war on crime and vice based on that perception.

sional criminals, and six hundred illegal lottery stores plagued the city. Reflecting prevailing sentiments, Crapsey attributed much of the increase in disorder to new immigrants. "The thrifty emigrants who came to us forehanded and determined to wring competence from the new republic, merely made New York their stepping stone to fortune," explained Crapsey. "The dregs settled in the metropolis where they landed."[2]

Charles Loring Brace—a Congregationalist minister, noted social reformer, and xenophobe—echoed these concerns. Poor immigrant stock, a lack of religious conviction, the rise of tenements, the breakdown of the family, alcohol, poverty, laziness, disease, and the inherent immorality of the lower classes were the causes of New York's decline. "The 'dangerous classes'," cautioned Brace, "are mainly American-born but the children of Irish and German immigrants." The new criminal classes were a potentially revolutionary force which had the potential to overthrow the nation's economic and political institutions. Armageddon was at hand:

Let but law lift its hand from them for a season, or let the civilizing influence of American life fail to reach them, and if the opportunity offered we shall see an explosion from this class which might leave this city in ashes and blood.[3]

Pathological gangs received blame for much of the city's crime. The Dead Rabbits, Plug Uglies, Forty Thieves, Gas House Gang, and Hell's Kitchen Gang terrorized the city. These gangs, which allegedly had up to fifteen hundred members, were involved in robbery, theft, confidence games, prostitution, and even murder. Organized on ethnic, religious, racial, and political lines, they were the products of the city's infamous slums: Satan's Circus, Five Points District, Murderers' Alley, Poverty Lane, Thieves Exchange, and The Morgue. Irish, Italian, Jewish, Chinese, and mainstream American gangs fought to protect their "business interests" and "turf." Members proudly displayed their "colors" and worked hard to cultivate their reputations. The Whyos required murder as a rite of initiation. The Reverend Brace and other respectable citizens had little doubt, especially following New York's Dead Rabbit Riot of 1857 and the Draft Riot of 1863, that these lower-class gangs were a major source of crime and a potentially revolutionary force.[4]

2. Crapsey, *Nether Side of New York*, 6. Ellis et al., *History of New York State*, provides an academic assessment of these changes.

3. Brace, *Dangerous Classes of New York*, 27, 29; on crime see 25–73. Other social critics were more sensitive to the plight of the poor, especially Riis, *How the Other Half Lives*; idem, *Children of the Poor*; idem, *Battle with the Slums*.

4. Asbury, *Gangs of New York*; Bernstein, *New York City Draft Riots*. Professional criminals were also an increasing concern during this period: Byrnes, *Professional Criminals of America*; Joselit, *Our Gang*.

Post-bellum New Yorkers were convinced that the state's criminal justice system was incapable of dealing with these gangs and the rising tide of crime and social disorder. New York City's police force was ineffective at detecting or preventing crime. It was common knowledge that policemen were unqualified, untrained, and corrupt. The court system was equally inefficient. Many judges, prosecutors, and defense attorneys were involved in city and state politics. Following the Tammany Hall tradition, bribery became widespread; it was common knowledge that justice was for sale in New York's courts. Crapsey's experiences as a police reporter led him to conclude that "as producers of travesties upon law and justice, the police courts of New York are unequalled."[5]

By the post–Civil War period, confidence in New York's correctional institutions—the pride of American penology in the first half of the nineteenth century—was badly shaken. The opening of the Auburn Prison (1817) and Sing Sing Prison (Ossining, 1826) marked the birth of the "congregate" or "silent system" of penal reform. The New York House of Refuge (New York City, 1825) was the nation's first juvenile reformatory.[6] But by the 1860s, the longstanding debate between proponents of New York's "silent" system and Pennsylvania's "separate" system—introduced at the Walnut Street Prison (Philadelphia, 1790), Western Penitentiary (Pittsburgh, 1826), and Eastern Penitentiary (Philadelphia, 1829)—had given way to a new realization: both systems might be ineffective.[7] Faith in the New York House of Refuge also de-

5. Crapsey, *Nether Side of New York*, 25, 13. Contemporary historians have supported Crapsey's notion that New York City's criminal justice system was ineffective and plagued with corruption: Richardson, *New York Police*; Reppetto, *Blue Parade*, 38–87; Miller, *Cops and Bobbies*; Fogelson, *Big City Police*; Walker, *Critical History of Police Reform*; idem, *Popular Justice*; D. Johnson, *Policing the Urban Underworld*.

6. New York's congregate or silent system was based on the aim of profit. Inmates worked in congregate shops during the day making a variety of products under the direction of contractors. Strict silence was maintained at all times. On adult prisons in New York see Klein, *Prison Methods in New York State*; W. Lewis, *From Newgate to Dannemora*; O. Lewis, *Development of American Prisons*; Barnes and Teeters, *New Horizons in Criminology*, 505–45; D. Rothman, *Discovery of the Asylum* and *Conscience and Convenience*, passim; McKelvey, *American Prisons*, passim. New York's juvenile justice system is analyzed by Peirce, *Half Century*; Pickett, *House of Refuge*; Schlossman, *Love and the American Delinquent*, 18–32; idem, "Juvenile Justice in the Age of Jackson"; Schlossman and Pisciotta, "Identifying and Treating Serious Juvenile Offenders"; Mennel, *Thorns and Thistles*, 3–31; Hawes, *Children in Urban Society*, 27–60; Pisciotta, "Saving the Children"; idem, "*Parens Patriae*"; idem, "Treatment on Trial"; idem, "Child Saving or Child Brokerage"; B. Smith, "Female Admissions." Holl, *Juvenile Reform in the Progressive Era*, examines New York's George Junior Republic movement.

7. Pennsylvania's separate system was based on the philosophy that inmates should be isolated in solitary cells. Silence, meditation, and Bible reading were the routes to reform. Pennsylvania's

clined. Post-bellum child savers increasingly opened "cottage-style" juvenile reformatories. In 1867, Governor Reuben Fenton declared that prisons were grossly overcrowded and only in "fair condition of internal management and discipline." In 1869, Governor John Hoffman declared that "the prison system of this state abounds in evils and errors."[8]

The New York Prison Association responded to this crisis in corrections by appointing two respected members, Enoch Cobb Wines and Theodore Dwight, to conduct an investigation. Wines and Dwight inspected New York's prisons, juvenile reformatories, county penitentiaries, and local jails. They also visited correctional institutions in seventeen states and Canada to develop a comparative perspective. Their *Report on the Prisons and Reformatories of the United States and Canada* (1867) was decidedly negative but offered recommendations to make New York's penal system once again "a model for other States." Rehabilitation, not punishment, should be the goal of each institution. The report called for reductions in sentence disparity, less emphasis on profit-oriented labor, and more emphasis on industrial education, academic education, religion, and post-release supervision. Wines and Dwight called for the opening of a new type of institution to separate hardened and novice offenders: an "adult reformatory." This institution would aim to "teach and train the prisoner in such a manner that, on his discharge, he may be able to resist temptation and inclined to lead an upright, worthy life."[9]

Governor Hoffman endorsed the Wines and Dwight report, and the legislature passed "An Act Authorizing the Appointment of Commissioners to Locate a State Penitentiary or Industrial Reformatory" in 1869. Five appointed commissioners selected a site and began planning the new "state penitentiary" or "industrial reformatory." The commissioners purchased a 280-acre tract of land in Elmira and hired an architect, W. L. Woolett, to design the institution. Woolett's plan called for a five hundred–cell facility on thirteen acres surrounded by a twenty-foot wall. Thirty acres were set aside for support buildings. The 1872 legislature approved the design and appropriated $500,000 for construction. Although Woolett was replaced in 1874, the original plan was

correctional system has received considerable attention: Barnes, *Evolution of Penology in Pennsylvania*; Teeters, *Cradle of the Penitentiary*; Teeters and Shearer, *Prison at Philadelphia*; Teeters, "Early Days"; Remick, "House of Refuge of Philadelphia"; Takagi, "Walnut Street Jail"; Dumm, *Democracy and Punishment*.

8. Lincoln, *State of New York Messages from the Governors*, 5:757, 6:17–18.

9. Wines and Dwight, *Report on the Prisons and Reformatories*, pp. 52, 47, 72–73.

followed. The construction of the new correctional institution made steady progress.[10]

At this stage, New York's penal reformers had no inkling that they were on the verge of building a model correctional institution which would capture the attention of the world and reshape the American criminal justice system. The commissioners charged with the responsibility of designing the institution received little direction and were, as a result, in a quandary. Wines and Dwight had called for the opening of an "adult reformatory" and the introduction of a new "science of punishment"—but their report was short on specifics. The 1869 state legislature authorized the commissioners to construct either a "penitentiary" or an "industrial reformatory." An 1870 legislative act provided some direction by restricting commitments to male first-time offenders between the ages of sixteen and thirty. This act also called for the new reformatory to provide "agricultural labor" and "mechanical industry."[11] But crucial questions remained: How should the regimen of this experimental adult reformatory be structured? How were the commissioners to develop a "science of punishment"? How was this new class of offenders to be reformed?

Events outside New York State shaped the regimen of the incipient Elmira Reformatory. Given the pessimism of post-bellum penologists, it is understandable that debates about new approaches to treating criminals took place across the country and around the world. Cognizant of the malaise in penology, Enoch Wines convinced his colleagues at the New York Prison Association that organizing an international conference to discuss these issues might reveal enlightened approaches to reform. The first meeting of the National Congress on Penitentiary and Reformatory Discipline was the product of Wines's efforts. Drawn in large part by the reported successes of European reformers such as Alexander Machonochie, Richard Whately, Frederick and Matthew Davenport Hill, Manuel Montesinos, and Walter Crofton, over 250 delegates from twenty-four states and a number of foreign countries traveled to Cincinnati, Ohio, in 1870.[12] A. J. Goshorn's opening address set the tone of the congress:

10. Elmira's construction is described by Brockway, *Fifty Years*, 162–65; McKelvey, *American Prisons*, 85–87.

11. "An Act in Relation to the State Reformatory"; "An Act Relating to the Building Commissioners."

12. I will not, due to space limitations, attempt to trace the European roots of the Elmira system. However, some of this system's key ideas were introduced by the famed "Irish system," which has received considerable attention: Osborough, *Borstal in Ireland*; B. Smith, "Irish Prison System"; idem, "Irish General Prisons Board."

With a rapidly increasing population and the disposition of the people to congregate in large cities, we have an alarming increase of crime, and legislation is obliged to be ever devising new remedies and imposing fresh penalties for the protection of society.[13]

With Goshorn's exhortation in mind, delegates delivered thirty-four papers. The pinnacle of the conference was the adoption of the acclaimed Declaration of Principles (reprinted in the appendix below). These thirty-seven principles—written by Ohio Governor Rutherford B. Hayes, Enoch Wines, Franklin Sanborn, and Zebulon Brockway—were grounded on the assumption that "the supreme aim of prison discipline is the reform of criminals, not the infliction of vindictive suffering." The Declaration of Principles called for individualized care based on "scientific treatment" and the "medical model." To foster reform, delegates recommended indeterminate sentencing, a carefully calculated mark and classification system, intensive academic and vocational instruction, constructive labor, and humane disciplinary methods. Intensive post-release supervision (i.e. parole) would, in theory, extend rehabilitation into the community. Wines was delighted: here was a new, enlightened approach to treating criminals. Here was the new penology—the ideological foundation of the Elmira system—and the solution to the malaise in American and international corrections.[14]

By May 1876, the Elmira Reformatory was nearly ready to receive its first inmates. However, the institution still lacked a clear mission, little effort had been made to develop a regimen of reform, and a superintendent had not been appointed. These problems were summarily dealt with when, on 11 May 1876, the commissioners offered the position to one of the nation's most respected penologists, Zebulon Brockway. Brockway did not hesitate; he accepted the superintendency on 12 May. New York was on the verge of introducing a revolutionary approach to the treatment of criminals. The American criminal justice system was on the verge of a paradigmatic revolution.

Building Elmira: The Economics of Penal Reform, 1876–1880

The opening of the doors of the Elmira Reformatory on 24 July 1876 to receive thirty inmates who were transferred from Auburn Prison marked the

13. In E. Wines, ed., *Transactions of the National Congress*, 1.

14. Ibid., 54. There seems to be some confusion regarding the authorship of the Declaration of Principles. Historians agree that Wines, Sanborn, and Brockway wrote the document. Some historians include Hayes, who was president of the convention. Sanborn stated that Hayes was an author in "Development of Reformatory Discipline," 19. These principles are briefly stated on pp. 541–47 of the *Transactions* with a fuller explanation on pp. 548–67.

beginning of a new era in American penology. William Phinney, Charles Forward, and Charles Mann had the dubious honor of serving as Elmira's first commitments. Phinney, Forward, and Mann were co-conspirators, convicted of grand larceny and sentenced to five years in the Auburn Prison. Similar to thousands of offenders who would follow them into Elmira over the next half century, these inmates were poor, unskilled, uneducated, unemployed, and exhibited bad personal habits (drinking, smoking, debauchery).[15] They were products of New York's dangerous classes—the new "floating population."

However, Phinney, Forward, Mann, and their Auburn cohorts did not go to Elmira for rehabilitation. Elmira's founding 1876 law did not call for indeterminate sentencing, parole, or other programs which would later become known as the Elmira system. The 1876 act appointed five "respectable citizens" to serve as the first board of managers, charged with the responsibility of hiring a superintendent, inspecting financial records, and making rules governing the operation of the reformatory. Most importantly, the law instructed the managers to finish building the institution, which was far from complete. Phinney, Forward, Mann, and the other Auburn inmates provided "the labor necessary for the construction of shops and the inclosures [sic] of the grounds upon which the reformatory is located, and for the completion of unfinished portions of the reformatory."[16] From 1876 to 1880, the Elmira Reformatory was, quite simply, a work camp.

A number of formidable tasks confronted Brockway; these needed to be addressed before prison science could even be contemplated. The central administration building, officers' quarters, and most of the twenty-foot security wall were finished when the institution was opened. However, only 312 of the institution's 504 cells were complete; there were locks on "some cells." Brockway later stated that, "During the initial twenty-six months, from July 24, 1876, to October, 1878, it was not practicable to enter upon the projected reformatory plans." The managers shared Brockway's assessment:

It is probably not expected, at this stage of the reformatory, we should have entered actively upon the work of improving the prisoners, as is only possible when the reforma-

---

15. New York State Reformatory, *Inmate Consecutive Register*, Case History #1, 2, 3. It should be pointed out that Elmira was not opened in 1877, as a number of works have stated: e.g., Rothman, *Conscience and Convenience*, 33; Barnes, *Story of Punishment*, 146; Walker, *Popular Justice*, 91; Johnson, *History of Criminal Justice*, 218.

16. "An Act to Provide a Government," p. 213. These inmates were also transferred to reduce crowding at Auburn and Sing Sing.

tory is completed and new legislation has giving [sic] us properly the special class [youthful offenders] for which it was designed.[17]

Elmira's work crew was steadily increased. One hundred ninety-four inmates were transferred from Auburn and Sing Sing by the end of 1876. Brockway kept his inmate-workers busy. They put in eighteen thousand hours of labor in 1876 and twenty-eight thousand hours in 1877. By the end of 1877, inmates completed the first cell house and constructed a chapel, barn, domestic building, workshop, tool shop, sewer line, and roads. By 1879, they had built a foundry building, furniture finishing shop, and brush factory and had finished grading the grounds. In 1880, the managers informed the legislature that their primary task was finished: the main structures were complete.[18]

The Auburn and Sing Sing inmates transferred to Elmira between 1876 and 1880 were not, however, enthusiastic workers. Brockway described the Sing Sing inmates as "city criminals ill-adapted for laboring work, besides being specially vicious and untamed men." The inmates from Auburn were a slight improvement, being "fairly suitable for the common laborers' work intended." Brockway suspected that the wardens of the Sing Sing and Auburn Prisons may have used the opening of Elmira as an opportunity to rid themselves of troublesome inmates or, he speculated, as a pretext for sabotaging his new institution. "Prison officials at the state prisons were antagonistic toward the reformatory, and their transferred prisoners came with only contempt for that which in their view the term reformatory signifies—the usual Sunday school notion."[19]

Irrespective of the motives of the keepers of the Auburn and Sing Sing Prisons, it is clear that Brockway's talents as a warden were fully taxed between 1876 and 1880. Although only eight men successfully "eloped" during this period, escapes caused constant concern. Brockway countered the inmates by placing a sharpshooter in the guard tower. The effect, he said, was "magical." But, added the superintendent, "Mr. Cook, the guard, soon resigned, disgusted, as he said, that he had wasted a full month of his time without a single shot."

Inmate revolts posed a serious threat. In one foiled plot, inmates planned to attack the guards with bricks and then escape. In another instance, twelve men attacked a staff member and tried to scale the wall. Brockway suspected a con-

17. New York State, Assembly Documents (1877), vol. 3, no. 15, New York State Reformatory, *First Annual Report* (1876), 3, 8. Brockway, *Fifty Years*, 174. Hereafter, annual reports are cited as *AR* and biennial reports are cited as *BR*.

18. New York State, Senate Documents (1881), vol. 1, no. 21, New York State Reformatory, *Fifth AR* (1880), 4. Pictures of the Elmira Reformatory and of inmates in the shops are in American Correctional Association, *American Prison*, 76–87.

19. Brockway, *Fifty Years*, 175.

spiracy at a Sunday religious service; a frisk uncovered knotted cords, weapons, and another escape plot. The superintendent's concerns about inmate violence were not unfounded: one inmate's throat was cut following an altercation; another inmate confrontation resulted in a crushed skull and death.[20]

Elmira's highest officials were not safe from the threat of violence. In 1880, inmate Edward Simmons murdered William McKelvey, Brockway's assistant superintendent. Simmons, a burglar committed in 1879, was a particularly difficult inmate. He refused to do his work, destroyed institutional property, and feigned illness and stupidity. When solitary confinement failed to promote compliance, Brockway ordered McKelvey to handcuff Simmons to the door of his cell. McKelvey attempted to administer the punishment on 6 May 1880; before he could apply the handcuffs, Simmons pulled a knife and stabbed McKelvey over the heart, killing him instantly. McKelvey's murder left a lasting impression on the superintendent and embittered him toward the Auburn and Sing Sing inmates: "More dangerous knives and improvised stilettos were in some way obtained, secreted, and offensively used by prisoners than had been known in all my prison experience."[21]

Despite difficulties with inmates and preoccupation with construction, the managers did not ignore the aim of reform during the 1876 to 1880 period. They required religious services, made an effort to start academic classes, and opened several workshops. However, the managers recognized that these programs were token, and that the 1876 governing legislation aimed to promote construction, not reform. They also recognized that they were inexperienced in corrections and unqualified to develop a new regimen of reform: William Wey, president of the board of managers, was a physician; Ariel Thurston, a retired judge; Rufus King, an attorney; Sinclair Tousey, the president of a newspaper company. Louis Pilsbury was a career penologist. However, he was engrossed in his new position as Superintendent of New York State Prisons and could not devote attention to the revision of Elmira's founding 1876 statute.

In 1877, the managers instructed Brockway to develop a new "science of punishment." He relished the task and used this opportunity to translate the Declaration of Principles into a systematic program of reform. His final plan impressed the managers, as well as the members of the state legislature. The

---

20. Ibid., 177. Brockway described his difficulties in the 1876-1880 period in ibid., 175–94.

21. New York State Reformatory, *Inmate Consecutive Register*, Case History #277. Brockway, *Fifty Years*, 188; the Simmons case is described on pp. 184–87. Simmons was convicted of second degree murder and sentenced to life in Auburn Prison. He later escaped and was never recaptured.

passage of Chapter 173 of the Laws of 1877 marked the first formal effort to translate the new penology into practice.[22] But Brockway's new penal plan could not be implemented until the buildings were complete. "Only very slow progress was made until ... October, 1880," reflected Brockway. "Up to this date the reformatory differed only in name from a common, rough, state prison with an unusual percentage of exceptionally bad prisoners."[23]

Georg Rusche and Otto Kirchheimer's classic work, *Punishment and Social Structure*, develops the thesis that systems of social control—galley slavery, fines, transportation, houses of correction, capital punishment, prisons, and prison labor—were designed to control the criminal elements of the working class and serve the economic and fiscal needs of the state. Academics have subjected Rusche and Kirchheimer's work to a wide range of logical, historical, and empirical criticisms, especially the charge of economic reductionism.[24] But for the Auburn and Sing Sing inmates who labored to raise the walls of Elmira between 1876 and 1880, I suspect that there was much truth to the Rusche and Kirchheimer thesis. Moving mud and mortar and using inmate labor to fill the coffers of New York state clearly took precedence over prison science and the reform of men during Elmira's early years.

Medicalizing Deviance: Building the College on the Hill, 1881–1882

The completion of the physical structure in late 1880 allowed Brockway and the managers to turn their attention from building structures to building men. Brockway characterized 1881–1882 as the "transitional epoch" in Elmira's history. The introduction of the Elmira system during this period made prison

22. "An Act in Relation to the Imprisonment of Convicts." This law includes ideas presented by Zebulon Brockway in "The Ideal of a True Prison System." Brockway, *Fifty Years*, 169–74, recounts the writing of this law.

23. Ibid., 174.

24. The observation that punishments reflected social structure and, in particular, the economic and fiscal needs of the state is the book's central theme. Works extending and testing this theme include Platt, *The Child Savers*; idem, "Rise of the Child-Saving Movement"; idem, "Triumph of Benevolence"; Miller, "At Hard Labor"; idem, "Sinking Gradually"; Shelden, "Convict Leasing"; Petchesky, "At Hard Labor"; Melossi and Pavarini, *Prison and Factory*; Adamson, "Punishment after Slavery"; idem, "Toward a Marxian Penology"; idem, "Hard Labor and Solitary Confinement"; Gardner, "Emergence of the New York State Prison System"; Conley, "Prisons, Production and Profit"; idem,"Revising Conceptions"; idem, "Economics and the Social Reality of Prisons"; Smith and Fried, *The Uses of American Prison*, esp. pp. 1–25. Weiss reviews this literature in "Humanitarianism, Labour Exploitation, or Social Control."

science a reality. Elmira soon became known, as Brockway was fond of putting it, as the "reformatory hospital" and "college on the hill."[25]

The task confronting the keepers was clear: youthful offenders were to be instilled with the Protestant ethic and prepared to assume their "proper place" in the social, economic, and political order. "The purpose of imprisonment and of treatment is to prepare such for industry, to train and transfer them from economic worthlessness to worthfulness," explained Brockway. The new Elmira system would, as Brockway concisely put it, instill inmates with "Christian character" and transform them into "Christian gentlemen." Inmates who internalized Brockway's vision of reform accepted full responsibility for their criminal act(s) and attempted to become responsible workers, husbands, fathers and citizens. On a more symbolic and macroscopic level, scientific reform aimed at taming and training New York's dangerous classes.[26]

Brockway's revolutionary treatment strategy rested on a new approach to crime causation: multifactor positivism.[27] Traditional fixed sentencing models and prison systems—including Auburn and Sing Sing—were premised on Beccarian classical theory and the assumption that criminals were free, rational, and hedonistic actors who needed and deserved punishment. Elmira's indeterminate sentencing model came from the belief that each offender's behavior was determined by a variety of unique environmental, psychological, and/or biological factors. Individualized diagnosis and treatment were, in theory, the key to the Elmira system. A new social control theme guided prison science: "Let the punishment fit the criminal, rather than the crime."[28]

25. Brockway, *Fifty Years*, 163, 212, 232. Governor Alonzo B. Cornell described Elmira as being still "in process of development" in 1881: Lincoln, *State of New York Messages from the Governors*, 7:527–28.

26. Brockway, "Abstract of Paper," 65. The notion of the "Protestant ethic" is, of course, borrowed from Max Weber, *Protestant Ethic and the Spirit of Capitalism*. Criticisms and applications of Weber's work as it applies to penology are discussed by Garland, *Punishment and Modern Society*, chap. 8. Brockway's vision of "Christian reform" is stated in "The Ideal of a True Prison System," 63, 65. The socialization and social control of the lower classes was not a uniquely American phenomenon. E. P. Thompson's classic work, *The Making of the English Working Class*, analyzes the taming and training of Britain's poor.

27. This is a term used by modern criminologists who believe that the search for "the cause" of crime is fruitless. Proponents of multifactor positivism, noting that no two criminals or types of crime are identical, call for an individualized diagnosis and treatment strategy for each offender. Brockway did not know the term, but he did use the approach—at least in theory—in dealing with his charges.

28. Beccaria, *On Crimes and Punishments*. Piers Beirne's revisionist interpretation, "Inventing Criminology," argues that Beccaria's work was the product of a deterministic view of man. My reading tends to support traditional interpretations. Rennie, *The Search for Criminal Man*, provides a concise overview of theories of crime causation during this period.

An overview of the 1881–1882 Elmira system demonstrates how Brockway and his staff used the medical model and the new penology to socialize their "patients." Brockway's "reformatory hospital" employed a three-stage "process of individualization" to transform the criminal elements of New York's working class into law-abiding and hard-working citizens.

The first stage in the treatment process, the "initial interview," followed a standard format. Every new arrival was bathed, issued a uniform, and then escorted to Brockway's office for a private interview. Brockway employed the case method to explore the social, economic, psychological, biological, and moral "root cause(s)" of each offender's deviance. The inmate was questioned, explained Brockway, "until the subjective defect is apparently discovered in each case." At the conclusion of the interview, Brockway assigned the inmate to an appropriate class in school and a suitable industry and sent him to a cell. The second stage in the Elmira system, the process of long-term in-house reform, was about to begin.[29]

Guards roused inmates out of bed every morning at 5:15 A.M., the approximate waking time for farm hands and factory workers. They had fifteen minutes to dress. They ate breakfast and then cleaned their cells, leaving them "scrupulously clean and in order." Inmates who did not conform to the "code of cleanliness" were corrected. Dirty and disorderly inmates, said Brockway, made poor citizen-workers and future career criminals.

The hours between 7:30 A.M. and 4:30 P.M. were spent at labor. Inmates learned skills designed to prepare them to join the honest working class. Inmates worked in the iron foundry, hollow ware works, shoe or broom factories, or the institutional farm or maintenance squad. The shops operated on the contract system during this phase of Elmira's history (contractors paid 56 cents for an eight-hour day). In theory, inmates learned a trade and the "habits of industry": punctuality, order, discipline, concentration, care in handling machinery, and respect for authority. Labor was stopped at noon for lunch; at 1:00 P.M. inmates returned to their jobs and worked until 4:30 P.M.; thirty minutes were then allotted for dinner.

Brockway granted interviews from 5:00 to 6:00 P.M. Meetings or special events also occasionally took place during this hour. Guest lecturers addressed

---

29. "An Act in Relation to the Imprisonment of Convicts"; Brockway, *Fifty Years*, passim. New York State, Senate Documents (1882), vol. 3, no. 26, New York State Reformatory, *Sixth AR* (1881) provides a detailed overview of the 1881–1882 regimen, 51–57. The 1892 regimen is described in New York State, Assembly Documents (1893), vol. 5, no. 25, New York State Reformatory, *Seventeenth AR* (1892), 149–66.

the inmates on a range of worldly topics, such as Cortes in Mexico, Chemistry and fire, Electrical communications. All inmates went to school at 7:00 P.M. The "college on the hill" offered seven levels of instruction in 1882.[30] Reading, writing, and basic math were taught in elementary classes; history, geography, and composition were available for advanced students. The inmates returned to their cells at 8:30 P.M. when classes ended.

Mandatory religious services took place on Sunday. In addition to delivering the Word of the Lord, the chaplain exhorted the Elmira boys to embrace the Bible and give up the evil habits which led them to crime: drinking, smoking, fornication, laziness, and dishonesty. Respect for God, law, family, work, and country were regular themes at these Sunday sermons. The chaplain reminded inmates that the Lord wanted them to abide by the rules of the Elmira system and work hard to become good citizens. The penalty for noncompliance was severe: inmates who fought their keepers and rejected the Elmira system were spurning God and risking eternal damnation and the flames of Hell.

Brockway introduced an innovative classification and mark system to promote personal and institutional order. Placed in the second grade, new inmates learned that they had a choice: to abide by the rules for six months and earn promotion to the first grade; or to fight the system and suffer the consequences of the third grade. Third-grade inmates wore coarse red uniforms, marched in lockstep, and were denied letters, library privileges, and visits. Their rooms were stark, consisting of a bed, blanket, and night bucket. In contrast, first-grade inmates wore comfortable blue uniforms and received spring mattresses and other accoutrements. They could write and receive letters on a daily basis and had extended library and bedtime hours and better food. These men had the privilege of serving as "monitors."

Theoretically, the mark system provided a "scientific-empirical measure" of each inmate's progress toward reform. The staff evaluated every inmate on a monthly basis in three areas: performance in school, at work, and general deportment. Three credits could be earned in each category. A monthly examination measured school achievement: students earning a score of seventy-five percent or higher received three marks; lower scores were penalized on a graduated basis. Performance at work was more subjective: inmates who worked hard received three credits; less diligent effort carried penalties. Compliance with institutional rules measured general deportment: three credits rewarded the absence of demerits; misbehavior was penalized. The path to release was

---

30. Brockway, *Fifty Years*, 212.

clear. Second grade inmates who earned six months of "nines" (three credits in each category) were promoted to the first grade. Six months of "nines" in the first grade earned the inmate the right to appear before the parole board. An obedient inmate could, then, earn release after just one year of confinement, irrespective of his minimum sentence.

Parole was the third and final stage in Brockway's Elmira system. The five managers sat as the parole board and considered a variety of factors in determining each inmate's suitability for early release: offense, offense history, institutional behavior, work record, academic progress, attitude, future plans, and most important, perceived threat of recidivism. Inmates appeared before the board to plead their case. Every inmate had to secure employment and find a place to live before parole could be officially granted. The final release criteria were clear: inmates who internalized the Protestant ethic and showed promise of working and obeying the law returned to the community; inmates who fought their keepers received an extended dose of the Elmira system.

Parole supervision extended the Elmira system and the new penology into the community. All parolees had to follow four rules designed to make certain that they became "good workers" and "good citizens." First, parolees had to remain with their employer for six months. Second, they submitted a monthly report, signed by the employer, stating

whether you have been constantly under pay during the month, and if not, why not, and how much money you have earned, and how much you have expended, or saved, together with a general statement of yourself and your surroundings.

Third, parolees could not quit or change their jobs. Finally, they were required to behave: "You shall, in all respects, conduct yourself with honesty, sobriety and decency; avoiding low or evil associations; and you shall abstain from intoxicating drinks."[31] Violation of one of these conditions subjected inmates to parole revocation and another trip to Elmira.[32]

Brockway was confident that the three-stage regimen of reform introduced in 1881 and 1882—diagnostic interviews, in-house treatments, and parole—

31. New York State, Senate Documents (1881), vol. 1, no. 21, New York State Reformatory, *Fifth AR* (1880), 42.

32. The rules governing parole revocations were complicated. Parolees who lost their positions through misfortune and voluntarily returned were received as "guests" and released as soon as a new placement was located. Parolees who "through fault, but without crime" lost their positions and voluntarily returned were required to serve at least three months in the second grade and six months in the first grade. Parolees convicted of a new crime, a "gross impropriety," or "on the way to commit crimes" served six months in the second grade and six months in the first. These requirements were modified at the keepers' discretion. Ibid., 39.

was a complete success. He announced that eighty-one percent of the inmates leaving Elmira in 1882 had "become with reasonable certainty and permanence self-supporting and law-abiding citizens."[33] The managers declared that "eighty-four percent of persons discharged from this institution have been reformed in the broadest sense of the word."[34] Elmira's keepers believed they had discovered the elixir for deviance and disorder and the solution to New York's crisis in crime and corrections.

However, there was a darker side to the Elmira system. The rhetoric of Elmira's keepers was kindly and benevolent. But the Elmira Reformatory, much like correctional institutions examined by Foucault—the French juvenile reformatory at Mettray, England's Panopticon Prison, and New York's Auburn Prison—was designed to build "machine-men, but also proletarians." The new penology introduced a new calculus of coercion which managed the souls of men by regulating each inmate's dress, speech, posture, thought, and action. The Elmira boys were exposed to a "world of details" aimed at transforming them into "meticulously subordinated cogs of a machine." This "collective coercion of bodies" changed the form but not the aims of state control.[35] Repression, not reform, was the central goal of New York's "college on the hill."

Public Relations and the Marketing of Prison Science, 1883–1899

The period from 1883 to 1899 was Elmira's "golden age of reform." During this sixteen-year span, Brockway introduced a number of experiments aimed at perfecting the Elmira system. But more important, he launched a public relations and marketing campaign aimed at selling the new penology. Elmira's effort to sound the trumpet of reform was marvelously successful. By the turn of the century, the Elmira Reformatory was the most important penal institution in the United States, Zebulon Brockway was the most respected penolo-

33. New York State, Senate Documents (1883), vol. 1, no. 8, New York State Reformatory, *Seventh AR* (1882), 16. While Brockway never hesitated to state that a high percentage of Elmira's inmates were saved, he did not approve of empirical surveys which contacted inmates to measure recidivism. He said that these contacts were "personal intrusions." My guess, based on the findings presented in chapter 2, is that he did not want potential critics to have uncensored contact with inmates.

34. New York State, Senate Documents (1882), vol. 3, no. 26, New York State Reformatory, *Sixth AR* (1881), 3. For a positive assessment of Elmira from an inmate's perspective, see Convict #6627, "Sentence as a Motive."

35. Foucault, *Discipline and Punish*, 242, 141, 169.

gist in the world, and national and international criminal justice systems were revising their aims and methods to embrace prison science.

Innovations in academic and vocational education were the centerpiece of Brockway's attempt to perfect the Elmira system. A summer school was started in 1882. A class in Practical Morality and an Experimental School of Industrial Arts opened in 1883. This school combined fine arts (e.g. painting, music) with mechanical arts (e.g. carpentry, bricklaying) to find an "immediate ground on which the lily fingers of intellect join with the horny hand of labor in bringing forth works, valuable both for use and beauty."[36] An inmate newspaper, *The Summary*, started in 1884.[37] The Industrial Arts School expanded in 1886. Elmira's inmates received instruction in carpentry, bricklaying, plastering, stone-cutting, blacksmithing, and even fresco painting. Elmira offered twenty-two trades in 1888, twenty-six in 1890, and thirty-six in 1896. Brockway maintained that the "graduates" of the "college on the hill" received instruction comparable to the best schools.[38]

Many penologists hailed an elaborate military system introduced in 1888 as a major breakthrough. Brockway was confronted with a crisis when legislators yielded to union and business interests and prohibited inmate labor. On the suggestion of an inmate, Brockway started a military system. The inmates were dressed in uniforms, assigned ranks, and divided into companies. A former military officer coordinated the men. The inmate-soldiers marched for five to eight hours each day under Upton's military discipline, the same system followed by West Point cadets. A garrison parade took place each day, complete with a military band and wooden guns. The managers declared that this "habituates the men to prompt and implicit obedience, deference to the their superiors, to the habit of command and to loyalty."[39]

36. New York State, Senate Documents (1883), vol. 1, no. 8, New York State Reformatory, *Seventh AR* (1882), 38; (1884), vol. 2, no. 15, *Eighth AR*, (1883), 44; Gehring, "Zebulon Brockway of Elmira"; Richards, "Manual Training."

37. New York State, Senate Documents (1885), vol. 4, no. 13, New York State Reformatory, *Ninth AR* (1884), 10–11.

38. New York State, Senate Documents (1887), vol. 2, no. 18, New York State Reformatory, *Tenth AR*, (1886), 52. This report is incorrectly labeled; it is Elmira's eleventh annual report. Warner, "Education as a Factor in Prison Reform," provides a glowing assessment of this program. Briggs, *Industrial Training in Reformatory Institutions*, explains how industrial training was applied at the Western House of Refuge.

39. New York State, Assembly Documents (1891), vol. 7, no. 33, New York State Reformatory, *Fifteenth AR* (1890), 7. *Infantry Tactics in Use at the N.Y.S. Reformatory Adapted from Upton's United States Army Tactics* describes the military system. B. Smith, "Military Training," links military drill to themes developed by Foucault in *Discipline and Punish*. See also Brockway, *Fifty Years*, 290–93 and Winter, *New York State Reformatory*, 145–48.

A wage compensation system began in 1889. Inmates earned their release by working their way through the classification system. The new system made one significant change: inmates received wages for labor, education, and general deportment instead of marks; and they were charged for room, board, and visits to the physician, and fined for misbehavior. The accumulation of money, rather than abstract credits, determined release date eligibility. The wage system was to prepare inmates for life in the real world. "The getting something for nothing ... contributes to the habit we are trying to correct, the very same habit, perhaps, that led the prisoner to crime," explained the managers.[40]

Elmira was also at the forefront of American biogenic research. Brockway and Elmira's physician, Hamilton Wey, were especially impressed with Cesare Lombroso's acclaimed study, *The Criminal Man* (1876). They shared Lombroso's belief that some criminals were biological throwbacks who could be identified by atavistic features (e.g. large jaws, high cheekbones, long arms, big ears).[41] Wey believed that "in physiognomy many of the men presented features indicative of criminal tendencies."[42] With Brockway's blessing, Wey started a Physical Culture class in 1886. Inmates who exhibited "stigmata" were exposed to baths, massages, calisthenics, and special diets. The Physical Culture class flourished: a gymnasium opened in 1890; a Manual Training class started in 1895 to "transform defective centers of the brain"; a nutritionist adjusted caloric intake.[43]

Elmira was one of the first correctional institutions in the United States to use recreational programs as a form of treatment. Baseball, basketball, track and field, and football became integral components of the daily regimen by the late 1880s. Brockway believed that physical activity strengthened bodies, sharpened minds, and taught the Elmira boys the benefits of cooperation, communication, and group coordination. A good team player would be an effective factory worker or farm hand; inmates who drank, smoked, or in other ways abused their minds and bodies learned that they would not be at their best on

40. New York State, Assembly Documents (1889), vol. 6, no. 32, New York State Reformatory, *Thirteenth AR* (1888), 26.

41. Brockway discussed the biological roots of crime in *Fifty Years*, 214–17. Lombroso was not a hard-core biological determinist. Later editions of his work gave increasing thought to environmental factors, especially Gina Lombroso-Ferrero's *Criminal Man* (1911), published two years after his death.

42. New York State, Senate Documents (1887), vol. 2, no. 18, New York State Reformatory, *Tenth AR* (1886), 61.

43. New York State, Assembly Documents (1896), vol. 5, no. 25, New York State Reformatory, *Twentieth AR* (1895), 14–15, 63–64; Richards, "Manual Training"; "To Measure Criminals," New York *Times*, 20 May 1896, 5.

the playing field of Elmira or on the playing field of life. By 1900, correctional institutions across the United States were using recreational programs to mold the "muscles and morals" of their charges.[44]

But the popularity and proliferation of the Elmira system over the last two decades of the nineteenth century was not based solely on the merits of these new programs, nor was it based on chance. In 1882 Brockway launched a carefully crafted public relations and marketing campaign to sell the new penology. "It had become evident that, as a city set upon a hill cannot be hid, our reformatory on the hillside at Elmira must henceforth be opened to American curiosity and public observation," explained Brockway.[45] Brockway's "policy of publicity" consisted of two key components: first, the systematic distribution of carefully written annual reports which dramatized Elmira's successes; second, opening the reformatory to visitors.

The distribution of the institution's annual reports was the centerpiece of the public relations campaign. "Pursuing the policy of publicity," explained Brockway, "the annual reports to the legislature were made more explanatory."[46] These reports were "extended" and "elaborated" and "illustrated." They described each component of the Elmira system in detail. Case histories were included to buttress Brockway's claim that prison science saved 80 to 90 percent of Elmira's "graduates." Three thousand copies of the annual report rolled off of Elmira's press each year. These reports went mailed to governors, legislators, judges, attorneys, libraries, and the keepers of penal institutions across the country and around the world.[47]

Brockway welcomed visitors and, in many instances, guided tours personally. "Visitors who came from curiosity were freely admitted and conducted over the entire establishment, and given painstaking explanations; and many

44. Cavallo, *Muscles and Morals*, demonstrates that recreation was used as a method of socialization and social control: "In short, control the muscles and you control the mind and conscience" (p. 5). Elmira's recreational programs also reflected these motives.

45. Brockway, *Fifty Years*, 236. The details of Elmira's public relations and marketing campaign are on pp. 236–41. Public relations and marketing are distinct, but at times overlapping, fields. This analysis is using the terms loosely in an attempt to suggest that they were essential components in proliferation of the new penology. Lovelock and Weinberg, *Marketing for Public and Nonprofit Managers*, provides a concise overview of these fields.

46. Brockway, *Fifty Years*, 236.

47. Elmira's report for 1892 was particularly thorough. This 277-page document gave detailed descriptions of every aspect of the institution's aims, organization, and programs. It also included the case histories of over a hundred inmates, including profile drawings, and assured readers that 79 percent achieved "probable reformation." New York State, Assembly Documents (1893), vol. 5, no. 25, New York State Reformatory, *Seventeenth AR* (1892), 172.

thousands of such visitors availed themselves of the privilege," noted the superintendent.[48] America's most important penologists traveled to New York to study the Elmira system. Prison inspectors from England, France, Italy, Canada, Germany, Switzerland, Spain, and many other countries were sent by their governments to learn how the new penology could be adapted to tame and train their criminal classes.

Brockway's public relations and marketing campaign was a complete success. P. Dorado, a visitor from Spain, declared that Elmira was a "great college rather than a prison and a penal institution" and that "hardly a defect is noted in the manner of governing the same." Frederick Hill, one of England's most respected penal authorities, reported, "Especially I have been pleased with the information about the Elmira Reformatory." Franklin Sanborn described Brockway as a "master of reformatory discipline" and a "man of genius in his profession." The Prison Association of New York did not exaggerate when it stated that "all the world is looking to this reformatory prison for a solution of some of the most involved problems of criminal treatment."[49]

Ohio reformers were so impressed by reports from Elmira that they boarded a train—sixty-five members of the state legislature, the state's lieutenant governor, prison officials, newspapermen—and traveled to New York to study the Elmira system. Their tour left them "highly pleased with everything connected with it."[50] When the Ohio Reformatory opened in 1896, there was one model to emulate: New York's "college on the hill."

Elmira's public relations and marketing campaign sparked a paradigmatic revolution which transformed America's approach to thinking about crime and treating criminals. First and foremost, Elmira's "miraculous success" led to the birth of America's third penal system and the invention of a new criminal class: the youthful offender. New adult reformatories for males opened in Michigan (1877), Massachusetts (1884), Pennsylvania (1889), Minnesota (1889), Colorado (1890), Illinois (1891), Kansas (1895), Ohio (1896), Indiana (1897), and

48. Brockway, *Fifty Years*, 237.

49. Dorado, "Elmira Reformatory," 9, 13; Hill, quoted in Prison Association of New York, *Thirty-ninth AR* (1884), 24; Sanborn, "Development of Reformatory Discipline," 1, 17; Prison Association of New York, *Thirty-ninth AR* (1884), 26. Elmira's admirers included "The Reform of Criminals," New York *Times*, 20 December 1890, 9; Langmuir, *Prison and Reformatory System of Ontario*, 164–68; Montanye, "State Reformatory at Elmira"; Barrows, "Introduction," 7–15; Warner, "A Study of Prison Management"; "English Opinion of Elmira"; Altgeld, *Our Penal Machinery*, 72; E. Wines, *State of Prisons*, 96, 102; Boies, *Science of Penology*, 133–92; F. Wines, *Punishment and Reformation*, 199–243.

50. "The Elmira Reformatory—Ohio Politicians Inspect It and Approve of the System," *New York Times*, 8 February 1891, 8.

Wisconsin (1899). These institutions provided a place of incarceration for thousands of "intermediate offenders" who were too old to be sent to juvenile reformatories but whose offenses and offense histories did not merit incarceration in maximum security adult prisons. The rise of the adult reformatory movement resulted in a wider, deeper, stronger, more sophisticated American network of social control.

The diffusion of prison science radically transformed the aims and structure of adult prisons and juvenile reformatories. By 1899, dozens of correctional institutions across the country had embraced Elmira's penal philosophy (rehabilitation, treatment, and reform), theory of crime causation (multifactor positivism), diagnostic methods (medical model, prison science), correctional vocabulary ("hospital," "patients," "college," "students"), and treatment programs (academic and vocational education, labor, religion, indeterminate sentencing, mark and classification system, military drill, recreation, biogenic treatments, and parole). These innovations enhanced the deteriorating image of prisons and juvenile reformatories and legitimized the claim that these institutions, much like Elmira, were making an important contribution to America's search for social order.

The spread of the new penology also laid the foundation for the birth of scientific criminology and the professionalization of penology. Late nineteenth-century superintendents were no longer viewed as glorified gatekeepers, merely concerned with maintaining order (preventing escapes, violence, riots). The keepers of "correctional hospitals," following Brockway's lead, assured the public that they were employing science, knowledge, and reason to diagnose and humanely treat their "patients'" deviance. The emergence of positivistic criminology and the medical model enhanced the prestige and power of superintendents and their staffs; it opened a new scientific discourse in the field of criminal justice; it sanitized human and social engineering.

The proliferation of indeterminate sentencing and parole extended prison science and the power and authority of correctional officals into the community. By 1900, every adult reformatory in the United States, with the exception of the Michigan Reformatory, had indeterminate sentencing and parole; twenty states had parole laws for state prison, penitentiary, or reformatory inmates.[51] Indeterminate sentencing resulted in longer sentences being handed out by courts; the introduction of parole extended surveillance and the disciplinary aims of the Elmira system into the community.

51. Lindsey, "Historical Sketch," 38–40, 69.

Zebulon Brockway: The Man and His Mission

An understanding of late nineteenth-century American corrections would be incomplete without examining the period's key actor: Zebulon Brockway. Brockway co-authored the Declaration of Principles, developed the Elmira system, fathered the adult reformatory movement, and introduced some of American penology's most significant and long-lasting reforms. Who was Zebulon Brockway? How and why did he become involved in penology? What were the ideological, philosophical, and cultural roots of his approach to explaining crime and treating criminals?[52]

Brockway's approach to thinking about crime reflected his early upbringing and environment. He was born on 28 April 1827 in Lyme, Connecticut, one of seven children born to Caroline and Zebulon Brockway, a successful merchant who taught his children to value hard work and public service. The elder Brockway served his community as a magistrate, county commissioner, state legislator, and, perhaps portending the future, as a prison inspector. The Bible was Caroline's "book of books" and the Protestant ethic was the moral foundation of the Brockway household. Traditional New England values—honesty, integrity, hard work, frugality, piety, sobriety, discipline, self-control, respect for authority and law—were drilled into the Brockway children. "My parents," reflected the superintendent, "maintained the noblest standard." Zebulon Brockway was raised to be a Christian gentleman.[53]

Young Zebulon did not always abide by the teachings of his parents. He was dismissed from school for "open insubordination" and truancy, an event which resulted in a flogging from his father. He kept late hours and participated in "feasts and frolicking." He once became involved in a game of poker and lost his own money as well as 40 dollars belonging to his employer. Fortunately, the winner was sympathetic and gave the money back; otherwise, reflected Brockway, his penal career might have had a less auspicious start. This brush with the crime was a pivotal event. Brockway eschewed his wild lifestyle and

---

52. Garland, *Punishment and Modern Society*, 209–11, provides a theoretical discussion of the dialectical linkage between social structure, "penal culture," and the background and training of criminal justice practitioners, such as Brockway.

53. Brockway, *Fifty Years*, 9. Brockway's early years are described on pp. 3–22 of his autobiography. Biographical portraits include Sellin, "Zebulon Reed Brockway"; Hawes, *Children in Urban Society*, 146–57; Pisciotta, "Zebulon Reed Brockway"; "Z. R. Brockway Dies at 93," New York *Times*, 22 October 1920, 15. Unfortunately, Brockway's personal papers have been lost. These records were on deposit at the Russell Sage Foundation but were moved with no record of their final disposition. The linkage between religion and social reform has been considered in other works, including W. Lewis, "Reformer as Conservative."

embraced the teachings of his parents. "That evening's experience ended forever for me all participation in games of chance with money staked."[54]

Brockway's career in penology began in 1848 when he left a job in a cheese shipping company to become a clerk at the Wethersfield Prison in Connecticut. Brockway gained valuable administrative experience in this position, keeping records and accounts, making purchases of supplies, and assisting in other managerial duties. Superintendent Elisha Johnson, and later Superintendent Leonard Willis, introduced him to the Auburn or "silent system" of penal reform.

Brockway's performance at Wethersfield was rewarded with a promotion to assistant superintendent of the Albany County Penitentiary in New York in 1851. Superintendent Amos Pilsbury was one of America's most respected penologists and one of the Auburn system's most ardent supporters. Brockway learned the "Pilsbury standard." High-profit industries, daily Bible reading, and strict discipline were the heart of the Albany Penitentiary. "The excellence of his discipline and the extraordinary financial results gave an impulse to the betterment of prisons throughout the country," said Brockway, reflecting fondly on his training.[55]

In 1853 Brockway became superintendent of the Municipal and County Almshouse in Albany, New York. Although he was only twenty-six years old, he was responsible for over a thousand men, women, and children who were committed for a variety of problems ranging from indigency to insanity. Brockway got a close look at the diversity of New York's "dangerous classes" while working in the almshouse. He left Albany to become the first superintendent of the Monroe County Penitentiary in Rochester, New York, in 1854. Brockway introduced the Auburn system and "Pilsbury standard" and was proud of the financial record of this institution.[56]

In 1861 Brockway left New York to become the first superintendent of the Detroit House of Correction. This assignment was instrumental in propelling him to the forefront of American corrections. Over the next eleven years, he introduced programs which took the form of a "rough-hewn model for the better perfected system afterward built at Elmira."[57] A profitable labor system, religious instruction, and educational programs were introduced. A "house of shelter" for women was opened in 1868. In 1869 he authored a bill—the "three

54. Brockway, *Fifty Years* , 21.
55. Ibid., 27; on his years at Wethersfield and at the Albany County Penitentiary, see pp. 23–50.
56. Ibid., 51–67.
57. Ibid., 81.

years law"—which provided indeterminate sentences and conditional release (i.e. an early form of parole) for some female offenders. Although the Michigan State Legislature passed the bill, the Michigan Supreme Court later nullified the act. Brockway's appointment to serve as one of the authors of the Declaration of Principles in 1870 reflected his emerging status as one of America's leading penologists.[58]

Brockway's experiences at Detroit were not wholly favorable. Disputes with Detroit's mayor and city council, the Michigan court decision terminating his indeterminate sentence law, several investigations of his management techniques, and family health problems sapped both his strength and interest in penology. Brockway decided to leave his calling. In December 1872 he accepted a position as vice president of the Michigan Car Company. An economic downturn prompted him to leave this position to become a partner in a furniture business. A subsequent economic downturn left Brockway on the verge of bankruptcy. In April 1876 he vacated his house, put his furniture in storage, and sent his wife and two daughters to live with relatives in Connecticut while he moved in with a friend in Michigan. "Thus at the age of fifty years I found myself out of employment; without the requisite capital for any suitable business venture; and with insufficient income for the support of my family."[59] The call from New York in May 1876 to serve as Elmira's first superintendent was more than a career change—it was salvation from financial and personal ruin.

Brockway came to New York with a clear vision of crime. His experiences led him to conclude that offenders were not cut from a single mold. Some criminals were free, rational, and hedonistic actors; a variety of forces determined the behavior of others: poverty, biological defects, laziness, liquor, pool halls, moral decay.[60] Brockway did not hold criminals in high regard. "It cannot too often be stated that prisoners are of inferior class and that our prison system is intended for treatment of defectives."[61] The typical offender was a menace: "They constitute a living, antisocial human mass, not easily resolved and brought into accord with the orderly life of a good community."[62]

58. Brockway's experiences at the Detroit House of Correction are recounted in *Fifty Years,* 68–150. Rafter, *Partial Justice,* 24–29, describes the significance of the "house of shelter" in more detail. McKelvey, *American Prisons,* 69–70 and 81–84, provides a favorable assessment of the Detroit institution.

59. Brockway, *Fifty Years,* 154–55.

60. Brockway's views on the etiology of crime are scattered throughout his writings: *Fifty Years,* passim; "The Ideal of a True Prison System"; "Prisoners and Their Reformation"; "Reformatory Prison Discipline"; "Crime"; "Abstract of Paper"; "Address."

61. Brockway, "American Reformatory Prison System," 463.

62. Brockway, "Reformatory System," 23.

Brockway's Elmira system was designed to "rehabilitate" salvageable offenders and protect the public from future transgressions. His ultimate aim was clear: "Each prisoner shall be trained and fitted for and introduced into his proper niche in the world's work and in the associated life of the community, there to be supervised and tested until he is completely established in self-sustained and orderly conduct."[63] Reformed criminals would embrace the Protestant ethic and act like "Christian citizens"—the same values that Brockway learned as a child.

Brockway's vision of crime and work at Elmira established him as the foremost penal authority in the United States, if not the world. Elected president of the National Prison Association in 1897, he became honorary president of the International Prison Congress in 1910. At a session of the 1910 American Prison Association Conference devoted to the Declaration of Principles, Amos Butler, president of the conference, described Brockway as the "Nestor of American Penology." R. W. McClaughry, warden of the United States Penitentiary at Leavenworth, described him as the "St. Paul of the new Movement." The Chief of Switzerland's Federal Bureau of Statistics described the Declaration as "a gospel over the whole world for those who were interested in penal law," adding that "if they wish to see a reformatory for men they should see Elmira." Frederick Wines summarized the sentiments of his peers:

Mr. Brockway is anything but visionary. He is a seer, a prophet. No man better understands human nature, and especially criminal human nature, than Mr. Brockway, or has adopted his methods more truly and conformed them more completely to the laws which govern the operation of human nature. Therein I find the secret of his great success.[64]

Conclusion

The impact of Zebulon Brockway and the Elmira Reformatory on the American criminal justice system was extraordinary. In the late 1860s and early 1870s, many penologists, politicians, and law-abiding upper- and middle-class citizens were convinced that the rising tide of crime and social disorder threatened the future survival of the nation—Armageddon was at hand. However, the implementation of prison science and the new penology at Elmira in the 1880s and 1890s offered new hope. Brockway's contemporaries believed that

63. Brockway, "An Absolute Indeterminate Sentence," 73.
64. Butler, "Introduction to an Address"; McClaughry, "Address," 169; Guillaume, "Address," 179, 181, 185.

he had discovered the final reform panacea and the key to America's crisis in crime and criminal justice.

Many criminal justice historians have echoed this positive theme, portraying the opening of Elmira and the diffusion of the new penology as one of the bright spots in the evolution of the American correctional system. My interpretation is decidedly less optimistic. The opening of Elmira, the development of the Elmira system, and the proliferation of the new penology were conservative "reforms" which legitimized the social control of the dangerous classes. Prison science and the medicalization of deviance buttressed existing economic, political, social, and class relations by attempting to instill the lumpenproletariat with traditional American values and to transform them into law-abiding, hardworking proletarians. Brockway launched the American criminal justice system on a false path to reform—a path which, unfortunately, we continue to follow to this day.

Chapter Two

Benevolent Repression:
The Reality of the Elmira System,
1876–1899

We know remarkably little about what actually went on inside Elmira during its "golden age of reform." This chapter extends our understanding of the new penology by examining the internal dynamics, problems, and practices of Elmira from 1876 to 1899. A number of questions are posed to contrast the rhetoric and the reality of America's new prison science: How did the Elmira system work in practice? Did scientific reform and the medical model build docile bodies and Christian gentlemen? How successful were the keepers of Elmira at balancing the conflicting aims of social control and social reform?

The 1893–1894 New York State Board of Charities investigation of Elmira provides a unique opportunity to address these questions. This inquiry—which includes thousands of pages of verbatim testimony on the institution's practices from the perspective of the keepers (Brockway, the managers, staff members), the Elmira boys (current and former inmates), and interested audiences (judges, parole officers, parents, and wives of inmates)—reveals a wide disparity between the promise and practice of the Elmira system.

The nation's model correctional institution was overcrowded, understaffed, and grossly mismanaged. Key treatment programs did not fulfill their stated goals and objectives. Violence, escapes, smuggling, theft, homosexuality, revolts, arson, and other forms of inmate resistance were serious problems. Inmates suffered extraordinarily harsh punishments—including severe whippings and months of solitary confinement in dark, cold dungeons—and deliberate psychological torture. Elmira was, quite simply, a brutal prison.

Rumblings of Discontent: The Roots of the 1893–1894 Investigation

The seeds of the 1893–1894 New York State Board of Charities investigation were planted when a former inmate, John Gilmore, took the rather unusual step of fighting his parole revocation in court. Gilmore testified that he was brutally beaten by Brockway and was afraid to return to Elmira. A series of articles in the Buffalo *News* featured letters from former inmates supporting Gilmore's charges of cruelty. The agitation created by Gilmore's trial and the Buffalo *News* articles did not escape the notice of *The World*, one of New York's sensational newspapers. Editor C. H. Jones attacked "Paddler Brockway" and encouraged the Board of Charities to look into the charges.[1]

The Board of Charities responded to pressure from the press and the public. Oscar Craig, president of the board, assumed the responsibility of serving as chairperson of the investigative committee. Dr. Steven Smith, a physician, and Edward H. Litchfield, an attorney, agreed to serve with Craig. In August 1893, Governor Roswell Flower officially endorsed the inquiry. Two general charges were specified. The first alleged "That the general superintendent, Z. R. Brockway, was guilty of unlawful, unjust, cruel, brutal, inhuman, degrading excessive and unusual punishment of inmates, frequently causing permanent injuries and disfigurements." The second was equally shocking:

That he was guilty of mismanagement, incompetency and neglect in his administration of the reformatory in the following particulars, among others, to wit: In the infliction of corporal punishment for unsatisfactory scholarship; in his particular method of using the inmate monitor system; in requiring the performance of unreasonable and excessive daily tasks in the shops; in allowing carelessness and neglect in the medical supervision of inmates; in countenancing brutality on the part of officers and keepers; and in various other charges which will not be repeated here.[2]

The severity of these charges, coupled with Elmira's vaunted status in the field of national and international penology, caused the commissioners to take

---

1. *The World* was owned by Joseph Pulitzer. News historian Mitchell Stephens concludes that this paper was sensational but was also known for "aggressive, intelligent news coverage" (*A History of News*, 208–9).

2. New York State Board of Charities, *Report and Proceedings*, vi.

extra care in planning their investigation. On 26 September 1893, commissioners Craig, Smith, and Litchfield discussed procedures with Brockway, Elmira's managers, and New York Deputy Attorney General Francis R. Gilbert. They agreed that the hearing would take the form of a military court martial, with Gilbert serving as the judge advocate. Attorneys John Staunchfield and T. F. Babcock would represent Brockway and the managers. The court was granted subpoena powers. All witnesses would be sworn and advised that their testimony was subject to charges of perjury. To protect the interests of the keepers, a list of witnesses would be provided at least three days prior to appearances. To protect the interests of current inmates, Brockway and the managers would be banned when they testified, but attorneys Staunchfield and Babcock would be present at all times. Auburn, Sing Sing, and Clinton inmates who testified on their Elmira experiences would not be returned unless they approved the transfer. Finally, a stenographer would record all testimony.[3]

The committee began to hear testimony on 7 October 1893; twenty-five days of hearings were held over the next five months. The commissioners spent twelve days at Elmira, two days at the Auburn Prison, two days at the Clinton State Prison, four days in Albany, and five days in New York City. Testimony came from inmates, former inmates, Brockway, the managers, Elmira's staff (including guards, monitors, work overseers, clerks, clergymen, medical staff), parents and relatives of inmates, volunteer parole officers, and judges. One thousand letters, most written by inmates, were received.[4] The committee collected 3,812 pages of material. The final report of the committee, released on 14 March 1894, was unequivocal; its findings were unanimously endorsed by the ten members of the New York State Board of Charities:

That the charges and the allegations against the general superintendent, Z.R. Brockway, of "cruel, brutal, excessive, degrading and unusual punishment of the inmates" are proven and most amply sustained by the evidence, and that he is guilty of the same."[5]

---

3. Ibid., 395, 413.

4. Eight hundred seventy-one letters were collected on 27 September 1893. The Elmira inmates were gathered in the chapel, with Brockway and the commissioners present. The superintendent informed the inmates of the purpose of the State Board of Charities inquiry. They were then given paper and sent back to their cells to comment on their treatment. These anonymous letters are included on pp. 2086–2438.

5. Ibid., xxxiii.

Benevolent Brutality: Punishment as "Treatment"

Much of the investigation focused on methods of punishment, which were rarely mentioned in Elmira's public relations campaign. Brockway maintained that his punishments had therapeutic value and were scientifically and professionally administered. The "spanking" of "patients" at "interviews," he explained, was only a last resort. Corporal punishments were "positive extraneous assistance" intended as "more direct appeal through bodily sensations." Spanking was "simple, altogether harmless, physical shock served to convince him [the "patient"] that a radical change in his personal behavior was indispensable and it perhaps made possible such a change by the incident molecular commotion in changing the channels for the flow of nervous energy." Corporal punishment was, quite simply, "harmless parental discipline."[6]

Reality was considerably different. The inmates had a clear choice: total submission or severe corporal punishment. Inmates who would not or could not conform to the rules experienced Elmira's "punishment ritual." The "patient" was escorted to an isolated bathroom in the southeast corner of the south wing of the south cell block—Bathroom #4—by two of Brockway's assistants. Following an "interview" (i.e. statement of charges, admonition, call for repentance), he received "physical treatment." Brockway paddled inmates with a leather strap which was twenty-two inches long, three inches wide, and nearly a quarter of an inch thick. The strap was attached to a fourteen-inch hickory handle. Although the paddle weighed over one pound when it was dry and was applied directly to the bare buttock, it was soaked in water before the punishment was administered. A rubber hose had been used in the past but this implement was abandoned, explained Brockway, "because of the added severity of the treatment."[7]

Inmate accounts of trips to the bathroom, which were given independently, are similar. In 1886, George Brown received two marks for failing to complete his work. His graphic description of Elmira's "punishment ritual" is revealing:

I knew I was in for a beating, and as I knew the terrible treatment received by others, I had a terror of what was coming. I refused to leave my cell. They stuck into the cell an iron rod with a two foot hook on the end, heated red hot, and poked me with it. I tried to defend myself with the bed, but my clothing took fire, and the iron burned my breast. My breast is deeply scarred to-day from the burn. They also had a shortened hot poker, which burned my hands. I have those scars, too. I finally surrendered, was handcuffed

6. Brockway, *Fifty Years*, 314, 356, 258.

7. New York State Board of Charities, *Report and Proceedings*, 184. Brockway made several appearances before the committee. His initial testimony (pp. 161–220) provides the most detailed overview of Elmira and the methods of discipline.

and taken to the bath-room. I asked Brockway if I had not been punished enough. He laughed at me, and said, "Oh, yes, we have just fixed you up a little, though." With that a hook was fastened into my shackles, and I was hoisted off the floor. I got a half dozen blows with the paddle right across the kidneys. The pain was so agonizing that I fainted. They revived me, and when I begged for mercy, Brockway struck me on the head with a strap, knocking me insensible. The next thing I knew I was lying on a cot in the dungeon, shackled to an iron bar. This was about 2 p.m. I stayed in the dungeon that night and the next day shackled, and received only bread and water. The following day I was again hoisted up and beaten, returned to the dungeon, and after one day's rest, beaten again. Then I was put in a cell in Murderer's Row, where I remained for twenty-one days on bread and water.[8]

Another inmate reported:

I have been treated in the most cruel manner and subjected to the most brutal punishment at the hands of Mr. Brockway. No later than the third of July last, I received a report for talking. I was taken down to the bath-room, better known among ourselves as Brockway's "slaughter house"; he stripped me to my skin and made me stand against the wall and beat me till the blood began to ooze from my waist with a raw hide about six inches wide. I turned in a dazed condition and begged for mercy. He then struck me several times over the head and face and told me, "If I turned around again he would knock my eye out," and remarked, "It is a pleasure for me to spank you fellows" ... But this is only a trifle to what I have seen the men getting at the hands of Brockway. I am here two years, have been in every grade, and know how the flogging is carried on.[9]

Harry Lablanche, a former Elmira inmate who was serving time at Clinton, worked outside of "Room #4" for several months and had an opportunity to see inmates as they left the interview.

He not alone paddles, but pounds, stamps, kicks, not alone the kidneys, but all over the head and body. To be cut, scarred, marred and beaten entirely out of shape is a frequent occurrence, and very often with a wide red mark across the face, resembling a birth mark. But the birth of the mark originated from Brockway's oiled strap.

Lablanche concluded, "I would by far rather prefer to remain here [Clinton Prison] my maximum five years than chance that place again."[10]

---

8. Ibid., 8–9.

9. Ibid., 2312.

10. Ibid., 95–96. Dozens of inmates reported receiving similar treatment in the bathroom: e.g., pp. 10, 40, 62–63, 81–82, 584–605, 605–22, 642, 829, 1384, 2072, 2093–94, 2137, 2193. Brockway's assistant in the bathroom, Irving Winnie, reported that some men cried during this treatment and that a number defecated and urinated. When asked why, he replied: "I can not explain why it occurred; my impression of it was the man done that sort of thing just to be disagreeable" (p. 1387). Other assistants offered similar accounts, pp. 322–48, 1463–67, 1568–1620. Inmates Christian Rhodes and Charles Cleare filed assault and battery charges against the superintendent and requested $225,000 in damages. A warrant for Brockway's arrest was issued but nothing came of the charges ("Order Issued for Brockway's Arrest," New York *Times* 20 September 1893, 8).

Respected staff members corroborated these inmate accounts. J. J. Bloomer, Elmira's Catholic chaplain for over a decade, was never present at the whippings; however, he described the condition of an inmate who came to him for protection. "I looked around and the boy pulled his shirt up from his pantaloons and exposed his whole back to me and I was astonished to see the condition presented." He continued, "there was everything there but a natural color; it was all black, purple, blue and discolored from his hips up to his shoulders."[11] William Searles, Auburn's Protestant chaplain, described his encounter with an inmate transferred from Elmira. Reverend Searles, noting that the inmate looked uncomfortable, asked if he was ill.

He turned about and dropped his pants and lifted his shirt, and his whole body was lacerated in the most fearful manner. ... They were festering; it was very offensive; I didn't get over it in a week. ... Across the top of his hips; the whole buttock; I should say twenty places abrasions of the skin festering; still bloody.[12]

The commissioners were troubled by other aspects of the punishment ritual, including Brockway's practice of punching inmates in the face and striking them with the club-like fourteen-inch handle of the whip. The superintendent explained that "quickening slaps" and "physical contact" were an essential component of professional-scientific reform:

Sometimes hit them a little butt on the wrist or on the shoulder or even under the jaw, not a severe one. I do not want to be misunderstood about this, because it is not a blow, an irritation, or passion; it is not a blow at random, it is an application, it is the making of physical contact between myself and the patient, as I might call him, that rouses his mind to active attention to that for which I wish to confer with him, and brings about the same result that would be had if I had, without this, sent him over under the window and applied a spanking.[13]

Brockway explained that quickening slaps were sometimes accompanied by an "explosion of voice" and an occasional profanity. "I have found the word damn exceedingly effective with certain classes of people occasionally (e.g. 'damn fool')." But he added, "I am not in the habit of using it."[14]

The commissioners did not share Brockway's views on the "therapeutic value" of physical contact. "The evidence shows that these blows are sometimes given with great severity, and that the convict is oftentimes greeted with them as he enters the bath-room, and before a word has been spoken to him by the

11. New York State Board of Charities, *Report and Proceedings*, 305.
12. Ibid., 672–73.
13. Ibid., 189.
14. Ibid., 191.

general superintendent."[15] Inmates who would not assume the "punishment position" received even harsher treatment:

That during the spanking the patient is required to stand with his fingers on the sill of the window above him and keep his head turned to the right away from the paddler, and that if for asking mercy, or from the anguish of the spanking, or any other cause, he turns his head, he is immediately struck a blow over the head or directly on the face by the general superintendent.[16]

Black eyes, bloody noses, and bruises frequently resulted. The investigators concluded that quickening slaps were unnecessary and cruel.

Inmates who were slow to disrobe, showed disrespect, or offered physical resistance in Room #4 received even harsher treatment. The commissioners described the dynamics of a "scrimmage" or "scramble":

In such cases, two or more powerful assistants seize the man and usually throw him to the marble floor, where he is kicked and pummeled into subjection, the blows being given on the face, in the head or in the stomach, or anywhere that can be reached. This is done in the general superintendent's presence and with his tacit approval, and is a regular practice and on instances a part of the punishment.[17]

Brockway's account of "scrimmages" confirmed the fact that many inmates did not appreciate the therapeutic value of his punishments, or his efforts to transform them into respectable citizens:

COMMISSIONER: When would the blow from the closed fist of the officer be given?
BROCKWAY: When the patient is on the floor, usually.
COMMISSIONER: There are two officers there?
BROCKWAY: Two officers are there always. ...
COMMISSIONER: What are the blows delivered in such cases?
BROCKWAY: Anywhere.
COMMISSIONER: In the face or on the head?
BROCKWAY: The face and head.
COMMISSIONER: The eye?
BROCKWAY: Anywhere.
COMMISSIONER: Nose and mouth?
BROCKWAY: Anywhere.
COMMISSIONER: Teeth might be knocked out?
BROCKWAY: It is possible a man's head might be injured seriously, but no case of that kind has ever occurred.[18]

15. Ibid., xxiii.
16. Ibid., xvii.
17. Ibid., xxi.
18. Ibid., 193.

Subdued inmates were, to the chagrin of the investigators, hung up: "A snap cord attached to the handcuffs and run through the bars of the window overhead, and then pulled upon his feet and the whipping renewed." The commissioners denounced hanging as "brutal and vicious."[19]

Corporal punishment was not the only method of discipline. Recalcitrant inmates were placed in solitary confinement where they experienced, in the words of the superintendent, "temporary inconveniences, deprivations," and "complete seclusion for a short time with or without artificial restraints as seemed suited to each case."[20] The medical and psychological value of "rest cure cells," as Brockway described them, escaped the commissioners. They concluded that these cells were medieval dungeons:

They are frequently manacled by the hand to a sliding ring on a bar on the wall, or to a ring in the floor, both day and night, so that they can not stand straight; or manacled by the hands during the day, for at least eleven hours at a time, to the iron gate of such cell, in a standing position with the hands at the height of the head, and that disgusting conditions [defecation, urination] frequently follow this method of restraint; that said cells are sometimes made totally dark by the closing of certain shutters in the adjacent windows, which absolutely excluded all light; that such punishment is extremely severe to the health, particularly if continued for more than several days at a time.[21]

The punishment of Moses Aaron was particularly horrifying. Aaron was chained in "rest cure" for five months on a diet of bread and water. He was eventually declared insane and transferred to a mental institution. (This case is described in the next chapter.)

Brockway used these punishments to terrorize his charges and maintain institutional order. Personalized notes were delivered each day warning of the consequences of protracted misbehavior. These notices, which Brockway described as "silly pleasantries," were fear-inspiring. One inmate was warned, "When you get enough reports after this date to lose a dollar I will take you down to the bath-room and spank you. Remember the experience of May, and avoid them." Another note read:

Ide, are you either a lunatic or a jackass? If the former, you should be sent to an asylum; if the latter, you should be knocked on the head; and if you don't improve your record, whatever you may be, I will knock you on the other end.

19. Ibid., xv–xvi, xxii.

20. Brockway, *Fifty Years*, 356.

21. New York State Board of Charities, *Report and Proceedings*, xi. One witness reported that he had seen an inmate three or four times in rest cure and, "Well, he was shit all over just as a cow or a horse would be; he couldn't stoop" (p. 284).

An inmate who was not working hard enough in school was warned: "unless you pass your examinations now I will apply to you every month physical treatment." Another note cautioned, "We will find you in the wilderness; that is to say, in more modern language, we will have you in the bathroom if you don't get on without reports."[22]

Other notices were even more unsettling. When Leopold Roseman told Brockway that he could not handle military drill, he was told, "If you don't get along I will kill you and send you home to your mamma in a box." The superintendent's parting words to Cornelius Houlihan were not consoling: "We could not kill you here, but I guess they can do it at Auburn." Dennis Lynch, who was in solitary confinement on bread and water, asked for food. "Yes; I will give you something to eat," replied Brockway. "I will either kill you or send you out in a box." John Witzman summarized the sentiments of inmates who received these notes: "I shivered, and I didn't know what to do."[23]

Elmira's Conduct Ledgers provided a foundation to quantify these punishments. The commissioners discovered that Brockway administered 19,497 blows to 2,578 inmates between October 1888 and September 1893. Corporal punishment was increasing: 261 inmates were paddled in 1889, 480 in 1890, 535 in 1891, 621 in 1892, and 681 in 1893. During this period, inmates spent 7,609 days in rest cure cells. Brockway sent out 18,681 notices and warnings.[24]

However, the commissioners suspected that the Conduct Ledgers were inaccurate. "Your committee think from the evidence before them that the records do not show the full extent of the paddling nor of the number of blows struck." They charged the keepers with deliberately concealing punishments. Elmira's annual reports, they noted, made no mention of whippings, and when corporal punishment appeared, it was carefully couched in scientific and medical terms which were aimed at obfuscation and public relations. They concluded:

22. Ibid., 1950, 2276, 58.
23. Ibid., 452, 29, 63, 645. Other inmates were told that they would be "killed" or sent home in a "box" or "wooden overcoat," e.g., pp. 9, 30, 642, 2097, 2103, 2193, 2204. Brockway did not view the death of some inmates with sympathy. When James Hart, sergeant of the guards at Clinton Prison, informed Brockway that a transferred Elmira inmate had died, he replied: "That is a good thing; that is the best I have heard in a great while." Hart was taken by the superintendent's response: "I didn't think the man understood what I said to him, and I repeated it to him, and he says: 'Yes; that is a good thing for him and the public at large, he ought to have been dead long ago;'... as much as to say it was a good thing and a relief to the public at large and to his family and himself that he was dead" (p. 500).
24. Ibid., 1956–60.

Furthermore, said [annual] reports contain no allusion whatever to the corporal punishment visited upon prisoners, but it is evident that the intention was to keep the knowledge thereof secret as far as possible, for the evidence shows that they were inflicted solely in the presence of a chosen few officers; that the managers themselves never witnessed them, nor knew the extent and severity thereof, and that the records made of them upon the books of the institution [the Conduct Ledgers] were in cabalistic letters and signs, unintelligible to the general reader.[25]

The conclusion of the State Board of Charities was unequivocal: "The brutality practiced at the reformatory has no parallel in any modern penal institution in our country."[26]

Inside the Elmira System: The Hazards of Building Docile Bodies

The 1893–1894 investigation also reveals major inconsistencies between the theory and practice of other aspects of Elmira's new penology. Inmate accounts of their diagnostic interviews with Brockway suggest that the medical model did not guide the first stage in the Elmira system. The superintendent did ask each new arrival about his background, heredity, and environment, but the questioning was less than delicate. Harry Lablanche was asked: "Your wife is some whore; an old prostitute; a Bowery street walker, is she?" William Facey was asked "if my mother was a fast woman, if my brother was a thief, the same of myself, and if my sister [who was six years old] was a fast woman." The interviewing of Natty Hausbaum was more direct: "I know your mother is a bitch."[27]

Testimony reveals that Elmira's administrative structure was seriously flawed. In theory, the managers had the responsibility of making regulations and supervising the operation of the institution. In practice, they were uninvolved and out of touch. The president of the board of managers, Dr. William Wey, was so distantly removed that he was unaware of the nature and extent of

25. Ibid., xxiv. The commissioners were correct in charging that record keeping was deliberately vague. Instead of recording blows received, the superintendent recorded letters: "A" = one blow, "B" = two blows, etc. The *Conduct Ledgers* are even more incomprehensible following the introduction of the wage system. I could not decipher these records.

26. Ibid., xxxiii. Glenn, *Campaigns against Corporal Punishment*, demonstrates that pre–Civil War reformers launched a movement aimed at reducing corporal punishments for prisoners, sailors, women, and children. Apparently, this movement never reached Elmira.

27. New York State Board of Charities, *Report and Proceedings*, 95, 47, 458. The commissioners discovered only one copy of Elmira's rules, which was last updated in 1884 (p. xiii). Could even well-intentioned inmates follow rules which were not clearly prescribed and circulated?

corporal punishments. Wey never attended a punishment ritual and admitted, "I was not aware of the number of stripes."[28]

The board's laissez-faire management style left the superintendent in charge. Testimony reveals that Brockway made an egregious error in turning over considerable power to sixty inmate monitors who were, in essence, correctional officers.[29] The superintendent assured the committee that his monitors were "quite trustworthy" and had given "very satisfactory service." Brockway maintained, "I think the reports of these monitors are quite as intelligent, where they have the average amount of education, as the reports of the civil service officers."[30] He reminded the committee that inmate monitors were less costly than civilian guards.

The evidence does not support Brockway's assertions. The committee concluded that the decisions of monitors—which determined punishments, marks, promotions, classification ranks, and ultimately eligibility for release—were often arbitrary and unfair: "He [the inmate] is at the mercy of any fellow convict who happens to be an inmate officer, keeper or monitor, and who bears malice towards him." The inmates supported this finding. "There is a great injustice done to the men by the system of inmate monitors," explained one inmate. "Old grudges can be paid up and it can be fixed for your friends." "I have tried to live up to the rules of the institution, which is a very difficult thing to do, considering the means of marking by those inmate officers," said another. An inmate who served as a monitor explained the potential for abuse:

I have been an officer in this institution and as such held the highest rank that an inmate can reach (senior captain) and I know that any inmate who wishes can keep another inmate, against whom he may have a grudge, almost to the end of his maximum term.[31]

---

28. Ibid., 1896.
29. Ibid., 229. The New York State, Assembly Documents (1893), vol. 5, no. 25, *Seventeenth AR* (1892), 117, of Elmira gives a breakdown of the institutional staff. There were ninety-three staff members, including the inmate officers and clerks: ten general officers and office clerks, twenty-two mechanical and trade instructors, eleven police and disciplinary officers, thirty guards, and twenty domestic and supervisory staff. Half these staff members were paroled inmates. The inmate population peaked at 1,506; hence, the inmate-to-staff ratio was 16 to 1 with all staff included. Deducting paroled staff members, the ratio would be 32 to 1; deducting domestic staff, accounting for shifts, staff illness, and staff turnover would inflate this ratio. The point: it would not be unreasonable to conclude that the inmates ran Elmira.
30. New York State Board of Charities, *Report and Proceedings*, 234–35.
31. Ibid., xxxii, 2167, 2324, 2320. Most inmates had a great deal of difficulty avoiding demerits and fines. In 1882, thirty-nine percent of the inmates earned promotion to the first grade in six months; in 1892, only five percent were promoted in six months. The commissioners viewed the introduction of the monitor system as one of the reasons for the increased stringency of the system.

Overcrowding exacerbated these staffing, management, and organizational flaws. The New York State Board of Charities had, for a number of years, adamantly opposed efforts to increase Elmira's population, but legislators continued to add cells. The final report of the commissioners, once again, denounced this overcrowding.

> The general superintendent should be able to have an intimate personal acquaintance with each prisoner, such as a physician must have of his patient before he can cure him, which personal knowledge he can use for the attempted reformation of the convict.

They argued that "it is absolutely impossible for any human being to remember the personal characteristics of one thousand four hundred and nine (1409) where the population is continuously changing."[32]

Curiously, Brockway did not agree. He maintained that he was able to subject each incoming inmate to a "very careful and minute diagnosis" and that he could, indeed, monitor each inmate's progress toward reform. He insisted that the Elmira system was so efficient that he could handle even more inmates. "With the requisite additional appliances and influences, of course, it is as easy for me to control 1200 as five."[33] Brockway called for more cell space. The commissioners recommended a population cap at one thousand inmates; six hundred would be preferable.

Overcrowding contributed to other problems, including "evil" homosexual activity. "The licentiousness shown to have existed in the reformatory at Elmira, and for which the system of 'doubling up' is largely responsible, is so vile as to be almost incredible of belief," reported the investigators.[34] Homosexuality was a major concern for Brockway and his staff. J. Sherman did not know what the words "sodomy" and "buggery" meant, but did acknowledge that he had been caught in a rather compromising position with a "colored boy ... pulling my privates." Peter Le Fleur, when asked whether he was aware of cases of sexual misconduct, replied: "Yes; I seen a great deal of it. ... Yes; this man I roomed next to I chalked him in myself two years ago for having connection with his room-mate." Other testimony revealed that licentious behavior frequently occurred. John McDonald testified that in one instance, "I saw the boy with his pants down; I couldn't say whether he was done or whether he was going to commence." One of the participants nonchalantly informed McDonald, "Go on, don't mind me at all."[35]

---

32. Ibid., xxxv.
33. Ibid., 187, 1940.
34. Ibid., xxxix. Brockway kept a chart of "N.D." cases in his office. "N.D." designated "no double bunking" for inmates suspected of homosexual tendencies.
35. Ibid., 469, 1965, 1978.

The discovery of a "homosexuality ring" was even more unsettling. In 1893, approximately seventy inmates were charged with sex offenses and brought before the institution's court. Forty-eight confessed; sixteen denied guilt but were convicted; the remainder were acquitted. The commissioners were shocked to learn that Brockway's trusted inmate officers were heavily involved in the sex ring. Monitors extorted sex from inmates in exchange for marks which would lead to a promotion and earlier release. "A new boy has to submit if he wants to get along," explained one inmate. "It was an every day occurrence, if he is a good-looking boy he has got to submit to an officer's [sic]." Another inmate explained: "The boys will submit to almost anything before they will get paddled. Therefore, the boys will submit to sodomy and crime against nature; that is an every day occurrence here."[36]

The investigation of homosexuality exposed other serious problems, including a lack of justice in the institution's court and an abusive transfer policy. The court—which consisted of two civilian officers, one paroled monitor, and one clerk (a former inmate)—showed little regard for facts. Inmates accused of homosexuality and other offenses could not confront their accusers, there was no record of the proceedings, and the court's final decision was conveyed to the superintendent orally. The court's conviction rate was high, and the superintendent exercised absolute authority in transferring "guilty" offenders to Auburn or Sing Sing. Transferred inmates served their maximum sentence unless Elmira requested their return. (Of the 608 inmates transferred to adult prisons between 1888 and 1893, only one returned to Elmira).[37] The commissioners denounced the court, the arbitrary transfer policy, and the extension of inmate sentences:

Thus the beneficent purpose of the indeterminate sentence law is frustrated, the young culprit is thrown into that very association of hardened criminals from which it was the purpose of the law to preserve him, and the penalty visited upon him is increased to several times that which the trial court in its wisdom and mercy would have inflicted; and all this autocratic-power is wielded by one man, the general superintendent, whose bare recommendation is at once carried out by his trusting and confiding board of managers.[38]

36. Ibid., 1835, 1978, 2124.
37. Ibid., xxxi. Governor Grover Cleveland denounced Elmira's transfer policy in 1884. He believed that transferring inmates to prison for minor misbehavior was unjust and led to longer sentences. The legislature did not support his recommendation to terminate transfer powers. Lincoln, *State of New York Messages from the Governors*, 7:955–56.
38. New York State Board of Charities, *Report and Proceedings*, xxxi.

Given Elmira's pioneering role in introducing the "medical model" into American corrections, it is ironic that basic health care was lacking. The institution's physician, Dr. Hamilton Wey, visited from 8:00 A.M. to noon and then returned to his private office. When Dr. Wey was absent, a hospital attendant (one of the inmates) handled emergencies. "The evidence shows that there is often occasion for the immediate presence of a trained physician both by day and night," concluded the committee.[39] Other aspects of medical care were deficient. Inmates were not examined when they arrived, or before or after corporal punishment. Dr. Wey did not seem to attend to other health matters, including the inspection of food, which was, in one inmate's words, "not good enough for a dog."[40] The commissioners failed to grasp the logic behind Elmira's "wage system," which required inmates to pay for visits to the physician and dentist. Hiring Dr. Hamilton Wey, the son of Dr. William Wey, president of the board of managers, to serve as physician smacked of nepotism.[41]

The commissioners were troubled by Hamilton Wey's use of "infibulation" to deal with masturbators. In this procedure, a ring was place through the foreskin of the perpetrator's penis, thereby preventing the dreaded practice. Inmate Herman Miller described the process:

They laid me out on a table and chloroformed me. I did not know what they intended to do. When I came out from the influence of the chloroform, I found a ring over the head of my penis. It was very painful to me. Dr. Wey told me that the superintendent had ordered the rings placed upon my penis, and that they would have to stay till he ordered them off. ... The scars are still on my penis where the rings were inserted.[42]

Dr. Wey assured the commissioners that this was an accepted medical procedure. Attorney Staunchfield explained, "This isn't discipline; this is surgical treatment to prevent masturbation." However, the testimony of Auburn's physician, Conant Sawyer, swayed the commissioners. Dr. Sawyer had never heard of this procedure; furthermore, he considered it inhumane. The commissioners' assessment was clear: that "the general medical supervision of the re-

39. Ibid., xii.

40. Ibid., 2094. Many inmates complained about the institution's food. One inmate summarized these feelings when he said, "I don't think a poor man would give it to his dog" (p. 2382). Another said, "There ain't a States prison, penitentiary or workhouse in this State that gives such bad eating" (p. 2324). Another reported that the "hash we get is not fit for [a] dog and soup we get is not fit for a pig" (p. 2102).

41. Ibid., xii.

42. Ibid., 54. New York State Reformatory, *Inmate Biographical Ledger*, Case History #4574. Dr. Wey describes this procedure on pp. 1807–8.

formatory is inadequately provided for, and that the appointment as physician of a relative of a member of the board of managers should not be tolerated."[43]

Religious instruction degenerated into crass proselytization. Although the institution's Jewish chaplain, Adolph Radin, had no complaints about his treatment, the Catholic chaplain, Father J. J. Bloomer, was clearly annoyed with the administration. Father Bloomer's requests to hold Sunday services were repeatedly denied. Given the history of religious conflict between Protestants and Catholics, as well as efforts by Protestants managers and superintendents to exclude Catholic priests at other New York penal institutions (especially the New York House of Refuge), it is understandable that Father Bloomer was suspicious. "I consider [it] an improper thing, compelling Catholic inmates to attend Protestant service on Sunday," complained Bloomer. "I have time and again expressed my sentiments against that practice."[44]

Inmates resisted the labor system and efforts to instill them with the habits of industry. The foundry foreman maintained that the work was not hard, but many inmates disagreed. "I have seen men in the foundry ... crying because they could not do their tasks," reported one officer. The Elmira boys resorted to extreme measures to avoid the shops: one inmate swallowed acid, another falsely confessed to being a masturbator, another jumped off the third tier when he heard that he would be punished for not completing a task. "I have seen men pour molten iron in their shoes in order to get out of there [the foundry] for a few weeks," reported one inmate.[45] Inmates detested Brockway's highly acclaimed wage system (introduced in 1889 as an innovative reform). One inmate explained that he earned 45 cents per day but was required to pay 32 cents for room and board. "Now if a man gets fined sixty cents what is he to going to do? ... It does not take long before he gets enough reports to put him in a red suit."[46]

The third key element in the Elmira system, indeterminate sentencing and parole, was also seriously flawed. William Wey, president of the managers, described the aims of Elmira's highly touted experiment in community corrections. In theory, inmates earned their release by accumulating marks and working their way through the classification system. The managers, sitting as

43. New York State Board of Charities, *Report and Proceedings*, 264, 769, xxxiv.

44. Ibid., 303. In 1892 the legislature passed a law mandating religious freedom in all prisons and reformatories, "An Act to Provide ... Freedom of Religious Worship." Father Bloomer obviously did not feel that Elmira was complying.

45. Ibid., 46, 453, 1293, 9–10, 96; for other inmate accounts on work, see pp. 29, 41, 2090, 2124, 2181.

46. Ibid., 2305.

a parole board, met four times each year to consider cases. The board interviewed each inmate and reviewed his record to give "an account of the man's name, age, place and time of conviction, his offense, period in the reformatory, his grade, his position in the school, his maximum under the old law and so on." These records, Wey explained, are examined "quite rapidly but thoroughly."[47]

However, further questioning revealed that the theory of parole decision-making bore little resemblance to practice. At their four annual meetings the managers heard, in addition to all prospective parolees, the cases of "bummers" and "malcontents." Two hundred cases came up at the board's last meeting. The managers spent an average of one minute forty-eight seconds on each inmate, hardly a thorough assessment of reform. The commissioners discovered that release decisions "are granted mainly, if not wholly, upon the recommendation of the general superintendent, and that no proper investigation is made by the board of managers themselves."[48]

When confronted with this evidence, Wey conceded that release decisions were, indeed, essentially made by Brockway. "He has to do it; that is true," said Wey. "It arises from this very fact, under the superintendent's direction the whole history of the man, his progress in school work has been marked oat [sic] and made out." Wey reminded the board that "the superintendent is like a great schoolmaster, whose recommendations are regarded." The commissioners discovered that arbitrary decision-making by the parole board and the superintendent contributed to sentence disparity: "Some can be detained for but one year and others for five, ten or twenty years."[49]

Parole supervision was ineffective. The institution's "transfer officer" (parole officer), Hugh Brockway—the superintendent's brother—was grossly overworked. He transported inmates to and from courts, handled the monthly reports for six hundred parolees, and tracked down parole violators. Volunteers from the New York Prison Association, Buffalo Charity Organization Society, police chiefs, and an assortment of citizen-volunteers carried the burden of supervision. These amateur, part-time "parole officers" received no training and little guidance and served a policing rather than social work function. The commissioners were distressed to learn that revocation decisions were arbitrary, often based on insignificant technical violations. These practices contributed to sentence disparity, lengthened terms of incarceration, and fostered inmate hostility toward Elmira's keepers and the state.

47. Ibid., 1886, 1901.
48. Ibid., xxxii.
49. Ibid, 1901, xxxviii.

Many inmates denounced the parole revocation system. One inmate reported that he was returned for simply using tobacco. Another explained that he was laid off during a business slowdown, found a new job, and worked diligently, but was returned to Elmira for not reporting a change in employment. Yet another parolee was arrested for burglary, tried, and found innocent; he was revoked on "suspicion of breaking the law." Peter Lefleur expressed the sentiments of many of his peers: "I was returned from parole without cause of any kind, and was returned without a word of explanation or interview of any kind." The commissioners shared his opinion: "The evidence further shows that men who are released on parole are frequently rearrested and reincarcerated in the reformatory for very frivolous and trivial reasons, and in a very arbitrary manner, with little or no opportunity afforded them for explanation or defense."[50]

The 1893–1894 investigation reveals that the Elmira system was particularly hard on minorities. "Colored boys" experienced a racist version of the new penology which was designed to prepare them to assume their "proper place" in the social and economic order: law-abiding, docile laborers in the lower echelons of the working class. "I would like to have a little manly principal shown to me if I am a black man," complained one inmate." Another succinctly summarized the sentiments of his peers:

Because a man is a negro he should not be treated worse than the rest. But that goes here for I am one of them. I don't get the same treatment a white boy gets in here. I will tell you here this is the worse [sic] plan the world ever knew."[51]

Elmira's staff members, reflecting broader societal prejudices, believed that black inmates were biologically, psychologically, and morally inferior and, as a result, less salvageable than their white counterparts. The institution's principal keeper, Irving Winnie, repeatedly referred to black inmates as "darkeys" in his testimony before the committee.[52] Entries made by Brockway under the "Condition on Admission" section of the Inmate Biographical Ledger indicate that he viewed "colored boys" as decidedly inferior. For example, William Jones was described as "Good health, low type, medium quality of colored race." Albert Thompson was "Low type. Good Enough of his race." Other inmates received less favorable assessments. Charles Williams was a "Medium type of mulatto. drooping thievish eyes, weak chin, puckering lips, extraordi-

---

50. Ibid., 1969, 2306, 2120, 1964, xxxii. For other questionable parole revocations, see pp. 2000–2001, 2051–52, 2081, 2306.
51. Ibid., 2438, 2168.
52. Ibid., 1380–81.

narily large hands and long fingers in one of his size." The superintendent went on to point out that he was "cunning—like rodents, smart enough, good enough." George Johnson was "Active but ignorant & illogical," an "ordinary type of Buckskin Darkey."[53]

Black inmates were not the only recipients of inferior care. Nineteenth-century nativism and xenophobia penetrated the walls of Elmira and guided the application of prison science. Brockway's diagnostic interviews and assessments of the "root cause(s)" of deviance were based upon ethnic stereotypes. Brockway described Edward Margretta as, "Good health - medium quality of Italian." John Nedes was a "medium type of Bohemian"; Rudolph Shoen, a "medium type of Hebrew."[54] The "Hebrew inmates" were particularly unhappy with their treatment at Elmira. David Morris resented being repeatedly referred to as a "damn Sheeny" by the officers. Max Reiss was distressed when an officer informed him that "I would be a dead Sheeny before I got out of here."[55]

Inmate resistance—escapes, theft, smuggling, rebellion, and violence—disrupted the "regimen of reform." Brockway admitted that fighting between inmates was "quite a common occurrence," and that over 370 inmate confrontations were recorded over the last five years. Constant vigilance was necessary because many inmates were armed and dangerous. "Hundreds of times; scores of times ... we discovered a weapon," reported former principal keeper Joseph Beach. Although Elmira's officers carried guns or clubs, these were not an absolute deterrent against inmate attack. "I have had a prisoner go for me with a knife," reported Beach, "when the revolver was cocked and held right on him."[56]

Inmate views of the Elmira system were not, however, uniformly negative. In fact, some inmates reported that they were quite fond of the superintendent. "I have looked upon Mr. Brockway as an honest, just and loving benefactor, no matter what he may have done to me it would have been for my own welfare," said one inmate. "I consider this institution the best penal institution in the world." Another employed a philosophical approach:

53. New York State Reformatory, *Inmate Biographical Ledger*, Case History #5174, 6000, 5537, 521.

54. Ibid., Case History #5132, 5155, 5141.

55. New York State Board of Charities, *Report and Proceedings of the State Board of Charities Relative to the Management of the State Reformatory at Elmira*, 1970, 1973.

56. Ibid., 1927–28, 340, 344.

Perhaps, I look at the matter in a different light than some of the other inmates. I feel that we have committed a crime, and can expect not to be treated as citizens. If we had all the delicacies of the season and were treated like lords in prison, why our prisons would be filled to overflowing capacity.

"I am sorry for Mr. Brockway," wrote yet another supporter,

for all the charges against him are as untrue as steel is cold. I have been here most five years and have ten, but I can't kick. ... Remember, Mr. Brockway has spent the best part of his life in the reformation of a lot of fools like myself."[57]

But many inmates recognized that the world's model reformatory was, quite simply, a prison in disguise. "The whole system is a sham," reported one inmate. "The treatment a man gets here is worse than Siberia," said another. "I have seen so much going on here that I am going crazy over it. This is a good place for murder." A number of inmates preferred a maximum security adult prison to Elmira; several asked the commissioners for assistance in securing a transfer.

The supt. can talk about such a good prison, but if he would draft me to any other prison in the United States I would be satisfied, as I can not get along here. ... I could have been sent to Sing Sing prison for two and a half years, but like a fool I came to this place.

Another expressed similar regrets: "If I had my choice again in court I'd say State's prison, or some other prison, and that is the opinion of many a man here." Another unequivocally stated, "I would rather do five years in Sing Sing than one in here."[58]

Some inmates were pessimistic about the outcome of the investigation. They cautioned the commissioners against blindly accepting the rhetoric of Elmira's carefully crafted public relations and marketing campaign—especially claims of benevolent reform. "I hope, most sincerely, you will not let Mr. Brockway pull wool over your eyes as he does over the board of managers," warned one inmate.[59] An inmate-poet summarized the sentiments of many Elmira boys:

Afraid to sign my name,
Elmira! Elmira! they break your nose

---

57. Ibid., 2258, 2297, 2382, 2393. Other positive assessments of Brockway or the institution can be found on pp. 1146, 1201, 1212, 1284, 1285, 2089, 2090, 2091, 2106, 2107, 2211.

58. Ibid., 2270, 2358, 2113, 2292, 2319–20, 2173. Other examples: 78–79, 2107, 2437.

59. Ibid., 2127. Other inmates shared this concern. One denounced writing letters as a "farce" and predicted that they would be opened by Elmira's administrators (p. 2091); another letter ended, "I suppose we will get punished for writing this" (p. 2189). Another warned the commissioners, "Don't let the old fellow pull the wool over your eyes as well as the public" (p. 2382).

And they give you red clothes.

At Elmira, Elmira, I'll never come here any more.[60]

Repackaging Punishment:
Public Relations and the Politics of Penology

The final report of the committee, which was unanimously endorsed by the ten members of the Board of Charities, called for sweeping changes at Elmira: replacing inmate-monitors with civilian guards; prohibiting the admission of recidivists; abolishing the institution's court; increasing the fairness of the mark and classification system; rewriting the indeterminate sentencing law to reduce sentence disparity; reducing excessive demands in the shops; improving health care and sanitation and appointing a new full-time physician; hiring a full-time chaplain and affording Catholic priests access to their flock; reforming the parole system; and most important, abolishing corporal punishment. Finally, a new reformatory was needed to eliminate overcrowding and its corresponding evils, particularly homosexuality.

The Board of Charities advised Governor Roswell Flower to fire Elmira's managers for neglect of duty. However, the commissioners did not call for Brockway's removal, as a number of historians have maintained.[61] Although the Board of Charities condemned Brockway's handling of the institution, their legal counsel advised them that his removal was beyond the purview of their authority.[62]

The handling of these recommendations had the potential to spark yet another paradigmatic revolution and redirect the aims, procedures, and character of the American criminal justice system far into the twentieth century. Acceptance of the commission's findings by Governor Flower, professional penologists, and the public would seriously damage Elmira's reputation, dampen enthusiasm for the new penology, and quite possibly short-circuit the proliferation of scientific reform and the adult reformatory movement. Rejection of the report, or at least discrediting its methods or key findings, would allow Elmira to maintain its position as the world's most important penal experiment. Brockway's reputation as the nation's foremost penologist and the personal honor of

---

60. Ibid., 2377.

61. Sellin's biographical account of Brockway makes this error. Sellin accepted Brockway's interpretation of the inquiry and concluded, "The investigation was apparently partisan in character, however, and Gov. Flower, acting upon the report of a special commission appointed by him refused to deprive Brockway of his post" ("Zebulon Reed Brockway," 61).

62. New York State Board of Charities, *Report and Proceedings*, xii.

the managers were also in jeopardy.[63] Given these stakes, it is not surprising that the keepers launched a concerted public relations and marketing campaign aimed at repackaging punishment and the reality of incarceration in Elmira.

Brockway spearheaded Elmira's counteroffensive and emerged as the key actor in the unfolding drama. The superintendent—who battled investigations in 1858, 1865, 1867, 1881, 1882, and 1887—remained undaunted by the charges leveled against him.[64] Close inspection of his testimony and subsequent rebuttals reveals that he did not deny the key accusations. Brockway admitted that he whipped inmates, punched them in the face, struck them with the club-like handle of his whip, chained them for months in rest cure cells on a diet of bread and water, used corporal punishment to extract confessions, and sent threatening notes to terrorize offenders into compliance. Inmates went to Auburn and Sing Sing solely to reduce overcrowding. He conceded that his trusted inmate-monitors were the backbone of Elmira's "sex ring" and that escapes and violence were, indeed, serious concerns.

Brockway offered a spirited and unwavering defense of his actions which was a continuation of the public relations and marketing campaign he had launched in 1882. Harsh methods were necessary because of the mental and moral deficiency of the inmates. "They are men without strength of character as a rule, creatures of instinct, unstable as water," he testified. "As a rule they have never known of healthful control, prompt obedience." Given this nature, "the habitual conduct of the man needs to be promptly arrested and new activities instituted." Brockway portrayed himself as the mayor of a "besieged town" who was administering Hobbesian "martial order" and "benevolent brutality" to maintain order. "As I stated in my original statement, I did not admit it, I affirmed it [corporal punishments and rest cure]; no admissions about it; it is sought to give the impression statements are drawn out of us; not at all; all I

63. The editors of the New York *Times* made this point in "The Elmira Reformatory," 11 April 1894, 5.

64. Brockway was investigated once at the Monroe County Penitentiary, twice at the Detroit House of Correction, and three times at Elmira on various charges prior to the 1893–1894 inquiry. These inquires provided good practice in dealing with investigators. Brockway discovered the value of public relations during the 1882 investigation and then launched his "policy of publicity" (*Fifty Years*, 232–41). Brockway's rhetorical techniques were basically the same in these earlier battles, see: New York State, Legislative Assembly Documents, *Report of the Joint Committee* (1881); New York State, Legislative Assembly Documents, Committee on State Prisons, *Report* (1882); Bookstaver, Blair, and Barnes, *Report of the Prison Labor Reform Commission* (1887). These investigations reinforce the findings of the 1893–1894 inquiry. I did not analyze them to avoid repetition.

have done is at your service."[65] Elmira was the last line of social defense against the dangerous classes. Brockway was a loyal public servant.

Brockway employed a variety of deceptive rhetorical techniques and called upon his status as a "professional penologist" to explain his approach to penology. He assured critics that the "treatment" of "patients" at the "reformatory hospital" was consistent with the emerging laws of scientific criminology.[66] Punishments might, he conceded, appear inhumane to the untrained amateur eye. Brockway explained that the "rest cure cell [solitary confinement on bread and water]," "positive extraneous assistance [whippings]," and "quickening slap [punches in the face]" were necessary components of the medical model: "It is to stimulate and regulate an instinctive mind and send him on in the course of improvement or reformation we seek to accomplish for him; I don't know as I can make myself plain to you."[67]

"Scientific whipping" even included an element of acting. "In the bathroom the superintendent is a very different man from when he is outside of it," said one inmate. "He seems to be unable to control himself, and acts more like an insane than a sane man."[68] Brockway explained that this "act" was carefully calculated to dramatize the ordeal and stimulate reform:

BROCKWAY: I do for the effect upon a man, often assume anger as I appear to a man. ...
COMMISSIONER: That is, in other words, you never allow a punishment to be inflicted when you are in passion.
BROCKWAY: I am not in a passion.
COMMISSIONER: Never?
BROCKWAY: Never.

The key to scientific whipping was the application of regular strokes. "You think you have such a complete control over your temper or passions that you can safely say that the last blow was no heavier than the first upon the occasion of that kind?" asked the commissioner. "Yes," responded Brockway. "The man who has any feeling spring up with the exercise of discipline should not exercise it at all."[69]

65. New York State Board of Charities, *Report and Proceedings*, 242, 243, 1943, 1917. Brockway's rhetoric supports Foucault's contention in *Discipline and Punish*, passim, that penal institutions were "cities of the wicked"—i.e., "punitive-plague cities."

66. Brockway was a master of the use of verbal misdirection. Professional language, explains JoAnne Brown, is used in occupations (e.g. law, medicine, teaching, psychology) to "define, organize and publicize their particular expertise and cultural authority" ("Professional Language," 35). On the power of language to persuade and deceive, see: Hayakawa and Hayakawa, *Language in Thought and Action*; Strong and Cook, *Persuasion*; Oliver, *History of Public Speaking*.

67. New York State Board of Charities, *Report and Proceedings*, 186.

68. Ibid., 2141.

69. Ibid, 199.

Brockway testified that his "patients" often thanked him after they had time to reflect upon their punishment. "They come to me at interview very often, the very next evening or the same week, and we have a pleasant, friendly and social chat about the matters constituting the purpose for which they come up." He cautioned the commissioners against being misled by the testimony of disgruntled inmates. "A prisoner usually over-estimates the treatment he receives; the largest possible impression with the smallest possible effort is the idea."[70]

Most importantly, Brockway maintained that scientific whipping resulted in no permanent injuries:

I will state that no blow has been inflicted upon the spinal cord; it is protected by the protuberance of the buttock; and allow me to add, in that direction, that *no injury serious or permanent* has ever been inflicted upon any man I have so treated, *no serious, permanent injury*; these little matters that I have described to you sometimes occur, but there has been no case in the institution of injury to the spine or kidneys (emphasis added).[71]

The managers—Dr. William Wey, M. H. Arnot, William Peters, Jason Rathbone, B. L. Swartwood—forcefully defended Brockway and escalated the public relations campaign. Wey testified, "Largely there is no foundation for those complaints."[72] The managers attributed the investigation to "ruthless press marauders," especially the editors of *The World*. Elmira's 1894 annual report was used as a forum to publicly denounce the investigation. This report assured Elmira's supporters that their confidence was not misplaced:

[Corporal punishment] neither tends to physical degradation, nor, as it has been administered at this Reformatory, has it, in any instance, contributed to a sense of moral degradation or hurtful self-deprecation. On the contrary, the records are replete with instances when a *trifling spanking* has initiated a course of improved conduct and better character growth, wonderfully like what is ordinarily termed moral regeneration (emphasis added).[73]

The managers even mounted a counteroffensive, calling on Governor Flower to appointment an "unbiased" investigative committee.[74]

70. Ibid., 200.

71. Ibid., 190. Glenn, *Campaigns against Corporal Punishment*, points out that a distinction between "moderate" and "abusive" punishment emerged between the 1820s and 1850s. Moderate punishment was administered by a controlled hand and left no permanent injury; abusive punishment was administered in passion and left observable marks on the body. Brockway's defense and public relations campaign was clearly aimed at demonstrating that he employed the "scientific-moderate version."

72. New York State Board of Charities, *Report and Proceedings*, 1903.

73. New York State, Assembly Documents (1894), vol. 14, no. 84, New York State Reformatory, *Eighteenth AR*, (1893), 117.

74. The memorial is printed in "Gov. Flower to Investigate," New York *Times*, 13 April 1894, 5.

Newspapers became embroiled in the controversy. The editors of *The World* and the Buffalo *News* denounced Elmira and called for the removal of Brockway and the managers. The New York *Times* defended the institution and echoed the managers' call for an "investigation of the investigators."[75] The New York *Times* charged that the 1893–1894 inquiry was the product of a one-man committee—Edward Litchfield—and that it was "far from conclusive."

Certainly the reputation of men like Superintendent Brockway and the managers of the Elmira Reformatory should not be left to the peril of such an investigation and report as that of Mr. Litchfield, when his principal allegations are so vehemently denied.[76]

Respected citizens came to Elmira's defense. Israel Jones, superintendent of the New York House of Refuge, denounced the "absurd finding of the committee." Thomas Beecher, a well-known Congregationalist minister, endorsed Brockway: "He has struck men, it is said, many blows. Of course he has. So has the surgeon, after fifty years of practice, made many ugly cuts and amputated many limbs. This caused suffering. ... I approve of it." Franklin Sanborn, one of the country's leading penologists, declared that the investigation was "one sided" and "wholly misleading." Sanborn pointed out that Elmira was a model institution and that Brockway "stands confessedly at the head of prison reformers in this country—perhaps the world."[77]

75. Articles appeared in the New York *Times*: "Cannot Order Reformatory Inquiry," 5 August 1893, 2; "To Investigate Elmira's Reformatory," 2 September 1893, 4; "The Elmira Investigation," 27 September 1893, 9; "Elmira Reformatory Abuses," 8 October 1893, 8; "Evidence of Their Own Eyes," 9 October 1893, 4; "Elmira Reformatory Investigation," 19 October 1893, 1; "Brockway and His Paddle," 1 November 1893, 6; "More Complaints of Prisoners," 2 November 1893, 6; "Stories of Abuse at Elmira," 11 November 1893, 8; "More about Brockway's Paddle," 12 November 1893, 5; "Coerced with Red-Hot Iron," 19 November 1893, 8; "Men Whom Brockway Paddled," 13 December 1893, 9; "More about Brockway's Paddle," 14 December 1893, 8; "The Elmira Investigation," 15 December 1893, 9; "Brockway Relieves [sic] in Spanking," 16 February 1894, 5.

76. [no title], New York *Times*, 30 March 1894, 4. Most of the investigation was, indeed, conducted by Edward Litchfield and Deputy Attorney General Gilbert. Oscar Craig became ill on 31 October 1893 and died on 2 January 1894. Dr. Smith left the country on 1 January 1893 to attend a medical conference in France and did not return until March 1894. However, Litchfield did not and could not manipulate the testimony of the inmates. The evidence against the keepers of Elmira was overwhelming.

77. "In Mr. Brockway's Defense," New York *Times*, 3 April 1894, 3; "In Defense of Mr. Brockway," New York *Times*, 10 April 1894, 1; "Brockway's Elmira System," New York *Times*, 26 September 1894, 3. Other articles attacked the Board of Charities and defended the keepers: "All Declared against Brockway," 3 April 1894, 9; "The Board of Charities Framed Brockway," 5 April 1894, 5; "Superintendent Brockway the Victim of Prejudgment," 6 April 1894, 5; "The Case of Superintendent Brockway," 10 April 1894, 4; "The Elmira Reformatory," 11 April 1894, 5; "Mr. Brockway and Governor Flower," 12 April 1894, 4; "The Elmira Reformatory," 14 April 1894, 5.

Governor Flower faced a serious political quandary. The Board of Charities inquiry, which he called for, concluded that there was a wide disparity between the promise and practice of Elmira and that the managers should be dismissed. New York's attorney general concurred with these findings and recommendations. Unfortunately, the managers were gubernatorial appointments, some of the state's wealthiest and most powerful citizens.[78] Additionally, Elmira's status as the nation's model reformatory reflected well on the governor. Flower followed his political instincts; a new committee was appointed to reconsider the findings. The New York *Times* observed that this action "enables the Governor to creep out of a very uncomfortable position, as it is well known that he has been loth [sic] to proceed to any radical steps if the Legislature could be persuaded to take up an investigation."[79]

The governor appointed William Learned, a former state supreme court judge, chairman of the new investigative committee. Austin Flint, a physiologist, and Israel Deyo, an attorney, agreed to serve. Unfortunately for Governor Flower, an even more confusing portrait of Elmira emerged when their final report was issued. A "majority report" submitted by Flint and Deyo rejected the board of charities investigation; a "minority report" submitted by Judge Learned supported their findings and recommendations.

The Flint and Deyo majority report conceded that Elmira was overcrowded, medical care was "defective," and Brockway's treatment of Moses Aaron (the inmate locked in rest cure for five months and later judged insane) was severe. However, they did not support other negative findings, including the charges of cruelty. They acknowledged that Brockway whipped and punched inmates and that these beatings caused "discolored faces, bloody noses and swollen eyes." But these injuries were "accidental" and "temporary" and "leave no perceptible effect." They concluded that Brockway did not technically break the rules because the managers did not prohibit these punishments. Flint and Deyo concluded:

---

78. Matthias Arnot was a banker. His obituary described him as a multimillionaire "captain of industry." James Bailey Rathbone married an Arnot and was also a wealthy banker. William Peters, an active Democrat, was a railroad executive, partner in a coal company, and president of a mining company. William Wey was a prominent physician who served as president of the New York State Medical Society in 1871. B. L. Swartwood, the fifth manager, is not included in any of the biographical compendiums. ("Matthias H. Arnot Dead," New York *Times*, 16 February 1910, 9; "Elmira's Noted Banker and His Life: Career of Matthias H. Arnot," Elmira *Telegram*, 20 February 1910; "James Bailey Rathbone," in Sullivan, *History of New York State*, 448–49; *Biographical Record of Chemung County*, 450–53; Towner, Our County and Its People; Byrne, *Chemung County*.

79. "Another Elmira Investigation," New York *Times*, 30 March 1894, 5.

As it is organized and conducted, however, it is a model reformatory. Its results have been extraordinary as regards its success in the reformation of criminals. It probably stands pre-eminent among the reformatories of the world. These results are due to the extraordinary qualities of Mr. Brockway as an organizer and executive officer, added to his intimate knowledge of the criminal character.[80]

Judge Learned's minority report did not share this glowing assessment.[81] "Looking at all the proof, I feel satisfied that the punishments have been excessive in number and in severity, and therefore have been cruel."[82]

Governor Flower pursued the politically expedient course: Flint and Deyo's "majority report" was accepted and Learned's "minority report," along with the findings of the 1893–1894 Board of Charities inquiry, was rejected. Flower's final report conceded that medical care at Elmira was "inadequate" and inmates had been whipped, punched, and chained in solitary confinement on bread and water. But following Brockway's logic, he said that "no permanent injury" resulted. The governor concluded: "The charges are in the main not proven, and are, therefore, dismissed."[83]

The final impact of the 1893–1894 investigation was minimal.[84] Brockway and the managers maintained their positions, and Elmira's reputation emerged

80. Flint and Deyo, "Report of the Majority," 33, 30, 40, 18, 45.

81. New York State Board of Charities, *AR, 1894,* lxiv.

82. Quoted in Flower, "In the Matter of the Charges," 438. The New York *Times* followed the investigation of Judge Learned, Austin Flint, and Israel Deyo as closely as they followed the board of charities inquiry: "Convicts Testify Falsely," 26 July 1894, 8; "Convicts Admit They Lied," 27 July 1894, 8; "Convicts Aid the Defense," 28 July 1894, 5; "Same as Former Witnesses," 1 August 1894, 8; "Hearsay Evidence Rejected," 2 August 1894, 9; "Ex-Convicts Seek Revenge," 3 August 1894, 8; "Charges False and Malign," 31 August 1894, 8; "An Assassin of Reputation," 31 August 1894, 4; "Cruelty Charges Disproved," 6 September 1894, 9; "Glaring Untruths Exposed," 7 September 1894, 9; "Medical Treatment at Elmira," 9 September 1894, 21; "Tales of Convicts Denied," 11 September 1894, 9; "Few Blows, Many Warnings," 12 September 1894, 9; "Prison Discipline," 12 September 1894, 4; "Mr. Brockway Was Never Abusive," 13 September 1894, 9; "Mr. Brockway on the Stand," 14 September 1894, 5; "Discipline at Elmira," 15 September 1894, 4; "A Judge's Praise of Elmira," 29 September 1894, 2; "Mr. Ivin's Argument," 31 October 1894, 4; "An Almost Perfect Institution," 1 November 1894, 3. However, their reporting was clearly biased. The paper praised Judge Learned and Flint and Deyo as being fair and unbiased in "A Warning to the Governor," 15 September 1894, 8. The article analyzing the final report of the committee was less than balanced. Flint and Deyo were described as "two men of such intelligence, impartiality, character and special knowledge" and their majority report was described in detail. Judge Learned and the minority report were not even mentioned ("The Elmira Reformatory," 11 December 1894, 4).

83. Flower, "In the Matter of the Charges," 426, 446.

84. The annual report of the Board of Charities for 1894, lxv, identified three changes which came out of the investigation. Corporal punishment was temporarily suspended. The legislature rejected an application for $200,000 to add five hundred cells at Elmira. A bill authorized the construction of a second adult reformatory, the Eastern Reformatory (Napanoch), to relieve overcrowding.

unscathed. New adult reformatories opened across the country and the new penology, medical model, and scientific reform continued to transform American and international corrections. The politics of penology and a carefully crafted public relations and marketing campaign had succeeded in repackaging punishment and altering the reality of incarceration in Elmira. Brockway's final assessment of the 1893–1894 investigation was essentially correct: "The attack upon us proved to be an effective advertising instrumentality and greatly increased the influence of the reformatory which the attack was intended to defame."[85]

Conclusion

This overview of the 1893–1894 New York State Board of Charities investigation provides compelling evidence that the Elmira Reformatory did not provide benevolent reform. However, this inquiry also raises questions about the repressive class control agenda of the new penology. Elmira did, indeed, deliver benevolent repression, but Brockway's efforts achieved, at best, mixed results. Elmira's highly acclaimed three-stage "regimen of reform"—diagnostic interviews, in-house treatments, parole—did not effectively manage the minds and souls of men. Many Elmira boys battled the Protestant ethic and resisted the state's efforts to transform them into "good citizens" and "good workers." Balancing the conflicting aims of repression and reform proved to be a difficult, if not impossible, task.

85. Brockway, *Fifty Years*, 343.

Chapter Three

Revisiting Elmira: The Defects of Human Engineering in Total Institutions

Clearly, Elmira was a brutal prison, and the proliferation of the new penology across the United States and around the world was largely a product of Brockway's public relations and marketing campaign. This chapter addresses corollary questions: Why were there so many disparities between the promise and practice of prison science? Why did the Elmira system fail in its effort to build Christian gentlemen? Why did Elmira's keepers tout the institution as a reform panacea, despite its dismal record of achievement?

These questions can be addressed from a variety of theoretical frameworks. This analysis is based on perspectives which have been overlooked in prior correctional histories: organizational and social systems theory. Drawing heavily from classic studies—Gresham Sykes's *The Society of Captives: A Study of a Maximum Security Prison* and Erving Goffman's *Asylums: Essays on the Social Situation of Mental Patients and Other Inmates*—this study argues that the failure of the Elmira system to achieve benevolent reform or benevolent repression was, in large part, an expected product of the inherent deficiencies of the medical model and "total institutions."[1] The keepers of Elmira, much like

1. Goffman states: "A total institution may be defined as a place of residence and work where a large number of like situated individuals, cut off from the wider society for an appreciable period of time, together lead an enclosed, formally administered round of life" (*Asylums*, xiii).

keepers of other asylums, were plagued by the "defects of total power." That is, despite Elmira's rigid daily regimen, strict surveillance, and extensive use of corporal punishment, the authority and control of Brockway and his staff was far from complete. This lack of control, coupled with the complexities of Elmira's covert class control agenda and the inherent inadequacies of the medical model—inaccurate diagnoses, ineffective treatments, incompetent staff, and a fundamental lack of understanding of the root causes of crime and human behavior—doomed the Elmira system to fail.

Correctional historians have, with a few isolated exceptions, paid scant attention to the role career of individual offenders and the question of "prisoner resistance."[2] The 1893–1894 New York State Board of Charities investigation demonstrates that Elmira's inmates were active rather than passive recipients of prison science. Elmira's inmates responded to the "pains of imprisonment" —deprivation of liberty, autonomy, goods and services, heterosexual relationships, personal security—by following Goffman's primary and secondary adjustments. An inmate adopting the course of "primary adjustment" accepted responsibility for his actions, cooperated with his keepers, and worked hard to become a "normal" and "programmed" member of society. An inmate following the path of "secondary adjustment" battled his keepers and used unauthorized means for "getting around the organization's assumptions as to what he should do and get and hence what he should be."[3]

These themes develop in two sections. First, the case histories of seven inmates who played an important role in the 1893–1894 Board of Charities inquiry are reviewed. These case histories reflect, as C. Wright Mills concisely puts it, the "human variety."[4] They demonstrate how individual offenders exhibited unique primary and secondary adjustments in responding to the Elmira system and in adjusting to the "pains of imprisonment." A second section explores the inherent defects and limitations of the medical model and the Elmira system. Inmate secondary adjustments—coupled with the defects of knowledge, power, scientific criminology, and total institutions, as well as the impossible mandate of state social control—doomed Brockway's effort to manage his charges and socialize New York's dangerous classes.

2. Garland, *Punishment and Modern Society*, 172.
3. Goffman, *Asylums*, 189.
4. Mills, *Sociological Imagination*, 132–42.

The Elmira Boys: Seven Biographical Portraits

Between 1876 and 1899, 9,346 inmates went to Elmira on indeterminate sentences. Fifty-six percent of these inmates were between sixteen and twenty years old; thirty-five percent were between twenty and twenty-five; nine percent were between twenty-five and thirty. Ninety-three percent committed property offenses; seven percent acts of violence. The Elmira boys were from the lower class. Eighty-four percent of their parents were "pauperized" or had "no accumulations." Eleven percent left their impoverished homes before the age of fourteen; thirty-five percent left "soon after 14 years of age." Sixty-three percent were "without any education, illiterates" or "simply read and write (with difficulty)." Lower-class occupations were the norm: eighty-one percent worked as "common laborers" or "clerks." Ninety-nine percent of their associations were "positively bad," "not good," or "doubtful." Brockway described his charges as an "anti-social mass" and the "dependent and dangerous classes."[5]

This aggregate demographic profile masks one crucial point: the Elmira boys were not statistics—they were individuals. As a collective they shared many common traits; they were young, poor, uneducated, unskilled, living on the verge of subsistence, and ergo, property offenders. An examination of the case histories in the Inmate Biographical Ledger presents a more complex view. The 9,346 inmates had unique personalities. They came from different homes and backgrounds, committed different crimes, compiled different offense histories, and, following their release from Elmira, confronted different problems. Herein lies the essential tension of the Elmira system and the medical model: How were Elmira's keepers to transform this diverse and uncooperative group of the lumpenproletariat into productive citizens?[6]

5. These statistics are in New York State, Assembly Documents (1900), vol. 2, no. 24, New York State Reformatory, *Twenty-fourth AR* (1900), 30–40. A cautionary caveat: Measures of age, offense, and other demographic variables are fraught with problems. The Inmate Biographical Ledgers indicate that a surprising number of inmates used aliases and lied about their ages and prior records to avoid prison. Inmate duplicity was difficult to detect prior to the introduction of fingerprinting and centralized offender tracking systems. Recorded offenses often did not reflect the actual crime committed. Plea bargaining was a common practice. Other problems: measures of nationality, race, and prior record were not included; and, offense categories were vague (e.g. "pauperized") and overlapped (e.g. 16–20 and 20–25 age groups).

6. New York State, Assembly Documents (1896), vol. 5, no. 25, New York State Reformatory, *Twentieth AR* (1895), 61. Monkkonen, Dangerous Class, argues that increasing crime and the growth of the "dangerous classes" was not, as many historians have suggested, positively correlated with urbanization and industrialization. Whether this thesis applies in New York is unclear.

Luke Halpin: Making a Christian Gentleman. When Luke Halpin arrived at Elmira on 30 October 1887, his background did not indicate that he would rise to the highest rank in the military system, lieutenant colonel, and one day serve as principal keeper, the second highest position at the institution. Halpin, who was nineteen years old, received a twenty-year indeterminate sentence for first degree burglary. His family history did not portend success. Brockway's diagnostic interview revealed that Halpin's father was intemperate and could "read only and that with difficulty." Mr. Halpin, a mason, had "no accumulations." Although Luke's mental status was rated as "good," his physical status was rated, "Low type. Coarse good health." Luke left home in 1885 to live the life of a vagabond. His personal associations were "bad" and the superintendent judged his "moral susceptibility" at "0," the lowest rating. He was assigned to learn bricklaying and plastering. Luke Halpin was a product of New York's dangerous class—by any means, not a promising prospect for reform.[7]

Halpin's exemplary adjustment to the Elmira system surprised the superintendent. Halpin showed little inclination for bricklaying and was transferred to the broom factory. He enjoyed this work, followed orders, took pride in his assignments, and later said that he was grateful to the keepers for teaching him a trade. Although he was not a strong student, he made a concerted effort in the classroom. He paid close attention to the chaplain's calls for Christian behavior and worked hard to internalize the Protestant ethic. His conduct was perfect, with the exception of a loss of marks for study (failing to get 75 percent correct on several monthly exams). Brockway promoted him to the first grade on 1 May 1888. On 1 January 1889, he was paroled and hired as "paroled officer."[8]

Halpin's performance as a paroled officer was outstanding. He followed orders and was immune to the temptations which led to the downfall of other officers (e.g. selling tobacco, accepting bribes, overlooking rule violations, engaging in homosexual activities). He was promoted to hall keeper and soon rose to the rank of lieutenant colonel in the military system. Brockway appoint-

---

However, Brockway, Brace, and other New Yorkers were not concerned with empirical relationships. They were convinced that social disorder and crime were increasing, and they were certain that the lower classes were responsible. Pearson, *Hooligan*, also deals with the artificial discovery of "dangerous classes."

7. Records of the New York State Reformatory, *Inmate Biographical Ledger*, Case History #2788.

8. Records of the New York State Reformatory, *Conduct Ledger*, Case History #2788. Halpin testified in New York State Board of Charities, *Report and Proceedings*, 1445–63, 1468–14.

ed Halpin principal keeper in 1891. Halpin was responsible for the custody of the inmates and the supervision of subordinate officers. When Brockway was absent, Lieutenant Colonel Halpin, still technically a paroled inmate, was in charge of America's most important penal institution.

Brockway had complete faith in Halpin. He served as a judge on the institution's court, assisted in disciplining inmates, and proved to be an important witness at the 1893–1894 investigation. Halpin assured the commissioners that inmates were not abused in the bathroom. He acknowledged that uncooperative inmates were struck during scrimmages, but denied that they were abused: "They were simply subdued; whatever force it took to subdue them—only necessary force." Halpin admitted that Brockway punched inmates and hit them with the paddle, but the punches were "just a slight tap" and the blows with the strap to the head and face were "a proper blow, a proper thing for Mr. Brockway to do." The inmates received this treatment when they would not assume the punishment position, used profane language, or offered other forms of resistance. In short, they deserved what they got. Some, he added to stress his point, defecated while receiving punishments; others fainted "to escape the punishment." These inmates were hung up and the punishment was resumed.[9]

Halpin assured the commissioners that other aspects of the Elmira system were effective. The mark and classification system did not place excessive demands on inmates, the inmate-monitors were fair, and cooperative Elmira boys had little difficulty earning release under the indeterminate sentencing plan. Inmates who violated institutional rules received justice from the military court. Halpin emphatically denied allegations that inmates charged in the 1893 sex scandal were unjustly transferred to Auburn Prison. "The evidence was so overwhelming in each one of the cases; where there was the slightest doubt there was not a conviction." Halpin was an ardent supporter of the superintendent: "I would say he has treated every inmate first rate, fairly and justly."[10]

The "Tarrytown burglar" was officially released on 20 April 1893. The historical record does not reveal why Halpin resigned his position as principal keeper and left Elmira, but Brockway clearly lost his key advisor and confidant. Luke Halpin was Elmira's most outstanding case of "primary adjustment" and, from the keeper's perspective, living proof that the Elmira system could instill the dangerous classes with the Protestant ethic.

9. Ibid., 1447, 1504, 1476, 1508.
10. Ibid., 1452–53, 1503.

Fighting The System: The Case of John Gilmore. When John Gilmore arrived at Elmira on 17 November 1891, Brockway had no inkling that he would prove to be Elmira's most troublesome case of "secondary adjustment" and the source of the 1893–1894 State Board of Charities investigation. Gilmore, who was twenty-one, received a five-year indeterminate sentence for third degree burglary. Brockway's interview did not reveal anything exceptional in Gilmore's family history. His father died when he was an infant, leaving "no accumulations." He was raised by his mother, a religious woman who tried to give her son a proper home, but John was rebellious and incorrigible. Brockway noted that Gilmore kept "bad associations" and acquired venereal disease. Gilmore confessed to one prior arrest for assault. He lived at home until the time of his arrest, working as a cart man and, less promisingly, as a clerk in a "wine place." Although Gilmore's education was limited, Brockway rated his mental status as "good to excellent."[11] Gilmore appeared to be a malleable member of the lumpenproletariat—a good prospect for prison science and reform.

Gilmore's adjustment to the Elmira system was fair. He earned a perfect record during his first month of incarceration. The Conduct Record reveals a number of transgressions in subsequent months, such as shouting from room to room, contraband, maliciousness, insolence, disturbance, profane language, talking. These offenses were not particularly serious. On 1 July 1892, after just over seven months of incarceration, he was promoted to the first grade. On 11 February 1893, after just over seven months in the first grade, he was paroled.[12]

Gilmore did well on parole from February to July 1893. He supported himself working as a mover, bricklayer, and plumber. In July 1893 he was hired to do a plumbing job for Henry Zinke, a butcher. Gilmore apparently did the work, received partial payment, and was instructed to return for final settlement. Zinke was not home when he arrived. Gilmore was invited in by Mrs. Zinke and had, by Gilmore's account, a pleasant conversation. Gilmore was shocked when Zinke's daughter informed him several days later that two watches were missing and that he was the prime suspect. She delivered an ultimatum: Gilmore could return the watches or her father would contact the police. Gilmore visited his former employer the next day to plead his innocence,

---

11. *Inmate Biographical Ledger*, Case History #4955. Elmira's keepers attempted to discredit Gilmore for initiating the 1893–1894 inquiry in New York State, Assembly Documents (1894), vol. 14, no. 84, New York State Reformatory, *Eighteenth AR* (1893), 9.

12. *Conduct Ledger*, Case History #4955.

but Mr. Zinke was not moved. Gilmore was arrested and appeared in the Tombs Police Court on July 22, 1893.[13]

From this point on the case became complicated. Mr. Zinke decided not to press charges and did not attend the court hearing. Hugh Brockway, Elmira's transfer agent, found out about the arrest from one of Gilmore's disgruntled cousins and was in attendance. Despite the facts that Mr. Zinke decided not to press charges and there were no witnesses, Brockway insisted that Gilmore was guilty and could be returned as a parole violator. Brockway maintained that Gilmore did not even have the right to present his case in court. When Gilmore attempted to explain his story to the judge, Brockway cut him off: "Be quiet. The Judge has no time to listen to you." Judge Martin thought otherwise: "Yes, I have. Go on, young man, and let me hear what you have to say."[14] Brockway and Judge Martin continued their debate following Gilmore's testimony. Brockway insisted that he had the right to revoke Gilmore's parole, even without evidence. Judge Martin maintained that proof was necessary for revocation and remanded Gilmore to the Tombs. Brockway promised that he would return with evidence.

Gathering evidence was more difficult than Brockway had anticipated. When the court reconvened the next day, Brockway admitted that he had no proof. However, he continued to insist, speaking for his brother and Elmira's managers, that "the law gives us the right to take him back with us."[15] Gilmore's attorney had, in the meantime, secured a writ of habeas corpus transferring the case to the New York Supreme Court.

The case was heard on 10 August 1893. Despite Gilmore's testimony that he had not committed an offense, despite the fact that no witnesses were produced, despite Gilmore's rather surprising testimony that Elmira's inmates were subjected to cruel punishments, the court ruled in favor of Brockway and ordered Gilmore returned as a parole violator.[16]

Gilmore's attorney did not quit. A federal writ of habeas corpus was obtained, moving the case to United States Circuit Court. A petition containing over a thousand names calling for Gilmore's release was presented to the governor, but again the courts ruled against Gilmore. On 2 December 1893 he was returned to Elmira, where he remained until the governor released him by order of executive clemency on 15 November 1895.[17]

13. "His Liberty is Imperiled," New York *Times*, 22 July 1893, 9.
14. Ibid.
15. "No Evidence against Gilmore," New York *Times*, 23 July 1893, 8.
16. "John Gilmore's Fight for Freedom," New York *Times*, 11 August 1893, 9.
17. "Gilmore Returns to Elmira," New York *Times*, 26 August 1893, 9.

Gilmore fought the Elmira system and lost, but Hugh Brockway, Zebulon Brockway, and the managers won a pyrrhic victory. They won the legal authority to revoke parole on limited evidence and the right to extend the Elmira system and the new penology into the community, but the 1893–1894 State Board of Charities investigation and corresponding negative press coverage sparked by Gilmore's testimony ultimately revealed that the faith of the court was misplaced. In fact, there was much truth in the charges of John Gilmore. Elmira was, indeed, a brutal prison.

A War of Wills: The Case of Frank Wallace. Frank Wallace was convicted of second degree grand larceny in the Court of Sessions in Buffalo and received a five-year indeterminate sentence. Wallace was admitted to Elmira on 22 October 1892. He was bathed, clothed, and escorted to Brockway's private office for a diagnostic interview. Wallace told the superintendent that he was twenty-one, but then refused to give his ailing mother's address. "I knew it would kill her," he later explained. [18] Brockway was not swayed by Wallace's noble aims. "Declines to give information about *himself* or relatives. Possibly to cover his previous criminal career; certainly he desires to hide something," wrote the superintendent in the Inmate Biographical Ledger. Brockway's response was stern: "He is consigned to screen room—2 rations a day—until he affords information necessary to determine a course of reformative treatment." [19] The interview was abruptly terminated.

Wallace was taken to the rest cure cell, chained to the floor, and fed bread and water. The next day he was brought back before the superintendent, but once again he refused to answer the key question: What was his mother's address? Brockway was miffed at Wallace. "I could take this out of you in about five minutes if I wished," warned the superintendent. "I will flog you within an inch of your life." Wallace returned to the rest cure cell; for the next six days he was chained to the floor and fed bread and water. Wallace was brought before the superintendent at the end of the week, but continued to refuse to give his mother's address. Brockway escalated the stakes promising "I will put you in a dark place, you won't live very long there." He added, perhaps hoping for the final mailing address, "What do you want done with your bones when you die?" Wallace, who took pride in his "good nerves," suggested donating his remains to medical science for dissection. Brockway was not amused: "He raised

18. New York State Board of Charities, *Report and Proceedings*, 77.
19. *Inmate Biographical Ledger*, Case History #5559; *Inmate Consecutive Register*, Case History #5559.

his foot and kicked me in the face so it nearly knocked me over; it hurt me considerable."[20]

The ensuing events marked an extraordinary test of wills between Wallace and Brockway. Wallace remained in rest cure on bread and water for four months for refusing to cooperate. "I prayed," he later recalled, "that I die to end my sufferings." On 26 January 1893, Wallace appeared before the managers to request a transfer to prison, but the request was denied. William Wey, president of the board, informed Wallace that he "would have to settle it all with Mr. Brockway."[21] Brockway, with an eye on crowding, finally relented and transferred Wallace to Auburn on 2 March 1893.

Wallace's transfer did not end the controversy surrounding this case. Wallace was shocked when Brockway informed him that Auburn did not have indeterminate sentencing; hence, he would serve his full five-year sentence. Wallace naively pled guilty on the advice of his attorney with the understanding that he would serve a shorter sentence and do "easy time" at Elmira.[22] Wallace took the rather unusual step of writing to his sentencing judge.

I was induced by Mr. John J. Colgan, a lawyer, to accept a sentence without a trial on the assurance that my sentence would not be greater than six months imprisonment in the penitentiary [Elmira] while, if I put the county to the expense of a trial, I might receive one year.

Wallace explained,

I gave him only six dollars, as I had but seven dollars, and was very foolish to expect any help for so small a sum, but he talked so well and expressed what seemed to me real sympathy for me, that I actually trusted him, intending to pay him as soon as I should be released.

Wallace implored the judge to "please write to me at least, and let me know what my sentence is." He added,

If I stay here five years I can not help but come out a wreck of no use to anyone, while one year might teach me at least never to leave home or go among strangers without being able to give a good account of myself."[23]

20. New York State Board of Charities, *Report and Proceedings*, 680, 76, 681.

21. Ibid., 75, 681.

22. Other inmates plea-bargained with the understanding that they would receive shorter sentences and do "easy time" in Elmira. Plea bargaining was not unique to New York: Langbein, "Plea Bargaining"; Haller, "Plea Bargaining"; Friedman, "Plea Bargaining"; Steinberg, "From Private Prosecution to Plea Bargaining"; Sanborn, "Plea Bargaining."

23. Wallace's letter to Judge Seaver was written on 26 March 1893 and is on pp. 686–87 of New York State Board of Charities, *Report and Proceedings*.

Judge Seaver was moved. On 29 March 1893 he wrote to Brockway requesting an explanation of the case. The superintendent informed the judge that Wallace was a liar. "He put it on the ground that he wished to shield his parents from disgrace, but we believe it is really to cover his previous record." Brockway assured Seaver that Wallace was placed in solitary "for security's sake, not for punishment, he was handcuffed awhile [over four months] to a side of the room." Brockway added that Wallace "may be returned to Elmira, at any time."[24] (This reassurance was clearly misleading: of 608 inmates transferred to state prisons between 1888 and 1893, only one came back—the rest served their full sentence).

Judge Seaver's testimony before the Board of Charities reveals that he was not pleased with Wallace's treatment or with Elmira's indeterminate sentencing and transfer policy. The judge did not view the theft of a ring and a watch valued at 41 dollars as meriting five years in Auburn.

LITCHFIELD: If the prisoner had plead [sic] guilty and you had not a reformatory to send him to, how long a sentence would you have given him out of the five years; would you have given him the whole term?

SEAVER: Oh, not at all; I would have sent him so he would have gotten out of the workhouse, the Erie county penitentiary, about the middle of the next summer; about a year's sentence.

The Wallace case changed Judge Seaver's opinion of Elmira:

LITCHFIELD: Have you sent other prisoners to the reformatory?

SEAVER: Up to this case of Wallace's we have sent a great many; we thought a great deal of the institution before, the district attorney and myself; since then we have not.[25]

Frank Wallace was an extreme example of Goffman's "intransigent line" of secondary adjustment; that is, "the inmate intentionally challenges the institution by flagrantly refusing to co-operate with staff."[26] Wallace was fortunate. On 30 September 1895 he was released by order of the governor and saved from a five-year sentence, but his case troubled the members of the Board of Charities. It was clear that Elmira's indeterminate sentencing and transfer laws were misunderstood, misapplied, and extended terms of incarceration. It was also clear that inmates who challenged the authority of the keepers paid a painful price.

---

24. Judge Seaver's letter is on p. 687; Brockway's response is on pp. 687–89.
25. Ibid., 690.
26. Goffman, *Asylums*, 62.

Hazards of the Medical Model: The Case of Moses Aaron. Moses Aaron entered Elmira on 1 April 1892. Convicted of second degree grand larceny in the New York County Court of Sessions, he received a two-and-one-half-year indeterminate sentence. The superintendent's initial impression was favorable. Aaron's parents were "German-Hebrew" immigrants. There was no reported history of insanity, epilepsy, or dissipation in the family, and his parents could read and write. Aaron's father was a peddler, but like many immigrants, the family had "no accumulations." Aaron, who was then twenty-one, had lived on his own for seven years, working as an office boy and taking odd jobs. His associations were "bad" but he was temperate and Brockway recognized some potential for reform. He was, in the superintendent's estimation, "Good health, good quality of Hebrew, pointed chin and jaw." Aaron was assigned to type-setting, one of the more intellectually demanding trades.[27]

Aaron's adjustment to the pains of imprisonment was extremely poor. On 4 April 1892, just three days after entering the institution, he was demoted to the third grade for "insubordination-like conduct." The demotion did not cure his belligerent behavior. Aaron continued to disrupt the institution. His activities covered a variety of offenses ranging from "talking" to "creating disturbances" to "threatening duty man" and "studying escape." Although the Conduct Ledgers did not record all punishments, Brockway clearly resorted to "physical treatment" to mend Aaron's ways. He received eight strokes of the whip on 13 April 1892. This had little effect. Aaron received eleven strokes on 14 April, and eleven more on 27 April. He was whipped on 18 May, and on 27 May and 16 June was interviewed with "admonition deferred." On 26 June he received nineteen blows. Aaron was chained in the "rest cure cell" from 1 April 1892 to 8 September 1892 on a diet of bread and water.[28]

The superintendent was slow to recognize the root cause of Aaron's misbehavior: he was insane. Aaron was finally transferred to the Mattawan Insane Asylum on 8 September 1892, after serving a record five months in solitary confinement. The superintendent's treatment of Aaron was condemned by the Board of Charities, and even Brockway's most ardent supporters admitted that he was badly abused. Governor Flower conceded that his treatment was "clearly a blunder which should have been avoided by a greater harmony between the Superintendent and the physician."[29]

27. *Inmate Biographical Ledger,* Case History #5229; *Inmate Consecutive Register,* Case History #5229.

28. *Conduct Ledger,* Case History #5229.

29. Flower, "In the Matter of the Charges," 7.

Brockway's mishandling of Moses Aaron highlights the hazards of attempting to apply the medical model without understanding the causes of crime and human behavior. It also reflects Goffman's secondary adjustment of "prison psychosis."[30] For Moses Aaron, Brockway's treatment had long and painful consequences. He was still in Mattawan on 1 October 1900, the final entry in his biographical record.

The Misguided Genius: The Case of Charles Paravicini. Charles Paravicini was one of Elmira's most promising prospects for reform. Paravicini received his early training at a German seminary and graduated from Heidelberg University. He spoke German, English, French, Greek, and Latin and played the piano and organ. Paravicini's father was a judge in Germany with a sizable estate. Paravicini emigrated to America on his own and supported himself as a painter. Flowers on canvas and silks were his specialty, but when art sales were slow he supported himself by painting artistic scenes for theaters and, as a secondary choice, by working as a house painter—interiors only. Paravicini attended church regularly and played the organ at Sunday services. Unfortunately, he fell in with "bad associations" and was committed on 26 May 1891 to serve a ten-year indeterminate sentence for second degree forgery.[31]

Paravicini was so talented that the superintendent assigned him to work as an instructor in the fresco shop and as an assistant to the musical director. Paravicini adjusted well. He was promoted to the first grade on 1 December 1891 and earned his parole on 1 August 1892. Paravicini reported directly to his employer, worked hard, and obeyed the conditions of parole. He was laid off by his employer due to a shortage of work in December 1892 and, unfortunately, resorted to his old habit to generate income: check forgery. On 18 February 1893 he was returned to Elmira and placed in the lower first grade. Showing signs of maturity and promise, Paravicini assumed full responsibility for his actions and parole revocation: "I was treated fair: I can't complain."[32]

Paravicini's second stay at Elmira indicated that he may have learned his lesson. He was promoted to the first grade on 1 December 1893, continued to do well, and earned parole on 11 December 1894. For the next ten months he worked as an inmate officer. On 1 October 1895 he was granted permission to take a job outside the institution. Paravicini obeyed the conditions of parole for three months, but in January 1896 left his job and disappeared. The last entry

---

30. *Asylums*, 61.
31. *Inmate Biographical Ledger*, Case History #4657.
32. *Conduct Ledger*, Case History #4657; *Report and Proceedings*, 1149.

in the *Inmate Biographical Ledger*, 1 April 1898, reported that Elmira's most promising inmate was still wanted as a parole violator.

Charles Paravicini proved to be one of Elmira's most disappointing failures. Given his high intelligence and solid middle-class background and upbringing, he was an ideal prospect for primary adjustment, but Paravicini squandered his enormous talents and yielded to temptations of alcohol, forgery, and vice. The Elmira system, the medical model, and Brockway's exhortations could not save him from crime.

Sex, Scandal, and Reform: The Cases of James Crumby and James Nicholson. One of the most striking findings of the 1893–1894 inquiry was the sex scandal. While the keepers were publicly projecting an image of benevolent reform, they were privately battling a homosexuality ring which netted dozens of inmates, including Brockway's trusted monitors. This is the story of two inmates who were caught in that scandal: Major James Crumby, one of the institution's highest ranking inmate officers, and James Nicholson, an inmate who testified against Major Crumby and a number of other sex conspirators.

James Crumby showed little potential for reform when he entered the institution on 9 May 1888. Crumby, who was twenty years old, received a twenty-year indeterminate sentence for first degree robbery. His parents were intemperate Irish immigrants with limited educations; Crumby's father was a garbage collector and the family had "no accumulation—very poor." His associations were "bad." He served time in truant school and lived the life of a vagabond, "travelling to and fro from Bost. and New York to Montana: but for the past few weeks running a night ferry to Ward's Island and while in this occupation he committed this robbery." The superintendent concluded that Crumby was in "good" mental condition but that he was a "low convict type."[33]

James Nicholson was convicted of second degree forgery and given a ten-year sentence. His mother committed suicide and his father was sent to an insane asylum when James was four. He was raised by his uncle, a college president, who provided a good home, leaving Nicholson with "no inducements to steal." But Nicholson was difficult to control. In 1881 he was committed to the New York House of Refuge. In 1887, at the age of sixteen, he moved to a rooming house and worked as a clerk. The superintendent noted that his mental con-

---

33. *Inmate Biographical Ledger*, Case History #3004.

dition was "good to excellent" and assigned him to learn stenography, a challenging occupation.[34]

Crumby got off to a slow start. He received an "imperfect record" for his first month and over the next several years received many demerits: study, disobedience, lying, quarreling, idleness, talking, careless malingering, laughing, laziness, shortage in labor, inattention, and unfaithfulness. He apparently reformed and, despite his rather checkered record, caught the attention of the superintendent. Crumby was granted parole on 24 February 1892 and began work as an inmate officer. By 1893 he earned the rank of major, one of the highest inmate-officers at Elmira.[35]

Nicholson's adjustment to Elmira was poor. He received an "unimproved" rating in his first month and went on to break a wide range of rules: talking, creating disturbance in room, carelessness, lying, gross inattention, neglect of duty, lack of table etiquette, laughing, fooling. The managers granted him parole in October 1891, but before he was released he was implicated in "school marking frauds" and the parole was revoked. Nicholson's performance after this demotion remained poor. He did not earn promotion to the first grade again until October 1892, and his stay in the first grade was brief. In January 1893 Nicholson was charged with sodomy, including contacts with Major Crumby.[36]

The charges against Nicholson and Crumby were similar to the charges leveled against other inmates. Nicholson was accused of dozens of improper relations, including:

Receiving vile propositions from Major Crumby, one offense of sodomy with Major Crumby, hugging and kissing Captain Burke, one offense of sodomy with Major Valentine, one offense of sodomy with Night Watch Kelso, sodomy with Thayer and receiving

---

34. *Inmate Biographical Ledger*, Case History #4107; *Conduct Ledger*, Case History #4107.

35. *Conduct Ledger*, Case History #3004.

36. *Conduct Ledger*, Case History #4107. Nicholson was technically reduced to the "new second grade." Researchers examining Elmira's annual reports or the Inmate Biographical Ledgers after 1889 will find references to the upper first grade, lower first grade, second grade, and third grade. Brockway introduced these grades, by his own admission, to circumvent the 1889 law ordering industrial education for the first grade of prisoners, industrial training and labor for the second grade, and profit-oriented labor for the third grade. The new classification system extended the presumed benefits of industrial education to more inmates. To avoid confusion, I have translated these new grades to the old system for the seven case histories analyzed in this chapter. Upper first grade was designed to be the equivalent of the first grade under Brockway's old system. Lower first grade corresponded to the second grade. Only a few inmates were placed in the new third grade; as a result, the new second and third grades were, in essence, the old third grade.

tobacco from the same, being hugged and kissed by O'Donnell and receiving vile propositions from him, numerous offenses of sodomy, about fifty, with Major Dougherty.

The charges against Crumby were equally serious: "one offense of sodomy a year ago with Ogden, one offense of sodomy with Nicholson, one offense of sodomy with Woodworth, admitted by Woodworth, one offense of sodomy with Shortell, admitted by Shortell."[37]

These allegations were reviewed by the institution's court, which consisted of Colonel Bryan, a civilian officer in charge of the military system; Mr. Van Etten, the school secretary; Oscar Hoppe, the institution's clerk; and Lieutenant Colonel Luke Halpin. The verdict of the court was unequivocal: Crumby and Nicholson were guilty. On 11 January 1894, Crumby's parole was revoked and he was placed in the lowest classification grade. Nicholson was also reduced to a red suit. Both inmates were transferred to Auburn Prison on 14 January 1893.

When the commissioners visited Auburn Prison to hear inmate testimony, Nicholson and Crumby provided a different perspective on the sex scandal. Nicholson confessed that he had fabricated the charges against Crumby and that he did not even know him. Nicholson explained that he was "nervous" and "never was punished in my life." Elmira's institutional court was intimidating:

I was taken down to the solitary, and I was confronted by Mr. Hoppe and Colonel Bryan and Mr. Van Etten; I was taken from the shop by Mr. Sample; I was taken in; I sat down in a chair, Colonel Bryan sat on a chair on my left; he asked me if I didn't expect to be chalked in; I says: "No, sir;" he says: "Your conscience is clear?" I says: "Yes, sir;" he called me an infernal liar and punched me with his fist.[38]

Nicholson continued to deny the charges until Mr. Sample, the guard who escorted him, suggested, "Take him to the superintendent; he will flog the truth out of him." For Nicholson the choice was now clear: "I had either to confess it; the only other alternative was to go to the bath-room and have the truth flogged out of me, and I knew they would make me admit it in the end, and I preferred to admit it without going there."[39]

Crumby adamantly denied the charges against him. He did not know Nicholson, let alone engage in sexual relations with him. Crumby described his "hearing":

I was called down to the solitary myself, and a fellow officer, Dougherty; we were told we were convicted and charges made against us of sodomy; I wanted to know if I was convicted; yes, I was convicted, without being present I was convicted; I asked to see

37. New York State Board of Charities, *Report and Proceedings*, 641.
38. Ibid., 637, 629–30.
39. Ibid., 630.

my accusers and I was told it wasn't necessary, thereupon being locked up that night; the next morning I requested to see the superintendent, and he came down and we had a little talk; it was altogether a noisy harangue, to make the best of it; the first man, Nicholson, was called in there; he told the superintendent that I made him masturbate me.

The burden of proof at these inquiries was clearly on the accused. "Prove what this man [Nicholson] says isn't so," said the superintendent. Crumby recognized that he was at a distinct disadvantage. "I can't prove it, I can only give you my word it isn't so. Why don't you make him prove it is so."[40]

But the die was cast, and both inmates were found guilty. Fortunately, they did not serve their maximum sentences. Nicholson was released on 30 September 1895. Crumby, perhaps fearing the prospect of being forgotten and serving the remainder of his fifteen-year sentence at Auburn, consented to being returned to Elmira on 7 May 1894. He worked his way through the ranks and was paroled on 26 February 1896.

The cases of James Crumby and James Nicholson demonstrate that some secondary adjustments were products of institutional injustice. The testimony of Crumby and Nicholson, combined with the accounts of other witnesses, places Elmira's keepers on the horns of a dilemma: Crumby and Nicholson may have been telling the truth when they maintained that they were innocent of the charges against them, in which case they were framed by the institution's court and administration. Or, Crumby, Nicholson, and the other inmates may have been guilty as charged, in which case the institution was rife with vice. Were Brockway's paroled officers—half the institution's staff—as trustworthy and effective as he maintained?

The Defects of Knowledge, Power, and Total Institutions

These case histories provide a foundation to consider three final questions: Why were there so many disparities between the promise and practice of prison science? Why did the Elmira system fail to socialize New York's youthful offenders? And finally, why did Brockway and the managers launch a public relations campaign which wildly exaggerated Elmira's record of success?

The obvious temptation is to simply blame Zebulon Brockway for the failings of Elmira. Brockway developed the Elmira system, maintained an iron grip over the daily operation of the institution, and personally wielded the

---

40. Ibid., 624, 625. The court hearings of other inmate officers who faced sodomy charges were equally brief, e.g., 584–605, 605–22.

whip. His public relations and marketing campaign set the American criminal justice system on a false path to "reform." But simply blaming one person, even one as influential as Brockway, for the deficiencies of prison science oversimplifies the complexity of penal reform and leads to a myopic interpretation. The failures of Elmira were the product of a variety of dynamic and dialectically interacting factors which, in large part, reflect the defects of total institutions and the hazards of human engineering.

To begin, the obvious should not be taken for granted. The Elmira boys, much like other asylum inmates, were not willing subjects. Some inmates, like Luke Halpin, did follow the course of primary adjustment. They accepted responsibility for their crimes and cooperated with their keepers. But other inmates—like John Gilmore, Frank Wallace, Moses Aaron, Charles Paravicini, James Crumby, James Nicholson—battled the Elmira system and responded to the pains of incarceration by adopting disruptive secondary adjustments. These findings reflect Sykes's contention that correctional institutions are "not simply the social order decreed by the custodians, but also the social order which grows up more informally as men interact in meeting the problems posed by their particular environment."[41]

The "defects of total power" magnified the disruptive impact of "prisoner resistance." Elmira used strict rules, harsh punishments, and a rigid daily regimen to maintain order. However, the power and control of Brockway and his staff were far from complete. Inmates did not blindly accept the authority of their keepers. Elmira's severe punishment system did not deter many inmates from engaging in prohibited secondary adjustments; conversely, the incentives offered by the reward system (marks and classification) were often insufficient to foster primary adjustment. Elmira's inmate-monitors and civilian guard staff—the key to surveillance, rule enforcement, and control—were incompetent and untrustworthy. "Far from being omnipotent rulers who have crushed all signs of rebellion against their regime," explains Sykes, "the custodians are engaged in a continuous struggle to maintain order—and it is a struggle in which the custodians frequently fail."[42]

The defects of total power, coupled with the problem of inmate resistance, disrupted the regime of Elmira's custodians and generated goal conflict and confusion. In theory, Elmira was the world's model correctional institution, committed first and foremost to the noble aim of the new penology. In practice, Elmira was like any other maximum security prison; its keepers were preoccu-

41. Sykes, *Society of Captives*, xii.
42. Ibid., 42.

pied with escapes, violence, rebellion, and other secondary adjustments. Brockway and his staff, like their counterparts at other total institutions, placed custody, control, and internal security before reform in the interests of personal and organizational survival. Prison officials, explains Sykes, "are relatively indifferent when it comes to saving their prisoners from sins in the future." However, custodians preserve the myth of reform: "Allegiance to the goal of rehabilitation tends to remain at the verbal level, an expression of hope for public consumption rather than a coherent program with an integrated, professional staff."[43]

The failure of the Elmira system to effectively manage New York's youthful offenders can also be traced to the defects of the medical model and its underlying theoretical foundation: multifactor positivism. An inspection of Elmira's Inmate Biographical Ledger—for instance, the case histories of Luke Halpin, Moses Aaron, Charles Paravicini—leaves little doubt that these offenders did, indeed, reflect the Millsian "human variety" and that their behavior was determined by a variety of psychological, sociological, economic, and biogenic factors. But the intuitive strength of the multifactor positivist approach was also its greatest weakness. Brockway was not capable of identifying the root causes of crime at his diagnostic interviews; and the 9,346 inmates committed between 1876 and 1899 did not receive individualized treatments. Brockway and other proponents of scientific criminology promised far more than they could possibly deliver. Reforming Elmira's human variety was, quite simply, a game of chance.

However, research on total institutions reveals that Elmira's failures are not unusual. Goffman maintains that "people work" is difficult and the medical model is, at best, a "tinkering service." The medical model increases the power, authority, and respect accorded "experts"; however, the professionalization of "treatment sciences" does not necessarily improve the care afforded inmates. Asylums routinely promise humane care but deliver "personal defacement" and "role dispossession"—in short, a "process of mortification." Sykes concludes: "Unfortunately, the advocates of confinement as a method of achieving rehabilitation of the criminal have often found themselves in the position of calling for an operation where the target of the scalpel remains unknown."[44]

---

43. Ibid., 34. Cohen, *Visions of Social Control*, 161–96, 273–81, demonstrates that contemporary penologists use euphemisms, medicalisms, psychologisms, psychobabble, technobabble, and other forms of "controltalk" to legitimize "treatments" and enhance their professional status; much modern jargon sounds disturbingly similar to that used by Brockway.

44. Goffman, *Asylums*, 74, 326, 13, 14, 21, 43; Sykes, *Society of Captives*, 11.

Organizational and social systems theory also provides a unique perspective on Brockway's use of severe corporal punishments. Historians have demonstrated that corporal punishment was a standard practice at many nineteenth-century juvenile reformatories and adult prisons. However, Goffman reveals that harsh punishments are also used in other asylums to maintain order and control. "In some penal institutions we find the humiliation of bending over to receive a birching," notes Goffman. He goes on to explain:

Just as the individual can be required to hold his body in a humiliating pose, so he may have to provide humiliating verbal responses. An important instance of this is the forced deference pattern of total institutions; inmates are often required to punctuate their social interaction with staff by verbal acts of deference, such as saying "sir." Another instance is the necessity to beg, importune, or humbly ask for little things such as ... a drink of water.[45]

Given the problem of inmate resistance, the defects of total power, deficiencies in the medical model—as well as Brockway's early training at the Wethersfield Prison and Albany County Penitentiary, where corporal punishment was widely used—it is easy to see how he could have resorted to the brutal disciplinary techniques. Brockway made it clear that the Elmira Reformatory was "analogous to American society." Inmates who resisted the Elmira system—such as Frank Wallace, Moses Aaron, and John Gilmore—were shunning God, law, and country. Brockway warned that any Elmira boy who failed to abide by the rules would "feel the odiousness of war with his fellow men and with God."[46] Brockway, acting as the arm of the state and the hand of God, kept his promise.

Studies of asylums also expose the roots of Elmira's public relations and marketing campaign. Organizational theorists have demonstrated that institutions resist change, reject outside criticism, and seek to further their well-being. The keepers of asylums, explains Goffman, have a vested personal and organizational interest in projecting a positive image to governmental officials and the public:

Many total institutions, most of the time, seem to function merely as storage dumps for inmates, but, as previously suggested, they usually present themselves to the public as rational organizations designed consciously, through and through, as effective machines of producing a few officially avowed and officially approved ends. It was also suggested that one frequent official objective is the reformation of inmates in the direction of some

45. Goffman, *Asylums*, 22.

46. New York State, Senate Documents (1885), vol. 4, no. 13, New York State Reformatory, *Ninth AR* (1884), 9; Assembly Documents (1893), vol. 5, no. 25, New York State Reformatory, *Seventeenth AR* (1892), 173.

ideal standard. This contradiction, between what the institution does and what its officials must say it does, forms the basic context of the staff's daily activity.[47]

Public relations and marketing campaigns—including "open house," tours, and embellished annual reports—are integral components of the image-making process at asylums.[48] Elmira's public relations and marketing campaign was not, then, exceptional. Brockway was merely the greatest salesman of his time.

Conclusion

This chapter probes and dissects the inner workings of Elmira. But it also raises serious questions about the depth and utility of some of the most respected interpretations of the history of social control, including the work of Michel Foucault. Foucault has argued that nineteenth-century penal institutions were "perfect disciplinary institutions" which were designed to make "obedient subjects" and "docile workers"—quite simply, "meticulously subordinated cogs of a machine."[49] This thesis is appealing but simplistic.

Rothman has correctly observed that

Foucault's analysis never enters into the everyday world of criminal justice. It is one thing to claim that the goal of surveillance dominated the *theory* of punishment, quite another to examine what actually happened when programs were translated into *practice.*

Much of Foucault's abstract intellectual history, notes Stanley Cohen, is grounded on "stories, visions and plans," fantasized relationships, and "leaps of imagination." Similarly, Garland faults Foucault for ignoring the role career of individual offenders and the question of prisoner resistance. A biographical perspective would have exposed the hazards of human engineering and forced Foucault to "revise this account in some important respects." Garland believes that Foucault

might have been led to describe the operation of power upon individuals as being less of an "automatic" process and more a matter of micro-political conflict in which the individual subject may draw upon alternative sources of power and subjectivity to resist that imposed by the institution."[50]

47. Goffman, *Asylums*, 74. Perrow, *Complex Organizations*, and Hall, *Organizations*, discuss the conservative nature of organizations; for applications to corrections, see: Jacobs, *Stateville*, and Cohen, *Visions of Social Control*, 92–100.

48. Goffman, *Asylums*, 101, 103, 106.

49. Foucault, *Discipline and Punish*, 128, 169, 202, 208, 243.

50. Rothman, *Conscience and Convenience*, 11; Cohen, *Visions of Social Control*, 29, 208; Garland, *Punishment and Modern Society*, 173.

These findings do not bode well for the diffusion of the adult reformatory movement or the paradigmatic revolution which shook the foundations of the American criminal justice system in the 1880s and 1890s. The works of Goffman and Sykes—coupled with more general research on organizational theory—suggest that the "inherent pathologies" of total institutions, the hazards of the medical model, and many of the other problems which plagued Elmira are universal and enduring. Could the keepers of the adult prisons and juvenile and adult reformatories who followed Brockway in implementing the new penology succeed where "the master" had failed? Could other reformatory keepers balance the conflicting aims of social reform and social control?

Chapter Four

Searching for Reform: The Birth of America's Third Penal System, 1877–1899

Elmira's failure to achieve the promise of the new penology does not mean that other institutions necessarily followed a similar course. A number of questions must be addressed to understand the diffusion and impact of the adult reformatory movement: When, where, and why were other reformatory-prisons opened? How were these institutions similar to and different from Elmira? What problems did the keepers of these institutions encounter in their attempts to socialize America's newest criminal class, the dangerous youthful offender?

These questions are addressed in four sections. The first examines the origin, aims, structure, and programs of Elmira's ideological rivals, the Michigan House of Correction and Reformatory (1877) and the Massachusetts Reformatory (1884). The second outlines the contours of the American adult reformatory movement by analyzing the development of eight institutions which opened between 1889 and 1899. The third reviews the findings of investigations of the Pennsylvania Industrial Reformatory (1892) and of the Colorado State Reformatory (1895), drawing parallels with Elmira. Finally, there is an assessment of patterns of prisoner resistance and secondary adjustment to the pains of imprisonment.

The adult reformatory movement was, indeed, complex. Concerns with increasing crime and social disorder, the threat posed by the "criminal classes," dissatisfaction with adult prisons and juvenile reformatories, and Elmira's remarkable claims of success set the stage for the opening of ten new adult reformatories in the United States between 1877 and 1899. New reformatory-prisons shared Elmira's central goal: transforming the dangerous classes into good workers and good citizens. But these institutions did not blindly emulate the vaunted Elmira system. Legislators and penologists modified the prison science and the medical model to reflect state-specific needs and interests.

However, there was a wide discrepancy between the promise and practice of prison science at these institutions. New adult reformatories, much like Elmira, were ultimately burdened by the defects of total institutions and the hazards of human engineering. These institutions did not socialize the dangerous classes or contribute to America's search for order.

Competing Systems: The Michigan and Massachusetts Experiments

Diffusion-of-innovations theorists have demonstrated that the discovery, adoption, and spread of technological inventions and ideas—including those aimed at human engineering and social control—are the product of a variety of dynamic and dialectically interacting forces. But the diffusion of innovations does not, as Everett M. Rogers has observed, follow a rote linear path. Adopters of innovations may follow the lead of "inventors" (e.g. Zebulon Brockway) and replicate model "inventions" (the Elmira system). Or, they may adapt pioneering innovations to meet their own needs, interests, and circumstances.[1]

Late nineteenth-century penologists did not, as some historians maintain, blindly copy the Elmira system. Adopters of the new penology—legislators, penal reformers, the superintendents of the nation's new adult reformatories—shared Elmira's central aim: to instill the criminal classes with "Christian character." However, they exercised personal and organizational autonomy, modifying the Elmira system and the concept of the dangerous youthful offender to meet state-specific social, economic, political, demographic, and criminal justice needs and interests. By the late 1880s, three approaches to controlling criminals emerged: the "treatment-oriented" Elmira system, the "punishment and profit" Michigan approach, and an eclectic version introduced in Massachusetts.[2]

1. Rogers, *Diffusion of Innovations*, and Rogers and Shoemaker, *Communication of Innovations*, are regarded as classics in this field.
2. An analysis of the paths along which the adult reformatory movement traveled would require an extensive state-by-state analysis of social, political, economic, demographic, and criminal

Left: Fig. 1. Zebulon Brockway, superintendent of the Elmira Reformatory from 1876 to 1900, was the father of the reformatory-prison movement and the new penology. Brockway's treatment-oriented Elmira system revolutionized America's approach to dealing with crime and criminals. (The Chemung County Historical Society, Elmira, New York)

Right: Fig. 2. Otis Fuller, warden of the Michigan Reformatory from 1894 to 1918, was Brockway's chief ideological rival. Fuller's version of the new penology rejected the Elmira system and advocated punishment, discipline, and profit-oriented industries. (Reproduced from **Men of Progress**, [Boston: *New England Magazine*, 1896]; courtesy of the State Archives of Michigan)

Top: Fig. 3. The New York State Reformatory at Elmira, 1913. (The Chemung County Historical Society, Elmira, New York)

Bottom: Fig. 4. The New York State Reformatory at Elmira, c. 1910. (The Chemung County Historical Society, Elmira, New York)

Fig. 5. The Michigan Reformatory, 1890. (Courtesy of the State Archives of Michigan)

Top: Fig. 6. A closer look at the ornate entrance to the Michigan Reformatory. (Courtesy of the State Archives of Michigan)

Bottom: Fig. 7. The imposing walls and inside yard of the Michigan Reformatory. (Courtesy of the State Archives of Michigan)

Top: Fig. 8. The Massachusetts State Prison at Concord (pictured in 1878) became the Massachusetts Reformatory in 1884. Under the direction of Superintendent Gardiner Tufts, this institution introduced a third version of the new penology which borrowed elements of the New York and Michigan systems. (Courtesy of the American Correctional Association)

Bottom: Fig. 9. The Ohio Reformatory, which opened in 1896, was designed to replicate New York's famed Elmira Reformatory. (Courtesy of the American Correctional Association)

Fig. 10. New arrivals at the Elmira Reformatory. (New York State Department of Correctional Services)

Fig. 13. Inmates in the third (or punishment) grade at the Elmira Reformatory working outside their cells. (New York State Department of Correctional Services)

Fig. 14. The cell block at the Michigan Reformatory, 1890. (Courtesy of the State Archives of Michigan)

Fig. 15. Elmira's inmates engaged in recreational-therapeutic activity. (New York State Department of Correctional Services)

Fig. 16. The military regiment of the Elmira Reformatory in a full-dress parade. (The Chemung County Historical Society, Elmira, New York)

Fig. 17. Superintendent Brock-way reviewing his "inmate-soldiers" on 15 June 1895. (The Chemung County Histor-ical Society, Elmira, New York)

Fig. 18. A group of Elmira's officers assembled on the steps of the superintendent's residence. (The Chemung County Historical Society, Elmira, New York)

Fig. 19. Staff members at the Michigan Reformatory, 1890. (Courtesy of the State Archives of Michigan)

Fig. 20. The Board of Managers of the Elmira Reformatory in 1906. The socially elite managers, who were appointed by the governor, were charged with the responsibility of overseeing the operation of the institution. They also served as the parole board. (The Chemung County Historical Society, Elmira, New York)

Fig. 21. An Elmira inmate going out on parole. (New York State Department of Correctional Services)

Governor John Bagley provided the impetus for the founding of the Michigan State House of Corrections and Reformatory. In 1873, Governor Bagley delivered a message on the state's penal institutions. He was especially concerned with the practice of mixing innocent young offenders with hardened older criminals: "We would not treat our cattle on our farms in this manner." The governor urged the legislature to open an institution for "intermediate offenders" which would separate "old from young, new beginners from old offenders, the ignorant from the vicious criminal, and thus prevent the demoralization that prison life spreads like a pall over all who suffer for crime."[3] In April 1873, the legislature passed a bill authorizing the construction of a "State House of Correction."[4] The Michigan experiment was about to begin.

The Michigan State House of Correction and Reformatory, which opened in Ionia on 1 August 1877, did not copy Elmira. In fact, these institutions were antithetical in terms of aims, programs, and inmate populations. The Michigan institution was not simply a reformatory. As its name implies, it was a combined house of correction and adult reformatory. It received misdemeanants and felons. Inmates were incarcerated for murder, rape, robbery, and a range of less serious offenses: "drunkards, tipplers, gamesters, and other disorderly persons," and "all persons who have no visible calling or business to maintain themselves by." The founding legislation imposed no age limitations. "The test for admission to a reformatory should not be a man's years of age but his years of crime," explained Superintendent D. R. Waters. "If he is young in years of age but old in crime he should go to the Penitentiary with confirmed criminals."[5] Also, there were no restrictions on recidivists; some offenders had dozens of arrests. Consequently, first-time teenage misdemeanants were incarcerated with hardened career criminals.

justice–related factors. Such an analysis is clearly beyond the scope of this work. Researchers interested in analyzing the diffusion of adult reformatories from an empirical framework might begin by consulting Sutton, *Stubborn Children*.

3. Quoted in Michigan State House of Correction and Reformatory, *First AR* (1878), 1. On crime in Michigan, see Schneider, *Detroit and the Problem of Order*.

4. "An Act to Establish a State House of Correction." The aims and regimen of the institution are defined in "An Act to Regulate and Govern." In 1873 Governor Bagley appointed a committee, which included Zebulon Brockway, to examine the state's penal institutions. They supported Bagley's efforts to open an "intermediate prison" and called for indeterminate sentencing and "conditional release" (i.e. parole). But these recommendations were not heeded (Walker, Lord, Brockway, and Putnam, *Special Report*).

5. Michigan State House of Correction and Reformatory, *Fourth AR* (1880), 11; *Second BR* (1884), 8.

The regimens of the Michigan and New York reformatories were markedly different. Sentences to Elmira were indeterminate, while sentences to the Michigan Reformatory were fixed, ranging from ninety days to life. Parole was not used at Michigan. Inmates received a new suit of clothes, a train ticket, and up to 10 dollars when they were released; beyond that, they received no assistance or supervision. Elmira's mark and classification system was not copied. Michigan inmates earned good time and release by simply staying out of trouble. Classification meant, at best, half-hearted attempts to separate misdemeanants and felons. At Elmira, academic and vocational education took precedence over labor (particularly after the abolition of contract labor in 1884). At Michigan, labor took precedence over education. Inmates worked for over ten hours each day under the contract system with one aim in mind: profit.[6]

The New York and Michigan systems followed diametrically opposed views of crime causation. Both institutions attempted to instill their charges with the Protestant ethic. However, Brockway's Elmira system, following the tenets of the Declaration of Principles, was grounded on the notion of multifactor positivism: there was no single cause of crime. Hence, criminals were diagnosed and treated as individuals (at least in theory). Michigan's superintendents—John J. Grafton (1877–1881), E.C. Watkins (1881–1883, 1885–1891), D.R. Waters (1883–1885), E. Parsell (1891–1894)—employed a Beccarian classical approach. They viewed Michigan's lumpenproletariat as free, rational, and hedonistic actors. Punishment, discipline, and hard work were the keys to building human capital and deterring future transgressions.[7]

Michigan's punishment and profit approach became firmly entrenched under Otis Fuller, superintendent from 1894 to 1918. Fuller was openly hostile to Brockway and the Elmira system. His response to an inquiry from the California State Board of Prison Directors on the advisability of opening an adult reformatory reflects his sentiments:

---

6. The state constitution shaped Michigan's punishment and profit orientation, by prohibiting teaching convicts a trade. State appellate court judges, while disagreeing with this logic, felt obliged to employ a strict constructionist view and uphold this provision. They explained that the founding fathers intended to "lessen the probability that the honest mechanics of Michigan should be compelled to associate with discharged convicts because the latter had been taught a trade of the former in the State Prison of this State." Otis Fuller discussed the influence of this provision in Michigan Reformatory, *Thirteenth BR, 1904–1906* (1906), 7–9.

7. The Records of the Michigan Reformatory, *Register of Residents*, reflects the classical approach to thinking about crime. The superintendents recorded basic information—name, age, offense, sentence, residence—but did not explore the inmate's background.

The idea of modern prison reformers seems to be that when a young man blows a safe, steals a horse, or forges a check he at once enters a preferred class and is entitled to an education and all the comforts of life without any individual efforts on his behalf, such as the ordinary son of a laboring man who has never committed a crime has to put forth. That is the New York idea. ... The New York Reformatory entertains its check forgers, porch climbers, and safe blowers with military drills in a huge costly building, with lectures, study, trade school instruction in which the product of the prison labor is destroyed, and the various prison duties of the institution are divided up among five men where one man could do the work without working more than half the day.

He encouraged the California Board of Corrections to reject maudlin sentimental reform and adopt the Michigan system.

Our main idea here is that productive labor and plenty of it is the best of reforming influences, while the central idea of most of the reformatories seems to be that rest and culture at the expense of taxpayers are most to be desired. ... I think, therefore, that I have the right to enter a personal protest against adopting in California the tax-grabbing and treasury-looting reformatory policies of New York, Pennsylvania, and Massachusetts. Prisons should be business institutions, and should have a decent regard for the rights of the taxpayers.[8]

While New York and Michigan penologists debated the merits of their approaches, reformers in Massachusetts developed an eclectic system. When the Massachusetts State Prison at Concord became an adult reformatory in 1884, it appeared that it would copy Elmira. Superintendent Gardiner Tufts admired Brockway and hailed Elmira as the "pioneer and only reformatory for males in this country."[9] However, the 1884 law governing the operation of the institution combined elements of the Michigan and New York systems.[10]

The Massachusetts Reformatory followed Michigan by accepting misdemeanants and felons, irrespective of age and prior offense history. The institution's commissioners explained their broad view of a "youthful offender": "But to exclude, by law, all who have served previous sentences, would cut off a very large proportion of the most hopeful cases." Chronic inebriates were also

8. Fuller's assessment of the reformatory movement is in Ford, Sonntag, Clinch, Devlin, and Porter, *Report of the State Board of Prison Directors*, 13–14.

9. Massachusetts Reformatory, *First AR, 1885* (1886), 35.

10. The Massachusetts State Prison, which opened in 1805, moved from Charlestown to Concord in 1878. Michael Hindus traces the history of the institution from 1805 to 1878 in *Prison and Plantation*, 162–81. Hindus states that the Massachusetts State Prison became a reformatory in 1878 (p. 180)—it was 1884. Glueck and Glueck discuss the history of this institution in *Five Hundred Criminal Careers*, chap. 3. Crime in Massachusetts is also analyzed in Lane, "Crime and Criminal Statistics"; Ferdinand, "Criminal Patterns"; idem, "Criminality"; Hirsch, *Rise of the Penitentiary.*

welcome: "Many of them were good workers; and, as a rule, they respond to the spirit of the institution."[11]

Although the Massachusetts Reformatory emulated Michigan with regard to the nature of the immediate offense, prior record, and age, the institution's stated goals and daily regimen were more closely modeled on Elmira. Superintendent Tufts viewed rehabilitation, not punishment, as his primary objective. Massachusetts inmates worked on a piece-price contract system, but profits were not a central concern. A modified indeterminate sentencing system was in place in 1884, and Tufts introduced a mark and classification system similar to Elmira's. Academic, vocational, and religious instruction received more emphasis in Massachusetts than in Michigan. Although there were no provisions for a parole officer until the mid 1890s, Massachusetts inmates were released on "permit" or "ticket of leave."

Discipline was less severe at the Massachusetts Reformatory. Tufts was adamantly opposed to the use of corporal punishment, handcuffing, and the ball and chain. Solitary confinement without restraints in a lighted cell was the punishment of choice. His successor, Joseph Scott, also rejected corporal punishment: "I am persuaded that a much better discipline can be maintained without its use than with it."[12] Myron Maynard (AKA Maurice Mansfield), who was incarcerated at Concord in 1888, compared the two institutions in his testimony at the 1893–1894 Elmira inquiry.

The main difference, as I understand it, no inmate has any authority over another, no inmate officers at all. ... They treat you there [at Concord] more as a man, and not as a mere consecutive number, as they do here [at Elmira]; some way or another they seem to put a man on his honor, and if he does what is right he gets a kind word once in a while; they have no flogging there.

Maynard went on to explain that "there was a more healthy public opinion among the inmates than there are here; I never heard an inmate speak harshly against Colonel Tufts." Maynard concluded that the Massachusetts Reformatory was a "better place."[13]

11. Massachusetts Reformatory, *First AR, 1885* (1886), 18, 12; "An Act to Establish a Reformatory." Massachusetts's intermediate approach was also reflected in inmate case histories: they were more elaborate than Michigan's, but less elaborate than Elmira's. Records of the Massachusetts State Reformatory, *Case Histories.*

12. Massachusetts Reformatory, *Ninth AR, 1893* (1894), 116. Tufts's sentiments on punishment are stated in Massachusetts Reformatory, *Third AR, 1887* (1888), 15.

13. New York State Board of Charities, *Report and Proceedings,* 2049–50. Records of the New York State Reformatory, *Inmate Biographical Ledger,* Case History #5300. Steven Smith, one of the authors of the 1893–1894 Elmira investigation, viewed Massachusetts's disciplinary system as a model ("Methods of Discipline in Reformatories").

The Michigan and Massachusetts systems experienced a number of changes before the turn of the century. However, the keepers of both institutions were convinced that their approaches to prison science offered effective alternatives to the Elmira system. Gardiner Tufts reported that seventy-five percent of his charges reformed. In 1886 he predicted that the Massachusetts Reformatory was "destined to stand at the head of all institutions of this kind in this country." Otis Fuller maintained that over seventy percent of Michigan's inmates were deterred, adding, "It costs far less to maintain it than any other reformatory of like character and capacity in the United States."[14]

The National Movement, 1889–1899

The claims of success by Brockway in New York, Gardiner Tufts and Joseph Scott in Massachusetts, and Otis Fuller and his predecessors in Michigan, coupled with the nation's increasing crisis in crime, criminal justice, and social disorder, had predictable results. New reformatories opened in Pennsylvania (1889), Minnesota (1889), Colorado (1890), Illinois (1891), Kansas (1895), Ohio (1896), Indiana (1897), and Wisconsin (1898). But the opening of these institutions and the diffusion of the new penology raised new and difficult questions: How should the dangerous youthful offender—age, prior record, offense (felony or misdemeanor)—be legally defined? Which model—New York, Michigan, Massachusetts—offered the greatest hope of reform?

There is little doubt about the course pursued by the nation's fourth and fifth institutions, the Pennsylvania Industrial Reformatory and the Minnesota Reformatory. These were unabashedly Elmira clones. The managers of the Pennsylvania Industrial Reformatory paid homage to Elmira in their first report:

We, therefore, visited and inspected the New York State Reformatory. ... Having been well satisfied, by our inspection of the Elmira Reformatory, of the correctness of the system of imprisonment under the indeterminate sentence with conditional liberation, we decided to adopt the same for the new reformatory.[15]

The keepers of the Minnesota Reformatory shared this enthusiasm, peppering their annual reports with tributes to Elmira.

The organizational problems confronting Superintendent R. W. McClaughry when the Pennsylvania Industrial Reformatory opened at Huntingdon on 15 February 1889 were minimized. McClaughry was firmly committed to the

---

14. Massachusetts Reformatory, *Second AR, 1886* (1887), 18; Michigan State House of Correction and Reformatory, *Eighth BR* (1896), 10.

15. Pennsylvania Industrial Reformatory, *First BR, 1889–1890* (1891), 3.

"three great factors in prison management and reform; namely, labor, education, and religious training." Pennsylvania's penologists were multifactor positivists who believed that individualized diagnosis and treatment were the keys to salvation: "The object the Reformatory has in view, is to repair, to remodel, to rehabilitate for the full duties of citizenship—in a word to reform." T. B. Patton, McClaughry's successor, assured the public that his reformatory saved youthful offenders and that the Elmira system "has proven the wisdom of the undertaking."[16]

The Minnesota Reformatory, opened in St. Cloud on 15 October 1889, pursued similar aims. Superintendent D. E. Myers believed that offenders should be instilled with seven Christian habits: "punctuality, regularity, truthfulness, self-control, justice, kindness and industry."[17] Minnesota copied Elmira's indeterminate sentencing scheme, parole system, mark and classification system, academic and religious programs, and sixteen-to-thirty age restrictions. The most unusual aspect of the institution was its commitment to labor and, following the Michigan model, profit. The institution was deliberately built on a rock quarry, prompting the managers to predict that "eventually this institution will be self-sustaining." Protests from rock quarry owners, and most important, the failure of anticipated profits to materialize, resulted in a shift toward industrial education in the mid 1890s. Nevertheless, Myers claimed that seventy-eight percent of his charges successfully completed parole, "an excellent showing, and probably cannot be surpassed by an institution of like character in the United States."[18]

The nation's sixth and most westerly reformatory-prison, the Colorado Reformatory, opened in Buena Vista in 1890, was highly unusual. On paper (i.e. founding legislation and annual reports) this institution emulated Elmira. In theory, inmates were to be reformed. Prisoners were committed on indeterminate sentences, exposed to Elmira's treatment programs, and ultimately released on parole. Unlike Elmira, there was no maximum age for commitments, but recidivists were excluded.[19]

In reality, the Colorado Reformatory was little more than a shell institution and work camp. When the first inmates arrived there was no cell house, school

16. Pennsylvania Industrial Reformatory, *Second BR, 1891–1892*, 4, 43, 15; *History and Development*; Wistar, "Pennsylvania Industrial Reformatory."

17. Minnesota State Reformatory, *Fifth AR* (1892), 16. [The printer mistakenly labeled this the fifth report. It does cover 1892, but it is the fourth report.]

18. Minnesota State Reformatory, *Second AR, 1890* (1891), 3; *Sixth AR, 1893* (1894), 3; Wolfer, "Reformatory System in Minnesota"; Minnesota State Reformatory, *Laws, By-Laws, Rules and Regulations*.

19. "An Act to Establish the Colorado State Reformatory."

house, kitchen, hospital, or wall to prevent escapes. "In the matter of permanent buildings nothing has been attempted," admitted the institution's commissioners, "as the lack of funds for other than maintenance most effectively prevented a start in that direction." Inmates spent the first decade constructing basic buildings (much like Elmira from 1876 to 1880). The first cell house took five years to finish, and the construction was still not complete at the turn of the century. Warden A. C. Dutcher complained in 1900 that the physical structure was "wholly inadequate."[20] A commitment to the Colorado State Reformatory was, quite simply, a sentence to hard labor.

The Illinois State Reformatory was also unique. The legislature passed a bill in 1891 transforming the juvenile reformatory at Pontiac into a reformatory for young adults.[21] Although the managers of the Illinois Reformatory regarded the New York and Massachusetts reformatories as models, their own institution bore little resemblance to either system.[22] The most striking aspect of the Illinois State Reformatory was its attempt to serve as a combined juvenile and adult reformatory.

Although it accepted offenders between the ages of ten and twenty-one, boys and young adults were rigidly separated and exposed to different regimens of reform. Boys between the ages of ten and sixteen were in the juvenile department. The regimen was adjusted for their age and innocence: they attended school; recreational activities and religious services were stressed; and the boys worked at "lighter kinds of employment," such as gardening and carrying messages.[23] Offenders between sixteen and twenty-one were committed to the "young adult division." This group was "treated with greater sternness" and had a more rigorous regimen emphasizing military drill and labor. "Money consideration, on the part of the authorities, should not be the motive," reasoned the managers. "But there should be extracted from each of the latter class of inmates as large a quantity of work, and of as good quality, as would be, or ought to be, required of him if he were not a prisoner."[24]

The Kansas State Industrial Reformatory, opened at Hutchinson on 29 August 1895, was firmly committed to the "great success" of the New York sys-

---

20. Colorado State Reformatory, *Second AR, 1892* (1894), 3; Colorado State Reformatory, *BR, 1898–1900* (1901), 10.

21. "An Act to Establish the Illinois State Reformatory." The original bill set the age limit at twenty-five, but the age was lowered to twenty-one in "An Act to Amend an Act."

22. The debt to the New York and Massachusetts reformatories is acknowledged in Illinois State Reformatory, *Second BR, 1892–1894* (1895), 7.

23. Ibid., 13–14.

24. Ibid., 13; Fallows, "Illinois State Reformatory." This institution is also analyzed in Pisciotta, "House Divided."

tem.[25] Although Kansas legislators broke with Elmira by restricting age commitments to sixteen to twenty-five, they copied Brockway's indeterminate sentencing, parole plan, and mark and classification system. The Kansas regimen, reflecting the needs of that state's agrarian economy, trained inmates to work as farm laborers. The managers announced that seventy-five percent of their parolees "never go back to crime again, but will become useful and valued citizens."[26]

The Ohio Reformatory, like its Colorado counterpart, was structurally incomplete when it opened in Mansfield in 1896. "I am sure I can promise when the cell wing and wall, now in the process of construction, and the grading of the grounds are completed," noted Superintendent W. E. Sefton apologetically, "we will be able to make a more satisfactory showing to those to whom we are responsible for our stewardship."[27] The institution's plan—indeterminate sentencing, sixteen-to-thirty-year-old offenders, mark and classification system, parole—demonstrated that post-construction reform efforts would be modeled on Elmira.

Indiana followed the path of Massachusetts by converting an adult prison, the Indiana Prison South, into a reformatory for young adults on 1 April 1897. "The Reformatory Principle has undoubtedly passed out of its experimental stage," noted the managers in explaining the transition. "It is no more a question whether it will be a success."[28] Elmira was selected as an organizational model. The keepers implemented a wage system which was similar to the plan used at New York. Inmates earned wages for labor and good behavior but also paid room, board, and medical expenses. Offenders were not eligible for parole until they saved 20 dollars. Indiana was not, however, emulating Otis Fuller's profit-oriented Michigan system. In fact, Superintendent Alvin Hert believed that profits and reformation were incompatible. His aim was more noble: the inculcation of the Protestant work ethic. Hert was confident that this goal was

25. Kansas State Industrial Reformatory, *Second BR* (1898), 14; Kansas State Industrial Reformatory, *Rules and Regulations*.

26. Kansas State Industrial Reformatory, *Second BR* (1898), 9; "An Act Establishing a Reformatory."

27. Ohio State Reformatory, *Fifteenth AR* [1898], 19; Brinkerhoff, "Reformation of Criminals." The Ohio State Reformatory was opened in response to perceived failures in the state's juvenile reformatories and adult prisons: Resch, "Ohio Adult Penal System"; Mennel, "'Family System of Common Farmers': Origins"; idem, "'Family System of Common Farmers': Early Years"; "An Act to Change the Name."

28. Indiana Reformatory, *First BR, 1896–1898* (1898), 21; "An Act to Establish the Indiana Reformatory." Indeterminate sentencing and parole were extended to offenders over the age of thirty as well: "An Act Concerning the Manner of Procedure."

being achieved. He looked back on the first two years of the institution's operation and declared, "I am confident that the career of this Institution as a reformative element in the State has only just begun."[29]

The Wisconsin State Reformatory was the last adult reformatory opened in the nineteenth century. Apparently, Wisconsin legislators heard about the achievements of these institutions and did not want to be left behind. They hastily passed an act appropriating funds for a new reformatory-prison to be opened in Green Bay. James Heg was appointed superintendent on 15 April 1898. Heg later reported that when he was appointed, "The plans for the Reformatory had not been made, nor had a stroke of work been done on the property." This did not deter Wisconsin's penologists. Construction began on 1 June 1898, and within ninety days the first twenty-four inmates were received.[30]

The task confronting Superintendent Heg was formidable. The "institution" had no cell house, kitchen, hospital, or school room; the construction of the wall was not started. The inmates were not, as the institution's charter stated, first-time offenders between the ages of sixteen and thirty. (Seventy-seven of the 194 inmates committed between 1898 and 1900 were older offenders serving fixed sentences.) The Wisconsin Reformatory, like the Colorado and Ohio reformatories, was a work camp. However, Superintendent Heg was confident that his institution would be a success. He proudly observed that "it is the first instance on record where a prison has been built, equipped, organized and filled in the space of three months time."[31] The Wisconsin State Reformatory was, quite simply, a ninety-day wonder.

The opening of the Wisconsin Reformatory in 1898 marked the final stage in the formative years of the adult reformatory movement. Eleven adult reformatories, incarcerating thousands of offenders, were in operation by the turn of the century. Reformatories in Pennsylvania, Minnesota, Colorado, Kansas, Ohio, Indiana, and Wisconsin emulated Elmira. Reformatories in Massachusetts and Illinois developed eclectic regimens of reform. The Michigan State House of Corrections and Reformatory was an ideological and organizational outlaw—the antithesis of Elmira.

Although Zebulon Brockway, Otis Fuller, Gardiner Tufts, and their counterparts in other states often vehemently disagreed on the methods needed to

29. Indiana Reformatory, *Second BR, 1899-1900* [1900], 18.

30. Wisconsin State Reformatory, *First BR, 1896–1898* (1899), 339; "An Act to Establish a Reformatory."

31. Wisconsin State Reformatory, *First BR, 1896–1898* (1899), 339; *Second BR, 1898–1900* (1901), 336.

save offenders, America's new "professional penologists" shared one common belief: the adult reformatory movement was the most effective penal system and brightest hope for fighting crime and social disorder in the future. Superintendent R. W. McClaughry declared that "this system, when once generally adopted, when perfected by study, observation, and experience, with thoroughly trained officers at its command, will do more toward protecting society by checking the increase in crime than any scheme of imprisonment that has yet been devised." Alvin Hert, superintendent of the Indiana Reformatory, summarized the sentiments of his peers: "The Reformatory Principle has undoubtedly passed out of its experimental stage. It is no more a question whether it will be a success. The success is assured; it is an accomplished fact."[32]

Prison Science in Practice:
A Closer Look at America's New Adult Reformatories

Investigations of the Elmira Reformatory provide a unique opportunity to contrast the promise and practice of scientific reform. Unfortunately, the Elmira inquiries were exceptional. Adult reformatories that opened between 1877 and 1899 were in their early stages of development and, accordingly, were granted a period of grace from criticism and scrutiny.

However, there were two exceptions: the Pennsylvania Industrial Reformatory was investigated in 1892 and the Colorado State Reformatory in 1895. These inquiries reveal that the policies, practices, and problems of the Elmira Reformatory were not unique. These institutions experienced difficulties in managing the minds and souls of men. Much like Elmira, they were brutal prisons.

The Pennsylvania Reformatory. The Pennsylvania State Board of Charities investigation started when ten inmates who were being transferred from the Pennsylvania Industrial Reformatory complained of physical abuse. At the same time, the governor received a letter from a state senator charging that several managers made illegal staff appointments and illegal profits by manipulating construction contracts. On 22 March 1892, the State Board of Charities began a three-day inquiry. Their final report, released on 1 June 1892, provided a mixed assessment of the Pennsylvania Industrial Reformatory. The

32. Pennsylvania Industrial Reformatory, *First BR, 1889–1890* (1891), 24; Indiana Reformatory, *First BR, 1896–1898* (1898), 21.

charges of corruption were unfounded; however, other aspects of the institution's regimen were unsettling.

The commissioners became alarmed at punishment policies which were, in essence, copied from Elmira. Disobedient inmates were "spanked" on the bare buttock with a leather "paddle" which was five inches wide and fifteen inches long. Superintendent T. B. Patton described Pennsylvania's "punishment ritual." Transgressors—referred to as "patients"—were taken to an isolated room:

Their pants were always taken down. Some of them, if they would stand without making disturbance, stood with their hands around the iron railing; else held their hands there. If they were inclined to kick up, their hands were fastened into an iron staple there, to prevent them getting away.[33]

Inmates who would not yield to the spanking were placed in solitary confinement on bread and water. Pennsylvania's "solitary cell" replicated Elmira's "rest cure cell":

In "solitary" he is kept on bread and water. Sometimes such inmates in solitary are allowed free movement in the cell. At other times the consigned inmate is fastened by the wrists to a ring in the wall at the heighth [sic] of about the average man's shoulder. Such fastening necessarily keeps the prisoner on his feet during the time he is attached to the ring. At other times the wrists of the prisoner in "solitary" are attached to a bar running diagonally down the side of the cell, and upon this bar a ring (to which his wrists are attached), moves either up or down at his will.[34]

Inmates who would not respond to the paddle, solitary confinement, or bread and water were subjected to a more debilitating punishment: the ball and chain.

Crucial elements in the regimen of reform were lacking. The labor system was highly inefficient. One quarter of the inmates were unemployed, and three quarters were "only kept employed by a general distribution of work within short hours." The inmates received one hour of academic instruction each day, "which seems to your committee an insufficient proportion of time to be devoted to the department of education in an institution of the character of a reformatory." The Pennsylvania Industrial Reformatory copied Elmira's mark and classification, promotion, and monitor systems. Similar problems resulted. The marking decisions of inmate-monitors were arbitrary, unfair, and subject to

33. Records of the Pennsylvania Industrial Reformatory, *Transcript of Stenographic Notes*, 1:17. Superintendent R. W. McClaughry also described the punishment procedure in "The Spanking System," Elmira *Telegram*, 14 June 1891.

34. Pennsylvania Board of Commissioners of Public Charities, "Report of the Committee," 416.

abuse. "There appears to be a decided repugnance on the part of the average prisoner to any seeming authority on the part of a fellow-prisoner."[35]

The spirit of the institution differed little from a common prison. Some of Pennsylvania's youthful offenders were, in the words of the commissioners, "brutes rather than human beings," who were "disposed to conduct themselves in a manner disgraceful to humanity and deserving treatment." Frequent fights occurred, and inmates were caught "secreting sharpened, pointed knives." The commissioners concluded that "there are frequently cases of incipient revolt, combinations for insubordination and purpose [sic] to break the rules of the institution, and in many ways give trouble to the keepers and other officers."[36]

The final report of the Committee touched on a wide range of topics. The labor system needed improvement and the educational system required a major overhaul. The commissioners called for abolition of the whip and ball and chain, modifications in solitary confinement, and termination of the inmate-monitor system. However, they concluded that the administration was "well-meaning, honest and competent." The commissioners blamed the inmates for the institution's failures: "This institution is not filled with model children."[37] The keepers of the Pennsylvania Industrial Reformatory, like their counterparts in New York, emerged unscathed.

The Colorado Reformatory. An investigation of the Colorado State Reformatory in 1895 was even more devastating. This inquiry, which was ordered by the legislature, authorized the State Board of Charities to look into the charge that Deputy Warden Clarence Hoyt was "guilty of cruel and inhuman treatment of the prisoners; of using profane, foul and obscene language in their presence and in the presence of the officers, and of suffering vile and unnatural practices among the convicts."[38] The committee's final report left no doubt that the Colorado State Reformatory was one of the most ineffective and inhumane institutions in the country.

The commissioners expressed shock at the condition of the institution and the general health of the inmates. Bunkhouse #3 was a small, frame structure which was so poorly constructed that the commissioners "gathered up with our

35. Ibid., 417–18.

36. Ibid, 416. Records of the Pennsylvania Industrial Reformatory, *Conduct Ledgers, Record of Special Punishments,* and *Minutes of the Board of Managers and Board of Trustees, 1889–1899* make references to violent attacks and threats against the keepers.

37. Pennsylvania Board of Commissioners of Public Charities, "Report of the Committee," 430–32.

38. Colorado State Board of Charities, *Report on the Investigation,* 4.

hands the snow that had drifted in." The building was "filthy, uninhabitable, and unsanitary." The bunks were constructed of "undressed lumber of the rudest kind" and the bedding was "covered with filth and infected with vermin." Deputy Warden Hoyt admitted that the sheets and blankets had not been changed or washed in four years. The construction of bunkhouses #1 and #2 was "somewhat better," but these buildings were equally unsanitary.[39]

Inmates were not classified or separated: "sick and healthy, black and white, young and old, held promiscuously together, ranging from 16 to 29." Hoyt admitted that homosexuality was a common occurrence, leading the commissioners to conclude that "the vile and unnatural practices charged, seem not to be unnatural to such a filthy and degrading environment." Although Hoyt attempted to stop these practices, his staff appeared indifferent. As long as the inmates were orderly, the guards did not interfere.[40]

The institution was, in theory, modeled after Elmira. Its annual reports claimed that treatment programs transformed Colorado's youthful offenders into productive citizens. In fact, there were no programs. Elmira's mark, promotion, and classification system was ignored. Religious services took place intermittently, as volunteer chaplains became available. The institution lacked a schoolroom, there were no reading books, and voluntary attendance was low. The bookkeeper, Mr. Coe, was also the schoolmaster. Schoolmaster-bookkeeper Coe did not have assistants, did not receive release time, and did not receive additional pay for his new assignment. The commissioners concluded that Coe "did what little work he did do in this regard as a voluntary service."[41]

The commissioners were displeased with the disciplinary system. The legislature prohibited the use of corporal punishment or "any other brutal or inhuman punishment." However, it did not provide further guidelines. The keepers introduced "hanging up":

The prisoner is taken to a small log building, in the midst of the pig-pen, used as a slaughterhouse. Over a beam in this building is a block and tackle used for drawing up the animals that are butchered. A pair of handcuffs is put upon the wrists of the prisoner; the hook in the block and tackle just referred to is fastened to the handcuffs, and the man is drawn from his feet.

Inmates were hung for times ranging from four to nineteen minutes. Guards attended the spectacle with "morbid curiosity, often treating the matter lightly and with indifference." Hoyt defended the practice, explaining that he did not

39. Ibid., 5.
40. Ibid., 4–5.
41. Ibid., 23.

consider it cruel and could not think of a more effective method. The commissioners disagreed. After hearing inmate accounts of hanging on the meat hook, they concluded that this practice was an "instrument of torture" and "extremely cruel."[42]

Superintendent Smith's report to the legislature stated that "parole is the keystone of the reformatory system."[43] In fact, the parole system was a complete failure. Paroles were "granted in the most arbitrary manner, with no guide nor rule save the whim or wishes of the commissioners." The managers turned over to the warden complete authority to release inmates. In some instances, minimum release eligibility standards were disregarded. Charles May, for example, was released after serving only three months. Superintendent Smith was aware that he was not technically eligible for release but informed the parole board that "May was his man" and "I want you to let him out." The investigators were distressed to learn that impoverished inmates who were granted parole were not released if there was a financial shortfall. Several inmates were kept for over three months because "the commissioners did not have the money to give them, to-wit: $5 and clothes and railroad fare."[44]

Parole supervision was completely ineffective. The parole officer, George Loar, received 50 dollars a month to supervise parolees from the Colorado State Reformatory and the Colorado State Penitentiary. But the commissioners were "unable to find from the records that any duty of any kind that a state agent should perform was performed by Mr. Loar."[45] Loar was a phantom parole officer.

The commissioners condemned the institution's management structure. The legislature, with an eye on the state's limited financial resources, committed an egregious error by making the superintendent of the Colorado State Penitentiary, William Smith, responsible for the Colorado State Reformatory. Smith received no extra pay for the new assignment, rarely visited the reformatory, and effectively turned over control to his deputy warden, Clarence Hoyt. Hoyt tried to do a good job but had little experience in penology and was "unfit to have charge of such an institution." Hoyt's guard staff was "with one or two excep-

42. Ibid., 6.

43. Colorado State Reformatory, *Second AR, 1892* (1893), 6.

44. Colorado State Board of Charities, *Report on the Investigation*, 17–19, 24. Inmates at the Pennsylvania Industrial Reformatory were also at the mercy of business cycles. Inmates who were granted parole but could not get a job because of economic conditions "have been obliged to serve their parole period in the Reformatory, and be granted their final discharge therefrom" (Pennsylvania Industrial Reformatory, *Third BR, 1893–1894* [1895], 8).

45. Colorado State Board of Charities, *Report on the Investigation*, 20.

tions ... not competent and not of the character or education demanded by Reformatory discipline and methods."[46]

The Board of Charities report placed most of the blame for the institution's failure on the managers. Although they had responsibility for supervising the institution, like the managers of Elmira, they were detached and "never knew what the warden or his deputy was doing in the premises." Irrespective of blame, it is clear that the Colorado State Reformatory was little more than a primitive work camp. The investigators concluded that "the wise and beneficent act establishing the Colorado State Reformatory has failed to secure such an institution as was contemplated." They urged the legislature to increase appropriations to "save the fair name of Colorado from any blemish of barbarism or inhumanity."[47]

Saving Satan's Children: The Seven Deadly Inmate Sins

In chapter 3 we saw that prisoner resistance disrupted the internal regimen of Elmira, forcing Brockway and his staff to focus their attention on maintaining order and internal security. The keepers of the ten reformatory-prisons opened between 1877 and 1899 also confronted a wide range of uncooperative offenders and the nagging problem of disruptive secondary adjustments: violence, revolts, escapes, drugs, arson, homosexuality, and suicide. These misbehaviors sidetracked efforts to manage America's youthful offenders. They also left some superintendents wondering whether they had taken on an impossible task—namely, saving Satan's children.

Inmate violence was a constant concern at every reformatory. Although the records of other institutions do not contain tallies of confrontations as does Elmira's (370 fights between 1889 and 1893), data sources indicate that inmates had little difficulty in stealing or making weapons and many had few compunctions about using them. For example, the Journal of the General Superintendent at the Pennsylvania Industrial Reformatory in April 1892 reveals a number of attacks on inmate-monitors. An inmate named Lynch received a mark for talking from inmate-monitor Nolan. Lynch, reported the superintendent, "struck Nolan in the face with his fist." In the same month, Thompson attacked monitor Dooley, "striking him with his fist in the mouth." Other assaults were more deadly. An inmate named Cato snuck up behind a monitor and struck him over the head with a shovel yelling, "Let the son of a bitch die." William Larkin

46. Ibid., 21, 23.
47. Ibid., 8, 25–26.

stabbed a monitor with a knife, leaving a gash running from his jaw to his chest. Larkin showed little remorse: "I sent for him to spank him," reported the superintendent. "He fought like a tiger, made all manner of threats and tried to bite and kick the Deputy and myself."[48]

Inmate violence was also directed at civilian officers. Officer Harry Miller instructed Edward Egan to get in line and keep quiet. Egan was in a contrary mood. He told Miller to "keep his God damn mouth shut" and "stooping down caught the officer by the legs and threw him down on the cell house floor." In another instance, three inmates attacked Officer Neffs. Inmates Hutson, Roach, and Walton knocked Neffs down with a sandbag. "He was then jumped on by the men who had provided a heavy twine and belt lacing his hands were tied together and a gag made of rags tied his mouth. Hutson took the officers revolver and threatened him." Some attacks were even more serious. Inmate Aiken bragged that he was "tough as you make them" and threatened to "cut some bodys [sic] throat and then they would send him to the 'Pen.'" Officer Bookhammer heard him uttering these threats and entered his cell. Aiken kept his promise: he stabbed Bookhammer in the face. Five months after the stabbing, Bookhammer was warned of a plot to murder him. This time he was prepared. When Edward Woods attacked with a two-foot pipe, Bookhammer shot and killed him.[49]

Even the superintendent was not safe from attack. In November 1893 a guard overheard a plot aimed at "smashing the superintendent." An inquiry revealed that three inmates were planning to kill Superintendent Patton. One conspirator was making a knife in the machine shop. At chapel services, "Reeder was to throw a brick at Supt. during time of prayer and that Gorman was to use the knife." This was not an isolated case. Patton granted inmate Houghton an interview in April 1894. Houghton questioned a disciplinary mark which he received and apparently did not like Patton's explanation. "Houghton struck the Supt. a heavy blow on the face, knocking him down, as well as knocking him senseless. As he attempted to rise, Houghton made a second attempt to strike him." Several clerks saved the superintendent from serious injury.[50]

Inmate violence sometimes escalated into riots and revolts. A headline in the New York *Times*—"More Trouble at Huntingdon"—was unsettling to supporters of the new penology. The article reported:

48. Records of the Pennsylvania Industrial Reformatory, *Journal of the General Superintendent, 1891–1906*, 43, 47, 44, 28.
49. Ibid., 99, 181, 100, 120–25. Records of the Pennsylvania Industrial Reformatory, *Investigation of the Escape; Investigation of Edward Wood's Death.*
50. *Journal of the General Superintendent, 1891–1906*, 93–94, 105–6.

As Officer D. W. Beyer was marching a squad of sixty inmates to the schoolroom at the reformatory to-day, James Caul of Philadelphia hurled his slate at the guard's head, but without hitting him. Alonzo Billings, also from Philadelphia, acting on Caul's signal, also struck at the guard with his slate, but missed his aim. That was a signal for a general revolt among the inmates, and half of the 100 prisoners in the schoolroom engaged in a deadly attack on the defenseless officer.

The dynamics of the ensuing revolt demonstrate that the inmates were earnest and the guards were lucky.

Caul, who had precipitated the assault, drew a brick from his hat and dealt Guard Beyers a violent blow over the eye, knocking him down. After receiving a fusillade of kicks and blows Officer Beyer drew his cane, but this was speedily taken from him and turned on himself. In endeavoring to rescue his prostrate fellow-officer, James Kyle was also severely injured.

Reinforcements subdued the rioters. The guards survived the attack but were severely injured, and the inmate leaders were placed "in the dungeons."[51]

Escapes were a constant concern at every adult reformatory. The experiences of the Michigan Reformatory were not unusual. Between 1883 and 1884, twenty-seven inmates "eloped." Determined inmates resorted to a variety of creative techniques to secure their freedom. One inmate tunneled into a ventilator shaft, climbed over a roof, and then jumped the wall. Another inmate, no doubt unhappy at the prospect of incarceration, jumped off a moving train on the way to the reformatory; he died the next day. Others simply attacked the wall which, at seventeen feet, "is but little hindrance to getting away." Escapes were such a gnawing concern that the physician, E. F. Beckwirth, considered each inmate's escape potential in deciding who would be sent to the hospital, which was not secure. High-risk inmates were not hospitalized until "it was evident that they were too sick to run away." Dr. Beckwirth explained that "the possibility of losing a long-time man must always be taken into consideration."[52]

Security was weak at other reformatories. The main line of defense, institutional walls, were often porous. A "board fence" surrounded the Minnesota Reformatory. One hundred fifty feet of the wall surrounding the Massachusetts

---

51. "More Trouble at Huntingdon," New York *Times*, 13 October 1892, 3; Records of the Pennsylvania Industrial Reformatory, *Journal of the General Superintendent, 1891–1906*, 61.

52. Michigan State House of Correction and Reformatory, *Second BR* (1884), 13; *Seventh BR* (1894), 13. A concerted effort was made to catch escapees and parole violators. Several institutions sent out up to ten thousand "wanted" posters for each escapee or violator with rewards ranging from 25 to 50 dollars (Kansas State Industrial Reformatory, *Escaped Men*). "Wanted" posters are also in the Records of the Pennsylvania Industrial Reformatory, *Scrapbook, 1889–1929*. James Comfort, a chaplain–parole officer at the Indiana Reformatory, discusses search techniques in "Return of Escaped Prisoners."

Reformatory blew down in an 1890 storm. The Illinois State Reformatory had a "frail board fence" which, the superintendent warned, presented "a standing invitation to the unruly to make an effort to escape." Apparently, he was correct: sixteen inmates escaped in 1892, twenty-six between 1894 and 1896. The Kansas Reformatory did not even have a wall when it opened in 1895. "Some of them were continually conspiring to escape; others had escaped and were recaptured," explained the managers in transferring eight inmates to prison. The wall of the Ohio Reformatory was unfinished when it opened in 1896. Although the guards would shoot to kill—they shot four inmates between 1897 and 1898, one fatally—thirty inmates attempted to flee between 1896 and 1899.[53]

Other inmates responded to the pains of incarceration by smuggling tobacco and making "prison brew." Tobacco was prohibited at every institution, with the exception of the Colorado Reformatory. Corporal punishments and solitary confinement were used to combat these "evil habits," but many inmates continued to steal, smuggle, or buy tobacco whenever they could; others made stimulating but deadly "prison hooch." Thomas Hardiman and Eugene Powers, inmates at the Massachusetts Reformatory, died in 1891 after drinking stolen methyl alcohol. "Finding the first effects to be exhilarating, they drank to excess," explained the physician. In 1898 William Spellman and James Murphy, also Massachusetts inmates, died after drinking another experimental concoction.[54]

Opposition to tobacco use was not solely based on health concerns. Tobacco required matches; matches could be used to burn down buildings. Incendiarism was, with good cause, a major concern. Despite concerted efforts to prohibit matches, disgruntled inmates were sometimes successful in obtaining them, with devastating consequences. A fire of "suspicious origins" destroyed the hospital, laundry, kitchen, bakery, and shoe and tailor shops at the Michigan Reformatory in 1884. A fire destroyed the brush, carpenter, tin, and paint shops at the Pennsylvania Industrial Reformatory in 1892. The upper floor and roof of the Minnesota Reformatory's main administration building burned in 1899.[55]

53. Minnesota State Reformatory, *First AR* (1889), 3; Massachusetts Reformatory, *Sixth AR, 1890* (1891), 149; Illinois State Reformatory, *Fourth BR, 1896–1898* [1898], vii; Kansas State Industrial Reformatory, *First BR, 1895–1896* (1896), 10; Ohio State Reformatory, *Fifteenth AR* [1898], 24.

54. Massachusetts Reformatory, *Seventh AR, 1891* [1892], 170; *Fourteenth AR, 1898* (1899), 141.

55. Michigan State House of Correction and Reformatory, *Second BR* (1884), 12–13; Pennsylvania Industrial Reformatory, *Second BR, 1891–1892* (1892), 9; Records of the Pennsylvania In-

Homosexuality presented another serious problem. The historical record does not reveal "sex rings" comparable to the one formed at Elmira in the late 1880s and early 1890s. However, the keepers of reformatories were forced to resort to extreme measures to prevent "crimes against God and nature." When the Kansas Industrial Reformatory became crowded in 1898, the managers paroled undeserving inmates to avoid double bunking. They explained:

Prison men everywhere know to what brutal extent sexual perversity is carried by the inmates of penitentiaries, when congregated together, and we are compelled to admit that reformatories are no exception to this rule, and cellular associations afford about the only opportunity for these detestable practices.[56]

Inmates who could not cope with the pains of incarceration sometimes resorted to the ultimate form of secondary adjustment: suicide. Superintendent Tufts suspected that Patrick Sullivan was insane and made an effort to have him transferred to a mental institution, but on 10 May 1888, "He eluded attention long enough to take his own life." G. W. Parker, a larcenist committed to the Michigan Reformatory in 1891, swallowed a fatal dose of a furniture finishing stain. When Charles Lang committed suicide at the Minnesota Reformatory in 1896, Superintendent Houlton was puzzled. "The coroner's inquest showed no cause; that there had been no sign of melancholy, ill-health, or mental unsoundness, and that he had no trouble here, having never been reported." Superintendent R. W. McClaughry faced two suicide attempts within a forty-eight-hour period in January 1891. William Dickerson "tried to hang himself to the door of the cell, by tearing his shirt to pieces and using it as a rope." A guard found Charles Reichner "hanging in his cell to an improvised gallows which he had made using his bedstead—standing it on end." The superintendent attributed both attempts to "extreme self-abuse" (a commonly cited explanation) and ordered Dickerson and Reichner placed in restraints.[57]

Complicating matters, many inmates were versatile and prolific rule violators—experts at "prisoner resistance." Charles P., a sixteen-year-old inmate committed to the Minnesota State Reformatory in 1891 for grand larceny, re-

dustrial Reformatory, *Investigation into the Fire*; Minnesota State Reformatory, *Second BR, 1898–1900* (1900), 8.

56. Kansas State Industrial Reformatory, *Second BR* (1898), 6. Reports of "immoral practices" are also in the Records of the St. Cloud [Minnesota] State Reformatory, *Misconduct Records* and *Inmate History and Record*.

57. Massachusetts Reformatory, *Fourth AR, 1888* (1889), 139; Michigan House of Correction and Reformatory, *Sixth BR* (1893), 10; Minnesota State Reformatory, *Eighth and Ninth AR, 1896–1896* (1897), 31; Records of the Pennsylvania Industrial Reformatory, *Journal of the General Superintendent, 1891–1906*, 27, 28.

ceived forty misconduct reports during his stay. His transgressions included fighting, creating a disturbance, insolence, disobedience, destroying property, shirking work, and having a live gopher in his cell. John S., a sixteen-year-old committed in 1890 for grand larceny, committed thirty-three violations: smuggling tobacco, fighting, creating a disturbance, disobeying orders, insolence, abusive language, destroying property, shirking work, crookedness, and throwing stones at his fellow inmates. These inmates were placed in solitary confinement a total of eighteen times, but to no avail.[58]

The inmates at other reformatories were also individually and collectively troublesome. Between 1896 and 1897, inmates at the Illinois State Reformatory collected 8,334 reports for misconduct. Between 1896 and 1898, inmates at the Indiana Reformatory received 6,586 reports. The Record of Special Punishments at the Pennsylvania Industrial Reformatory includes hundreds of infractions which reflect considerable inmate creativity at rule breaking and secondary adaptation. Offenses included: fighting, smoking, sodomy ("licentious intercourse"), indecency ("exposure of person"), attempted riot and escape, talking, loudness, vile language, theft (e.g. food, clothes), refusing to obey orders, refusing to work, laziness, telling falsehoods, quarreling, crookedness, defiling cell house, spitting, feigning sickness and insanity, writing obscene notes, making obscene pictures, secreting dangerous weapons, obscene gestures to a female visitor, threatening officers, assaulting and attempting to kill officers, and "evacuating bowels on floor of cell."[59]

Conclusion

Zebulon Brockway was the most important penologist in the United States; the Elmira Reformatory was the world's model correctional institution. However, the keepers of ten adult reformatories opened in the United States between 1877 and 1899 did not blindly replicate the Elmira system. Three ver-

58. Records of the St. Cloud State Reformatory, *Misconduct Record, 1889–1897*, 2:8–9, 29. Inmate infractions are also traced in the *Conduct Ledgers, 1889–1891*, the *Record of Special Punishments*, and the *Solitary Register*. Other institutions also had prolific rule violators: e.g., "Case of William B..." (p. 259) and "Case of Roy D..." (p. 439) in Records of the Ohio State Reformatory, *Historical Conduct Record, 1896–1901*, and Case History #19 and #34 in Records of the Pennsylvania Industrial Reformatory, *Biographical and Descriptive Register*.

59. Illinois State Reformatory, *Fourth BR, 1896–1898* [1898], vi; Indiana Reformatory, *First BR, 1896–1898* (1898), 19; Records of the Pennsylvania Industrial Reformatory, *Record of Special Punishment, 1889–1897*, 1–17, and *Conduct Ledgers, 1889–1891*; Records of the Ohio State Reformatory, *Weekly List of Prisoners Punished for Infractions of Rules*, reflects similar behavior.

sions of scientific criminology emerged as legislators and reformatory keepers modified the new penology to reflect and serve state-specific needs and interests. However, the New York, Michigan, and Massachusetts models pursued a common aim. America's new reformatory-prisons, much like the institutions of social control analyzed by Foucault and Garland, were "punitive-pariah cities" which attempted to administer "bourgeois justice."

But America's new adult reformatories failed to socialize their charges and mold obedient citizen-workers. The keepers of Foucault's "carceral cities," like Brockway, were confronted with the defects of the medical model and total institutions. Inmates at every institution rejected the authority of their custodians and responded to the pains of incarceration by resorting to disruptive secondary adjustments. The seven deadly inmate sins—violence, revolts, escapes, drugs, arson, homosexuality, suicide—magnified the defects of total power and forced reformatory keepers to focus their attention on custody and control in the interests of personal and organizational survival. America's adult reformatories were—witness the investigations of the Pennsylvania and Colorado institutions—ineffective and brutal prisons. The pathology of the society of captives and the hazards of the "tinkering science" and "people work" were, quite simply, universal.

Chapter Five

The "New" Elmira: Psycho-eugenics and the Decline of the Rehabilitative Ideal

The Elmira Reformatory played a central role in the formulation of national penal policy during the Progressive Era; however, these policies were very different from those advocated between 1876 and 1899. Brockway's forced resignation in 1900 set the stage for the introduction of a new Elmira system. Between 1900 and 1920, physicians seized the reins of administrative power and, drawing on the latest developments in the fields of medicine, psychology, sociology, and social welfare, implemented eugenic prison science.

The discovery of a new type of criminal, the mentally defective offender, led to the adoption of a new goal (custody, control, incapacitation, social defense), a new theory of crime causation (biologically and psychologically based multifactor positivism), new tests (Binet-Simon and psychograms), a host of new criminal categories (feebleminded, morons, dullards, psychopaths), the rise of a new class of experts (correctional psychologists and psychiatrists), and calls for more draconian solutions to America's crime problem (penal colonies and sterilizations). Two versions of the Elmira system emerged: salvageable offenders participated in a variety of programs aimed at reform; mentally defective offenders were exposed to an incapacitative-custodial regimen aimed at protecting the public.

The Fall of the Master

In 1900, penologists celebrated the first quarter century of the adult reformatory movement by publishing a series of articles on America's third penal system. These papers, compiled by Samuel J. Barrows, commissioner of the International Prison Commission, heaped praise on Brockway and Elmira. Franklin Sanborn summarized the sentiments of his peers. Brockway was a man of "rare powers of observation and reflection" with "a mind for systematic thought and methodical direction," a "constructive genius." Elmira was a "great technological training school" and a "prison university." Sanborn concluded: "They have, in fact, developed a prison science while constructing a reformatory prison system."[1]

Ironically, Brockway was fighting for his job at the same time that Barrows published his collection. The battle began in May 1899 when Governor Theodore Roosevelt replaced three managers, all staunch supporters of Brockway; two remaining pro-Brockway managers resigned shortly thereafter.[2] The new managers began their tenure by evaluating every aspect of Elmira. Their findings, published in Elmira's 1901 annual report, reveal that they were not pleased with Brockway's stewardship. In fact, their criticisms echoed the findings of the 1893–1894 Board of Charities inquiry: America's "model reformatory" was still a brutal and ineffective prison.

The new managers discovered that the physical plant was in inexcusably poor condition. The heating system was "primitive," the lighting system was "extremely precarious," and the boilers were "fully dangerous." The water supply was "honeycombed with rust" and the sewer system was a "menace to health." They concluded that "the plant is old and rotten."[3]

The managers were even more distressed with the condition of the inmates. Tuberculosis was widespread. The managers blamed Dr. Hamilton Wey, the institution's part-time physician, for the plight of the inmates. Dr. Wey did not

1. Sanborn, "Elmira Reformatory," 28–29, 40, 42, 44. Others shared Sanborn's views: Warner, "A Study of Prison Management," 50; idem, "What Shall Be Done," 77; C. Lewis, "Indeterminate Sentence," 63.

2. In 1899 Roosevelt replaced James Rathbone, W. H. Peters, and C. T. Willis with Ainsley Wilcox, Henry Danforth, and Thomas Sturgis. Wilcox resigned shortly thereafter, to be replaced by Charles Beckett. The new majority elected Sturgis to serve as president of the board. Mathias H. Arnot submitted his resignation and Henry Danforth, following Wilcox, resigned after one year. Roosevelt appointed Charles Howard, a physician, and Justin Harris as replacements. In 1900, the last Brockway supporter, John Diven, resigned.

3. New York State, Assembly Documents (1901), vol. 2, no. 17, New York State Reformatory, *Twenty-fifth AR* (1900), 27–28.

examine new arrivals; inmates with tuberculosis were not segregated; medical record-keeping was poor; the milch cows were not tested (five were tubercular); and inmates with psychological disorders were neglected. The managers concluded that "Dr. Wey's private professional practice, and the nominal compensation paid to him, prevented his giving more than a perfunctory attention to his duties at the institution."[4]

Brockway's public relations and marketing campaign stressed the point that Elmira's inmates were malleable first-time offenders; however, the managers discovered that sixty percent of the "Elmira boys" were recidivists. Many were hardened offenders "whose life has been one violation of the law." They concluded, "It is a common misconception that Elmira is for boys or youths, and only for first offenses. The facts are quite different."[5] The mixing of hardened and novice youthful offenders was complicated by overcrowding. In 1899 the institution had 1,200 cells and 1,474 inmates. "Such association brings in not a few instances moral contamination," warned the managers.[6]

The managers were highly critical of Brockway's continued use of inmate-monitors, as well as their detrimental influence on the mark, classification, and promotion system. Inmate-monitors and low-caliber civilian staff contributed to decadence and corruption. In March 1900 the managers uncovered "a widespread conspiracy to supply tobacco, opium and other contraband articles to prisoners." Monitors and inmates responded to the pains of imprisonment by creating an elaborate smuggling network; civilian officers were willing accomplices. Corruption spread to other parts of the reformatory. The managers discovered that the food was of a "very inferior grade." An investigation revealed that the cook was buying low-quality food for inmates and "providing a restaurant in the institution [with good food] for a part of the employees as a private business, the profits from which accrued to himself."[7]

Brockway's disciplinary techniques, which had changed little since the 1893–1894 inquiry, drew intense criticism. The managers denounced the practice of "flogging" (their term) as archaic and barbaric. "The time has gone by when we seek to punish the criminal. Punishment as a deterrent has had its day and has failed." Flogging, they concluded,

---

4. Ibid., 11, 13.

5. Ibid., 19.

6. New York State, Assembly Documents (1900), vol. 2, no. 24, New York State Reformatory, *Twenty-fourth AR* (1899), 11.

7. New York State, Assembly Documents (1901), vol. 2, no. 17, New York State Reformatory, *Twenty-fifth AR* (1900), 30, 25.

degraded and brutalized alike the man who received and the man who administered it [namely Brockway]; that while flogging would cowe [sic] an insubordinate spirit, it would not elevate it; that where flogging and only flogging would secure obedience, the man was incorrigible, under the law, and belonged in the State prison and not in the Reformatory."[8]

Governor Roosevelt's managers instituted a variety of changes in 1899 and 1900 in an attempt to correct these problems. Funding requests went to the legislature to rebuild decrepit buildings and improve the water, sewer, heating, and electrical systems. Health care improved: a full-time physician was hired; inmates received physicals when they were committed and released; dentist and oculist hours increased; food improved; the entire institution was cleaned and whitewashed; tubercular and mentally ill inmates were transferred. The managers made plans to dismantle Brockway's monitor system and hire more civilian guards, limit the size of the institution, and send recidivists to adult prisons. They reorganized the industrial and academic education programs and cut back labor hours which "produced too much mental and physical strain." And they abolished corporal punishment.

A number of staff members, including some of Brockway's most trusted confidants, were summarily fired. Brockway was most distressed when Dr. Wey submitted his forced resignation in February 1900. The managers ignored Brockway's protests and filled the position of assistant superintendent, which had remained empty since the murder of William McKelvey in 1880. Patrick McDonnell, the new appointee, did not receive a warm reception when he arrived in July 1900. In a final "insult," the managers revised Brockway's "outgrown" 1877 legislation. The new act, which passed the legislature on 11 April 1900, was designed to correct the "defects" in Brockway's famed Elmira system.[9]

Brockway was enraged. He vehemently denied all the criticisms leveled against his administration, condemned the firing of his assistants, and resisted the new "improvements."[10] The managers were, in Brockway's estimation, naive and misinformed amateurs. They did not understand the complexities of prison management and prison science; more important, they did not understand the inmates. Brockway defended all aspects of the Elmira system, including the use of corporal punishment: "The only harmless stimulating physical

8. Ibid., 20–21.

9. Ibid., 10; "An Act to Revise, Consolidate and Amend."

10. Brockway devoted a full chapter of *Fifty Years* to his 1899–1900 conflict with the new managers (pp. 363–76). He was also miffed at the managers for terminating two experimental dietary programs which, in his judgment, were successful.

treatment is, for such as must suffer it, the safest and surest, that which has always been used, rarely abused, the too-much contemned measure—spanking!" Brockway argued that he must be in "full command" and afforded "wide discretionary power." He cautioned that "To hamper and belittle his position is unwise":

Administrative details can not be well conducted by any remote non-resident authority or agency [the managers], and it is impossible to maintain with efficiency the numerous departments and the delicate adjustments of them in a well organized reformatory if there is divided executive authority.[11]

For the first time in his fifty-two-year career, the public relations, marketing, and propaganda techniques which had served Brockway so well in the past were ineffective. Governor Roosevelt and his successor, Benjamin Odell, wanted change, and the managers did not yield. Brockway, who was now seventy-three years old, lacked the spirit to fight the new board. After battling for control of his beloved institution for fourteen months, he finally conceded defeat. On 31 July 1900, Brockway quietly submitted his forced resignation. Elmira's "golden age" had come to an end.[12]

The New Elmira: Custodial Reform and the Napanoch Connection

Brockway's supporters were alarmed: What course would Elmira's new superintendent, Dr. Frank Robertson, and his administration follow? Would the new managers and superintendent tamper with the medical model and dismantle the Elmira system? Would they abandon what was still regarded by many penologists as America's most innovative and successful correctional experiment?

The new administration quickly assured its critics that they were not dismantling the Elmira system or abandoning prison science. The managers issued an emphatic "denial of any intent to destroy what he [Brockway] has built

11. New York State, Assembly Documents (1901), vol. 2, no. 17, New York State Reformatory, *Twenty-fifth AR* (1900), 37.

12. Brockway's forced resignation was not widely publicized and it certainly did not diminish his reputation. Brockway's retirement years were spent in Elmira, where he resided with his widowed daughter, Emma Blossom, her children, and his own wife. He served as a prison inspector for the Prison Association of New York, and continued to lecture, write, and attend prison conferences. He was Elmira's mayor from 1905 to 1907. In 1910 he was made honorary president of the International Prison Congress in Washington, D. C. Brockway remained active in the field of corrections until his death in Elmira, New York, on 21 October 1920 at the age of ninety-three (Pisciotta, "Zebulon Brockway," 137).

up." They softened their forced removal of Brockway by conceding that they "find in the system much to admire and uphold; something to criticize and modify, and something to condemn." The basic assumptions and programs of the Elmira system were, in their view, sound; delivery (i.e. management, personnel, funding) was the root of the institution's problems. The new managers wanted to introduce a less coercive Elmira system—a "truly Christian theory of treatment."[13]

Superintendent Robertson and the new managers focused their initial efforts on two pressing problems: improving inmate health care and repairing the buildings and infrastructure. As promised, the administration did not abandon the medical model. The new 1900 legislative act governing Elmira facilitated the transfer of inappropriate commitments but did not significantly alter key programs. Brockway's indeterminate sentencing and mark and classification system remained unchanged during Robertson's three-year tenure. Military drill continued. Trade school hours were modified and an effort was made to replace inmate-instructors in the schools and shops with civilians. A new full-time chaplain improved religious instruction. Solitary confinement, without chains, replaced Brockway's dreaded rest cure cell and corporal punishment.

Robertson made an effort to administer these programs in a more humane and less psychologically coercive environment. In 1902 the managers pointed out, "Two years ago the inmate population here was in a condition of chronic nervous excitement and unrest mingled with apprehension and fear. ... To-day the reverse is the case."[14] They concluded, "We are proud to say that the New York State Reformatory to-day stands first among similar institutions throughout the world. Its system and methods are copied wherever a new institution is founded."[15]

When Robertson resigned on 1 December 1903 to return to private practice as a physician, Joseph Scott, superintendent of the Massachusetts State Reformatory, became his successor. One of America's most respected penologists, Scott shared the new administration's goals and, following Robertson's example, did not alter Elmira's key programs. Reforms under his eight-year tenure were aimed at, first, making the disciplinary system (i.e. solitary confinement)

13. New York State, Assembly Documents (1902), vol. 1, no. 21, New York State Reformatory, *Twenty-sixth AR* (1901), 25. The new managers spent eight days listening to complaints and suggestions from eight hundred inmates. Unfortunately, the testimony was not recorded.

14. Ibid., 9.

15. New York State, Senate Documents (1903), vol. 6, no. 13, New York State Reformatory, *Twenty-seventh AR* (1902), 19. Arthur Call characterized Elmira as a "reformatory hospital" in "Education versus Crime," 601.

less psychologically stressful and, second, improving the quality of the civilian guard staff (higher pay, shorter hours, better benefits, raising the hiring age from twenty-one to twenty-five).

Brockway's departure did not, then, greatly diminish Elmira's stature. Prison officials from Denmark, England, Germany, New Zealand, Brazil, and other countries visited in 1905 to study the "improved" version of the Elmira system. Scott and the managers assured their visitors that eighty-five percent of the inmates were reformed and that their institution was "the best in the world."[16] In 1907 the New York State Board of Reformatories concluded that Elmira was "obtaining results which no institution in the world can excel."[17]

The optimism of Superintendents Robertson and Scott and the managers was not, however, solely due to the firing of Brockway and "improvements" in the Elmira system. External events, particularly the opening of the Eastern New York Reformatory, had a profound effect on the Elmira Reformatory.

Brockway's claims of remarkable success, coupled with overcrowding at Elmira, led in the late 1880s to calls for the opening of a second adult reformatory in New York. The 1892 legislature passed a bill authorizing the selection of a building site for a new institution. An 1894 act appropriated funds to purchase a site at Napanoch and begin constructing a five hundred–cell facility. Ground was broken in 1894, but inconsistent appropriations delayed the project. The nation's twelfth adult reformatory for males, the Eastern New York Reformatory, finally opened on 1 October 1900.[18]

From Elmira's perspective, the most significant aspect of the 1900 law governing Napanoch's operation was a rather obscure clause regarding commitments. The Eastern New York Reformatory did not receive offenders directly from the courts. All of New York's sixteen-to-thirty-year-old criminals were sent to Elmira, which served as a reception diagnostic center. Elmira's keepers, following a diagnostic interview, decided which inmates would stay and which would go to Napanoch.[19]

16. New York State, Assembly Documents (1906), vol. 2, no. 23, New York State Reformatory, *Thirtieth AR* (1905), 25. Rusztem Vambery, a Hungarian penologist, pointed out that the Elmira system had spread as far as Australia, South Africa, New Zealand, and Norway. German penologists, much to Vambery's dismay, still opposed the system because they thought that it was lenient ("The Indeterminate Sentence," 112–13).

17. New York State Commission of Prisons, *Thirteenth AR, 1907* [1908], 113. Case histories continued to serve as "proof" of the effectiveness of Elmira's new system. Inmate Peter Luckey was cited as an ideal case of reform ("Institutional Experiences," 71–111).

18. "An Act to Establish the Eastern New York Reformatory"; "An Act to Provide for the Construction"; "An Act to Provide for the Organization." An excellent dissertation, Hahn [subsequently Rafter], "The Defective Delinquent Movement," provides a detailed history of Napanoch.

19. Napanoch received sixty-nine inmates from the Sing Sing, Auburn, and Clinton Prisons from its opening in October 1900 to February 1901. Thereafter, inmates were committed from Elmira. Records of the Eastern New York Reformatory, *Receiving (Admission) Register.*

Elmira's keepers used this discretion to create unofficially two classes of youthful offenders, two versions of prison science, and two types of adult reformatories in New York. Recidivists, offenders over twenty-five, and parole violators—"troublemakers" and "incorrigibles"—were sent to the Eastern Reformatory, while younger, manageable, and more hopeful offenders remained at Elmira.[20] Elmira would, in theory, pursue the aim of treatment and reform. Napanoch would assume a custodial function, serving as the dumping ground for New York's human and social refuse.

The internal regimen of the Eastern New York Reformatory reflected its custodial-incapacitative mission. Napanoch was, much like Elmira during the 1876 to 1880 period, primarily a work camp.[21] Napanoch's superintendent, Silas Berry, was more of a construction foreman than a superintendent. In 1902 the inmates were kept busy "building, grading, ditching, road-making, breaking stone, farming, gardening, etc. ..."[22] Rehabilitative programs were not even contemplated: there was no academic instruction, industrial education, or military drill; religious services were held intermittently.

John Jaeckel, president of the New York State Commission of Prisons, expressed serious concerns about Napanoch's custodial mission following his 1903 inspection. Jaeckel concluded that the Eastern Reformatory was in "crude condition":

Why this institution should be designated as a reformatory is paradoxical. Certainly the arrangement, construction and plan of the building are illy adapted for the purpose implied by its title, and we cannot recognize in the treatment of its inmates any reformatory features; no educational progress; no development along the lines of industrial training, nothing, indeed, to advance the mental and physical condition of the inhabitants toward reformation. It is simply a prison, and a poor one.

Inspections by the New York State Commission of Prisons in 1904, 1905, and 1906 echoed Jaeckel's harsh criticisms.[23]

In 1906 the legislature created a new seven-member State Board of Reformatories to oversee Elmira and Napanoch.[24] The inclusion of Elmira's five managers on this board effectively placed the Eastern New York Reformatory under the direct control of Elmira's keepers. The bill made Joseph Scott the su-

20. "An Act Amending Section Sixteen"; Superintendent of New York State Prisons, *AR, 1903* (1904), 269; New York State, Assembly Documents (1910), vol. 26, no. 48, New York State Board of Reformatories, *Thirty-fourth AR of the New York State Reformatory and Ninth AR of the Eastern New York Reformatory* (1909), 10.

21. New York State Board of Reformatories, *Thirty-second AR of the New York State Reformatory and Seventh AR of the Eastern New York Reformatory* (1907), 12.

22. Superintendent of New York State Prisons, *AR, 1902* (1903), 270–72.

23. New York State Commission of Prisons, *Ninth AR, 1903* [1904], 81–82; *Tenth AR, 1904* [1905], 96–99; *Eleventh AR, 1905* [1906], 108–12; *Twelfth AR, 1906* [1907], 48–53.

24. "An Act to Provide for a State Board of Managers of Reformatories."

perintendent of both institutions, but the Eastern Reformatory's assistant superintendent, George Deyo, managed the daily operation of Napanoch. The Eastern New York Reformatory was now an official, but decidedly inferior, appendage of Elmira. (Napanoch maintained this status until it became the nation's first institution for defective delinquents in 1921.)[25]

Scott attempted to improve Napanoch's custodial–dumping ground status. But the institution continued to receive New York's less promising cases, and the construction of the physical plant clearly took precedence over reform. In 1909 the Board of Reformatories conceded that Napanoch was not nearly complete (including the wall, which was not started until 1907). The 1917 State Commission of Prisons Report noted, "This institution is being gradually constructed by inmate labor."[26] The keepers of Elmira-Napanoch faced a rather unusual situation in 1920: the physical plant was incomplete but deteriorating.

The opening of the Eastern New York Reformatory proved to be a mixed blessing for the keepers of Elmira. The transfer of troublesome offenders to Napanoch left Elmira with more manageable inmates. However, Superintendent Scott and his successors had the enormous problem of building and maintaining a branch institution which was more than 120 miles away. Despite its dismal record and peripheral status, the Eastern New York Reformatory had a major impact on Progressive Era penology. Napanoch's custodial-incapacitative mission set the stage for the introduction of yet another approach to "reform": eugenic prison science.

Eugenic Prison Science:
The Discovery of the Mentally Defective Offender, 1910–1920

A group of delegates to the International Prison Congress visited Elmira on 19 September 1910. They were led by Dr. Charles Henderson, professor of sociology at the University of Chicago and president of the Congress. The visitors toured buildings, inspected the Elmira system, and discussed with Superintendent Scott the progress of American penology since the completion of the 1870 Declaration of Principles. The selection of Elmira was not accidental. International Prison Congress delegates officially endorsed indeterminate sentencing, parole, and the rehabilitative ideal when they convened in Washington, D.C., in October 1910. Zebulon Brockway, the high priest of the new penology, was elected honorary president of the Congress.[27]

25. "An Act to Amend the Prison Law and the Mental Deficiency Law."
26. New York State Commission of Prisons, *Twenty-third AR, 1917* [1918], 26.
27. Papers from this conference are published in Henderson, *Correction and Prevention*.

Henderson and his colleagues did not know that Elmira-Napanoch was about to embark on a new course which was, in many ways, antithetical to the aims and spirit of the new penology. Exploratory psychological tests were uncovering an alarming finding: many of New York's youthful offenders were "mental defectives." Drawn from America's new dangerous classes—"Hebrew, Italian, Colored"—these offenders were considered biologically and psychologically inferior and not amenable to reform.[28]

Research by Elmira's physician, Dr. Frank Christian, sparked interest in the mentally defective offender.[29] In 1908 Christian studied data on eight thousand consecutive commitments and concluded that thirty-seven percent were mental defectives. A study of 1,035 inmates committed to Elmira in 1910 concluded that thirty-eight percent were defective. Christian believed that these offenders could be fitted into two broad categories: congenital and acquired defectives. Congenital defectives were the "offspring of degenerate or criminal parentage." Acquired mental defectives were the victims of poor environments, especially poverty, slums, and the temptations of America's decadent big cities.[30]

Christian was not terribly alarmed by the findings of his 1908 and 1910 studies. He was confident that the new Elmira system developed by Superintendents Robertson and Scott would reclaim a large percentage of these degenerate offenders. However, feeble-minded offenders presented a more vexing problem. They were "a residue who are of such low type that very little can be accomplished with them." These offenders were not amenable to prison science and threatened institutional and societal order:

They are never able to reach the standard of discipline of the institution and are a hindrance to all with whom they come in contact: the severe discipline of an institution of this character works a hardship upon them. They are unable to attain the standard for parole and in most cases serve their maximum sentences, when they must be released, unimproved to prey upon society. While they have committed crimes, it is usually due to

28. Elmira's Progressive Era keepers viewed Italian inmates as America's most threatening dangerous class. In October 1915, they began keeping a separate count: Records of the Elmira Reformatory, *Register of Italian Inmates, 1915–1930*. These records contain standard biographical data, which was repeated in the *Inmate Biographical Ledgers*. The separate register was, apparently, aimed at tracking and surveillance.

29. Dr. Christian did not "discover" the mentally defective offender. Rafter points out that Brockway used the concept of the defective offender to explain the failure of some inmates. However, Christian did make the defective offender an integral component of the Elmira system, and he emerged as an authority on the subject. The roots of this movement are traced in Hahn, "Defective Delinquent Movement"; Haller, *Eugenics*; and Gould, *Mismeasure of Man*.

30. New York State, Assembly Documents (1911), vol. 25, no. 35, New York State Board of Reformatories, *Thirty-fifth AR of the New York State Reformatory at Elmira and Tenth AR of the Eastern New York Reformatory* (1910), 13–19.

their imbecility, and they are better subjects for custodial care than reformatory treatment.

Christian called on the legislature to open a new institution (in essence, another Napanoch) to "give them custodial care and where they can be restrained beyond the limit of their maximum sentences."[31]

A number of administrative changes which occurred in 1911 facilitated Elmira's march toward eugenic prison science and social defense. In June 1911, Joseph Scott accepted appointment as New York State's Superintendent of Prisons, and Patrick McDonnell, Elmira's assistant superintendent since 1900, became its new superintendent. Frank Christian, the physician since 1900, became the new assistant superintendent, and Dr. John R. Harding became Elmira's new chief physician. Medical men, the primary advocates of mental defective theory and psycho-eugenics, were rapidly rising in Elmira's administrative and decision-making hierarchy.[32]

Dr. Harding continued Christian's research. A 1911 study of Elmira's population was alarming: seventy-three percent of the inmates had "poor" mental capacity; seventy-nine percent were "coarse" physical types; eighty-eight percent exhibited "poor" susceptibility to training; ninety-three percent lacked the "appreciation" to understand the consequences of their behavior. Only two percent had normal mental capacity. A Sicilian immigrant who did not speak English (and had never seen a pencil) was a prime example of the new breed of defective offender:

Much earnest effort has been put forth to teach him, and apparently he has made some effort to learn; but the sum total of his literary accomplishments at the present time, after ten months of reformatory treatment, consists of the ability to write his name (although he cannot spell it), and a knowledge of about fifty English words, but these he cannot spell. His mental equipment was insufficient to permit his learning the military work in the "Awkward Squad" and, in point of fact, he has been unable by reason of his defective mentality to sustain his part in the life of the reformatory. Why then should such an one be here?[33]

31. Ibid., 24. Goddard's *Kallikak Family* and *Feeble-mindedness* were regarded as definitive studies on this topic.

32. Medicine and psychology were emerging professions during this period, with their lines of expertise still unclear. Medical men had no qualms about being identified as authorities on the identification and treatment of defective offenders. The development of medicine is analyzed in Starr, *Social Transformation*. Grob, *Mental Institutions in America* and *Mental Illness and American Society*, deal with the emergence of psychology and psychiatry. On New York see Dwyer, *Homes for the Mad*. On European roots: Scull, *Museums of Madness*; Doerner, *Madmen and the Bourgeoisie*.

33. New York State, Senate Documents (1912), vol. 24, no. 34, New York State Board of Reformatories, *Thirty-sixth AR of the New York State Reformatory and the Eleventh AR of the Eastern New York Reformatory* (1911), 37.

Superintendent McDonnell, after consulting with Assistant Superintendent Christian and Dr. Harding, concluded that these inmates are "constitutionally unable, by reason of defective mentality, to respond to the reformative treatment given here." The school superintendent, Ivan Smith, confirmed this pessimistic diagnosis. Smith concluded that "we have in the past made too strong demands, educationally and otherwise." He concluded that defectives were uneducable and should be placed in colonies "where they would be trained to do the things they are capable of doing." Above all else, "They should never be permitted to become the fathers of children like themselves. In these cases, prevention is everything, and cure, impossible."[34]

The mentally defective offender quickly became the focus of attention, if not an obsession, at Elmira. In 1912 the managers concluded, "From what has been said as to the character of the reformatory population, it will be evident that in this sense we reform very few, because it is impossible." Superintendent McDonnell was equally pessimistic:

> It is this class that drive the courts to despair. They are not fully responsible for their acts and are not fit to be at large, but it is hard to tell what ought to be done with them. There is no institution exactly suited to their needs. At the present time the reformatories are selected as the most available places for getting them temporarily out of the way.[35]

The optimism which had dominated Elmira for nearly forty years, and which had been celebrated only two years earlier at the International Prison Congress, rapidly gave way to a new mind-set: mentally defective offenders were beyond salvation.

An important experiment took place in 1913 to manage this new group. Twelve inmates were selected to start a "Special Training Class for Mental Defectives." They were completely segregated from the rest of the population and exposed to a less rigorous regimen which included "useful institutional work" such as mending, janitorial duties, or shelling peas.[36] McDonnell concluded that the experiment was an unqualified success. Mentally defective inmates profited from the less rigorous demands placed on them, and "normal offend-

---

34. Ibid., 44, 31, 33.

35. New York State, Senate Documents (1913), vol. 22, no. 43, New York State Board of Reformatories, *Thirty-seventh AR of the New York State Reformatory and Twelfth AR of the Eastern New York Reformatory* (1912), 15, 13.

36. New York State, Senate Documents (1914), vol. 17, no. 40, New York State Board of Reformatories, *Thirty-eighth AR of the New York State Reformatory and Thirteenth AR of the Eastern New York Reformatory* (1913), 15; New York State, Senate Documents (1915), vol. 34, no. 55, New York State Board of Reformatories, *Thirty-ninth AR of the New York State Reformatory and Fourteenth AR of the Eastern New York Reformatory* (1914), 39.

ers" were not contaminated by association with this inferior class. The department was, accordingly, expanded. In 1915 McDonnell announced that the Special Training Class was "the most useful and effective aid to the reformation process in vogue here."[37]

The sudden death of Superintendent McDonnell on 29 August 1917 and appointment of Dr. Christian to take his place marked a new phase in Elmira's history. Under Christian's leadership, Elmira emerged as one of the nation's leading centers for the diagnosis and treatment of mentally defective offenders (along with the Massachusetts and Indiana Reformatories, which are discussed in the next chapter).

One of Christian's first acts was to organize a "Psychological Laboratory" under the direction of Dr. Harding.[38] Each new arrival was sent to the laboratory for a detailed physical examination, social history, and psychological assessment. Inmates were given the Binet-Simon intelligence test and a battery of tests developed by William Healy, one of the nation's leading experts on psychopathic research.[39] Test results were supplemented by information gathered from responses to twelve standardized letters sent to each inmate's parents, schoolteachers, wife, physician, minister, employer, relatives, friends, social service workers, and probation or police department.[40] The resulting "psychogram" laid the foundation for transfers to Napanoch and placements within Elmira.[41]

These psychograms did not produce hopeful results. Dr. Harding's reports to Superintendent Christian reflected his declining faith in the malleability of New York's dangerous classes. Harding's diagnosis of inmate #28,655 was typical:

37. New York State, Senate Documents (1916), vol. 14, no. 27, New York State Board of Reformatories, *Fortieth AR of the New York State Reformatory and the Fifteenth AR of the Eastern New York Reformatory* (1915), 26.

38. This was not the first psychological laboratory for criminals opened in the United States. Sing Sing Prison opened a laboratory under the direction of Dr. Bernard Glueck in 1916. Psychopath laboratories appeared as adjuncts to the juvenile court shortly after 1900. A number of nineteenth-century penal institutions, the New York House of Refuge, for example, did psychological profiles as they were taking anthropometric measures. However, Elmira's Psychological Laboratory achieved national prominence.

39. Healy, *Individual Delinquent*; Healy and Alper, *Criminal Youth*.

40. Christian, *How We Obtain Detailed Information*, provides an extended description of the content of these letters and their use.

41. The first report of the Psychological Laboratory is in New York State, Senate Documents (1918), vol. 12, no. 36, New York State Board of Reformatories, *Forty-second AR of the New York State Reformatory and Seventeenth AR of the Eastern New York Reformatory* (1917), 75–80. The regimen during this period is described in Allen, *Handbook*, and Masten, *Military Training*.

Cons. #28,655 ... is, in my opinion, a very dangerous character of the "thug" variety and who would hesitate at no possible end to secure freedom from imprisonment. He is also a constant menace to the morale of the general population, and I fear for his actions in the event of his becoming seriously involved in combat with other inmates, or more particularly officers, against whom he has considerable animosity. I therefore recommend that he be put under careful observation and transferred to Napanoch at the earliest possible moment.[42]

Harding presented a paper at the 1919 meeting of the American Association of Clinical Criminology which summarized the findings of Elmira's new Psychological Laboratory. The prognosis was "good" for only four percent of these inmates; the remainder were classified as "fair" (35%), "poor" (17%), "doubtful" (34%), or simply "hopeless" (13%).[43] Harding called for the establishment of custodial farm colonies and the sterilization of inferior offenders.

Why, in the name of reason, should the philanthropist use every means in his power to prevent sterilization of the confirmed criminal degenerate in the face of such statistics as these? In other words, why not reach out and deal directly with the most prolific source of crime—the prospective ancestor who has demonstrated his criminality beyond the shadow of doubt?[44]

Superintendent Christian, who was widely recognized as one of the leading "correctional psychiatrists" in the country, echoed Harding's findings. "This operation performed upon selected cases will produce excellent results and its value from the eugenic viewpoint merits careful consideration."[45]

Frederick Kuhlman, Director of Research at the Minnesota State School for the Feeble-Minded and Colony for Epileptics, was one of the few who dared to question these findings. Kuhlman charged that studies claiming that seventy to one hundred percent of inmates were defective were "extreme to the point of absurdity." He delicately charged his peers with being witch doctors and suggested that the popularity of eugenic prison science was due to the scientific aura of testing and the new "expertness" of the correctional psychologist/psychiatrist profession. Kuhlman concluded, "The detailed systematized clinical procedure gives the appearance and impression, though illusory, of a thorough-

42. Records of the Elmira Reformatory, *Examining Physician's Memoranda File, 1918–1928,* 83; *Inmate Biographical Ledger,* Case History #28,655.

43. Harding, "One Thousand Reformatory Prisoners," 429. Harding's "classification table" adds up to 102 percent and his "prognosis table" adds up to 103 percent.

44. Ibid., 432.

45. Christian, *Management of Penal Institutions,* 9; idem, *A Group of Youthful Robbers;* idem, *A Study of Five Hundred Parole Violators;* idem, *Statistics and Comments.*

going exhaustive examination that inspires respect, and a blind faith in the accuracy of the result to be obtained with it."[46]

The discovery of the mentally defective offender marked the dawn of another dark stage in Elmira's attempt to socialize New York's criminal class. Progressive Era inmates were free from the horrors of Brockway's whip, but the pain of corporal punishment was replaced by a more lasting danger: the threat of a stigmatizing mentally defective label and eugenic prison science.

Progressive Parole:
The Practice of Community Corrections, 1900–1920

The Progressive Era keepers of Elmira-Napanoch focused much, but not all, of their attention on developing strategies to cope with the threat posed by the mentally defective offender. Between 1900 and 1920 they also made a concerted effort to reform the parole system and to extend prison science and the disciplinary aims of the Elmira system into the community.

By 1905 Superintendent Scott and the managers became satisfied that the Elmira system was reformed and that their "Christian theory of treatment" was in place. The keepers turned their attention to Elmira's vaunted parole system and made a startling revelation: the system, which had not changed since 1877, was ineffective and badly out of date.[47] Parole supervision—the key to community corrections—was completely inadequate. One transfer officer and volunteer parole officers supervised 2,669 inmates paroled between 1901 and 1905. Could they cover 49,000 square miles of territory, including some of the world's foremost dens of iniquity—namely New York City?[48]

"Gate money" was woefully inadequate. Parolees who left Elmira in 1905 received $11.50. A train ticket to New York City, the destination of over half the parolees, cost $6.10, leaving $5.40 to buy food, clothes, and shelter.

It is subjecting him to far too severe temptation to force him to get along meanwhile on so small an amount [warned the managers]. To spend two or three hundred dollars on a man in the institution, trying to reform him, and then have him relapse into evil ways

---

46. Kuhlman, "Mental Examination," 136–37.

47. Brockway describes indeterminate sentencing as an "emasculated sentence" and legislative "bungling" in "An Absolute Indeterminate Sentence," 72–73. Brockway says very little about parole in his autobiography, *Fifty Years*. Community corrections was an afterthought to the "father of American parole."

48. New York State, Assembly Documents (1906), vol. 2, no. 23, New York State Reformatory, *Thirtieth AR* (1905), 37. Eugene Smith, president of the Prison Association of New York, also raised questions about the parole system in "Indeterminate Sentence," 64–71.

just because he lacks two or three dollars needed to get something to eat, is far from wise.[49]

Superintendent Scott charged the state with "economizing too much." He urged the legislature to appropriate funds to hire full-time parole officers, build a centralized parole staff, and increase gate money. However, these requests were ignored, and parole supervision continued to deteriorate: 1,016 inmates were paroled in 1906, 1,047 in 1907, 876 in 1908, and 1,063 in 1909. The managers were blunt: "The work could be more satisfactorily done if placed under a sufficient number of parole officers appointed and drilled by the reformatories."[50] The New York State Commission of Prisons echoed their plea:

The parole system has no justification unless there are enough competent parole officers to insure that each prisoner on parole shall frequently report in person to said officer, and shall receive his careful attention and discriminating counsel. Reports by letter are not sufficient.[51]

The 1910 legislature appropriated funds to hire more parole agents.[52] However, the keepers were dismayed to learn that these new officers must be civil service appointments; members of the New York Prison Association or Charity Organization of Buffalo could not automatically fill these positions. The managers appealed to friends in the legislature to repeal the law but to no avail. Elmira's parole staff was not, then, assembled until 1912. A chief parole officer, one assistant officer, and a stenographer monitored parolees in New York City; one assistant parole officer covered the Buffalo area; volunteers continued to monitor parolees in less accessible areas of the state.[53]

The managers were pleased with their new full-time parole staff. Of 903 inmates paroled between 1912 and 1913, they concluded that 640 (70.9%) "made good," 169 (18.7%) were "uncertain outcomes," and only 94 (10.4%) returned to crime.[54] Reports from the parole officers were cited as evidence that parol-

49. New York State, Assembly Documents (1906), vol. 2, no. 23, New York State Reformatory, *Thirtieth AR* (1905), 25. Samuel J. Barrows offered a more complimentary view of Elmira's parole system in "Safeguarding the Indeterminate Sentence."

50. New York State, Assembly Documents (1911), vol. 25, no. 35, New York State Board of Reformatories, *Thirty-fifth AR of the New York State Reformatory and Tenth AR of the Eastern New York Reformatory* (1910), 23.

51. New York State Commission of Prisons, *Fifteenth AR, 1909* [1910], 79.

52. Elmira was far behind many other institutions. In 1910, for example, the New York House of Refuge had a chief parole officer, four full-time assistants, as well as over a dozen volunteer officers. New York House of Refuge, *Eighty-seventh AR* (1911).

53. New York State, Senate Documents (1913), vol. 22, no. 43, New York State Board of Reformatories, *Thirty-seventh AR of the New York State Reformatory and Twelfth AR of the Eastern New York Reformatory* (1912), 26.

54. New York State, Senate Documents (1915), vol. 34, no. 55, New York State Board of Reformatories, *Thirty-ninth AR of the New York State Reformatory and Fourteenth AR of the Eastern New York Reformatory* (1914), 15.

ees were, indeed, assuming their "proper place" in society. Reports from the Buffalo agent were typical:

In regard to _____, I wish to state that I believe the young man is ready for his absolute release. He is working steadily at the _____ Works, from whom I have received very encouraging reports concerning him. His reports from home have also been favorable. He was married on Tuesday.

Another stated:

In regard to _____, since I wrote you last concerning this young man I have been watching him closely and have not been able to learn of his drinking to any great extent. He is working steadily, and I feel that it would not be fair to deprive the young man of his absolute discharge any longer.[55]

The parole staff expanded over the next several years. By 1917, the department had eight full-time members: the chief parole officer, H. B. Rodgers; an assistant officer based in Buffalo; four assistant officers who traveled around the state; a police lieutenant assigned to monitor parolees in New York City; and a stenographer. The staff's duties covered a wide range of activities. In 1917 Rodgers and his assistants investigated 1,400 offers of employment, made 1,600 home visits, wrote over 500 letters, and secured medical or legal advice for 150 parolees. The parole officers acted, in Rodgers's words, "not as policemen, but as advisers and helpers."[56]

Rogers and his staff made eugenic prison science an integral part of their supervision strategy. A study of five hundred parole violators published by Superintendent Christian in 1918 concluded that only three percent of the failures were "responsible offenders." Seventy-six percent of the parole violators were "sub-normal types" who fell into a variety of categories: defective delinquents (35%), psychopaths (23%), epileptics (11%), and an assortment of alcoholics, drug addicts, insane inmates, vagrants, and gangsters.[57] Two approaches to community supervision emerged: mentally defective and high-risk offenders were subjected to intense police-oriented supervision aimed at preventing illegal activity; "responsible offenders" received supervision aimed at helping them become "good workers" and "good citizens."

55. New York State, Senate Documents (1914), vol. 17, no. 40, New York State Board of Reformatories, *Thirty-eighth AR of the New York State Reformatory and Thirteenth AR of the Eastern New York Reformatory* (1913), 24–25.
56. New York State, Senate Documents (1918), vol. 12, no. 36, New York State Board of Reformatories, *Forty-second AR of the New York State Reformatory and Seventeenth AR of the Eastern New York Reformatory* (1917), 81–82, 89.
57. Christian, *A Study of Five Hundred Parole Violators*, 26–27.

But Elmira's "improved" parole system was not nearly so effective as the keepers claimed. Release decisions were still arbitrary, capricious, and plagued by the inherent defects of the medical model. Progressive Era manager/parole board members were upper-class, white males, appointed because of their social and economic status and political influence. They had little or no expertise in penology; they spent little time on each case; they were incapable of identifying the elusive "root causes" of crime; they could not assess reform or predict future misbehavior.

A 1917 evaluation of Elmira's parole system by the New York Prison Association (a decidedly friendly audience) concluded that there was still wide disparity between the theory and practice of community supervision. The Prison Association commended Elmira's managers for abandoning Brockway's laissez-faire attitude toward parole. "Through all the forty years since the opening of the reformatory [1876–1916,] the parole supervision has been notably inadequate," observed the report. But caseloads were still much too large: "far too few to have any save the most casual, and often most perfunctory, contact with the inmates." The report concluded that the parole system at Elmira was still an "inadequate working out of an excellent principle."[58]

Inside Parole: The "Cat and Mouse" Game

The Biographical Register of Returned Men, 1913–1937, of the Elmira Reformatory and Record of Returned Men, 1916–1920, of the Eastern New York Reformatory provide an opportunity to explore the problems of parolees and parole officers and expose the inherent defects of community supervision. An examination of three case histories, two from Elmira and one from Napanoch, reveals that each parolee's response to community corrections was unique. Some inmates followed the course of Goffman's primary adjustment: they obeyed the conditions of parole and accepted their "proper place" in the social and economic order. Others followed the path of secondary adjustment: they violated conditions of release with impunity and returned to crime. Parole supervision was a "cat and mouse game"—parole revocation a "game of chance."

58. Prison Association of New York, "Indeterminate Sentence and Parole," 51. This report heaped similar criticisms on parole at the state's adult prisons (pp. 52–55): the three-member State Board of Parole, which decided releases from prisons, was too small; too little time (on average, six to eight minutes) was devoted to each case; too many inmates (three-fourths) were released at their first appearance; the caseloads of the state's three parole officers (343 per officer) were too large. See also Prison Association of New York, "Parole System of the State Prisons."

Seventeen-year-old J. D. was committed to Elmira in 1914 for third degree burglary. He had a long arrest record and had served time in several juvenile reformatories. But before leaving Elmira on 20 August 1914, he assured Parole Officer Rodgers and the members of the parole board that he had learned his lesson. He was ready to work hard, obey the conditions of parole, and take his place in society as a law-abiding citizen.[59]

J. D. wasted little time in breaking his promise. He quit his job after one day, later explaining that he simply "did not want to work." Although he lived at home with his parents, they were unable to control his behavior. He spent his evenings in dance halls, gambling dens, and bars, where he would "drink anything on the calendar" until he had "enough to make me feel good." On 22 September 1915, J. D. was picked up by a detective for possession of stolen property but released for lack of evidence. On 4 October 1915 he was arrested for burglary. Rodgers had seen enough. J. D. was returned as a parole violator.

All parole revocations were sent to the Psychological Laboratory for a diagnostic interview. Dr. Harding concluded that J. D. was one of Elmira's new criminals: a mentally defective offender:

This boy is mentally defective—delinquent since 7 years old—already served several sentences. Hates work of all kind. Egotistical, and rather vainly, admits premeditating murder of an old enemy—took two revolvers—shot enemy at first opportunity—so he claims. Shows no remorse for his crime or return. Is intemperate, fond of gambling— proud of his crimes—sought out old associates—also loose women at once. Is morally imbecile. Is vindictive, mercyless [sic] and without conscience.

Harding's prognosis was not good: "Imbecile with all that term implies— should not be let out to prey upon society, and to propagate his kind. Should have permanent custodial care, is a menace to society and posterity."

G. R., who was twenty-one years old, was committed in 1914 on a charge of third degree burglary. He was paroled on 20 August 1915 and went to live with his mother. His monthly reports were promising. G. R. reported that he was working as a driver, saving his money, and spending his evenings home. G. R. said that he was avoiding the evil habits which contributed to his downfall: bars, gambling houses, and houses of ill fame. He even attended church on Sundays. G. R. was, according to his monthly reports, working hard to become a productive citizen.[60]

---

59. Records of the Elmira Reformatory, *Biographical Register of Returned Men*, vol. 2, p. 1, Case History #24,065. The keepers also kept a chronological list of returned men, *Summary Register of Men Returned for Violation of Parole, 1907–1948*, but this lacks interpretive depth.

60. *Biographical Register of Returned Men*, vol. 2, Case History #23,973, p. 40.

Rodgers received a letter from G. R.'s mother in March 1916 which offered a different view. She complained that he was keeping bad company and staying out late at night. Rodgers had a fatherly chat with G. R., which led to improved behavior, but another complaint from his mother soon followed. She was concerned with her son's bad habits and especially puzzled by the discovery of a vial containing a mysterious white powder. Rodgers submitted the substance for analysis and discovered that it was a drug which was sweeping New York: heroin.

When G. R. returned to Elmira on 13 March 1916, he denied that he was, as Dr. Harding put it, a "heroin habitual." He maintained that his mother had fabricated the charges against him:

Inmate exonerates himself of all wrong doing but admits former use of drugs. Accuses mother and brother of persecution—tells deliberate untruths about his actions without apparent realization that he is lying. He is in a "highly nervous state": has some facial tremor, only slight patellar reflexes & is anemic. Lost ten pounds while away. At present is emaciated and has gleet. Morally, he is a weak character. Heredity and home influences has [sic] played prominently in his down-fall. Father and all paternal family drank—brother was here & is now in Clinton Prison—bad associates "came back."

Harding's prognosis was unfavorable: "Is a drug habituate, who after leaving here went back to his old habits. Can make a good living but readily went back to his old ways without any effort to maintain the cure that his confinement has effected."

Many inmates paroled from the Eastern New York Reformatory were equally troublesome. J. C., a twenty-nine-year-old grand larcenist, arrived at Elmira in 1914. An analysis of his personality and prior record, which included fifteen prior arrests, led to his transfer to the Eastern Reformatory. J. C. studied farming at Napanoch and was paroled on 20 June 1917.[61]

J. C. secured a job as a longshoreman, earning an exceptional wage of $27.50 per week. He lived with his wife in New York City and seemed to be doing well until he began to suspect her of infidelity. J. C. stayed home every night—"had to watch my wife"—and eventually quit his job so that he could

61. Records of the Eastern New York Reformatory, *Record of Returned Men, 1916–1920*, Case History #3,841, p. 85; *Discharge Register*, Case History #3,841. Archival sources in other states reveal that the behavior of Elmira-Napanoch inmates and problems confronted by Rogers and his staff were not unusual: Records of the Illinois State Reformatory, *Parole and Pardon Index, Register of Prisoners*; Records of the Saint Cloud [Minnesota] State Reformatory, *Board of Control: The Agent's Correspondence, 1909–1910, Board of Parole Correspondence, Superintendent's Correspondence Regarding Fugitives, Inmate History and Record, Escapee Record*.

keep a full-time eye on her. Irrespective of the merits of his suspicion, it is clear that family tensions escalated. On 22 January 1918 Rodgers reported that:

[J. C.] appeared at his office on January 16th intoxicated, and on the morning of the 18th, his wife appeared with a 13 month old baby, complaining that he had not worked for several weeks, nor has he contributed to his support. She further states that [J. C.] forced an entrance into her mother's apartment, with whom she resides, and after punching her in the face, took her shoes and ran away with them [presumably to prevent a tryst].

J. C.'s wife filed charges of breaking and entering and assault. Rodgers did not wait for the courts to adjudicate the case; his parole was revoked. However, J. C.'s account of the events leading to his return did not match those of his wife. The physician reported that:

[J. C.] maintains that he would have made good if his wife had been true to him. Admits drinking but says he did so on account of the domestic trouble. A weak individual mentally and morally of sufficient intelligence to earn a living but easily depressed and welcomes all excuses for indulging in drink.

Harding concluded that J. C. had "too little moral fibre to succeed."

Erving Goffman suggests that the keepers of total institutions use parole to extend their power, authority, and "surveillance space" into the community.[62] David Garland maintains that the introduction of parole was an integral component of the new penology that was aimed at extending the "shallow end of penality" and "normalizing" the behavior of former inmates in natural settings: the home, workplace, school. "By means of the personal influence of the probation or after-care [parole] officer, they attempt to straighten out characters and to reform the personality of their clients in accordance with the requirements of 'good citizenship.'"[63]

These observations are thought-provoking but somewhat simplistic. Only three inmate histories have been examined here; however, these cases demonstrate that Rodgers and his staff faced an enormously complex task. Confronted with huge caseloads, prisoner resistance, and the defects of the medical model and "people work," Elmira's parole officers were asked to serve as policemen, detectives, social workers, psychologists, work supervisors, family and drug counselors, and in the case of revocations, as judges. Progressive Era parole officers, like their nineteenth-century counterparts, were marginally successful at helping or policing their charges. Extending prison science, surveillance, and

62. Goffman, *Asylums*, 227–38.
63. Garland, *Punishment and Welfare*, 238.

the disciplinary aims of the Elmira system into the community was a difficult if not impossible task.

Conclusion

The discovery of the mentally defective offender and the introduction of eugenic prison science introduced yet another social contract between criminals and the state. Elmira's new version of scientific criminology, like Brockway's multifactor positivist approach, worked on the premise that each offender's behavior was caused by a variety of forces. However, this new form of iatrogenic deviance located the primary roots of crime deep within the biological and psychological makeup of the offender. The diseased minds and bodies of mentally defective offenders were, quite simply, beyond redemption. Custody, control, incapacitation, and social defense—not rehabilitation—were the logical and necessary aims of Elmira's new psycho-eugenic approach.[64]

This new approach to human and social engineering served a wide variety of interests. The discovery of the mentally defective offender allowed physicians to bill themselves as correctional psychiatrists. And the mentally defective offender provided a convenient rationalization for failure. How could Drs. Christian and Harding be reasonably expected to probe so deeply into the bodies of their charges? How could they be expected to locate and treat a "bad seed" which was planted at birth by God?

The discovery of the mentally defective offender and introduction of psycho-eugenics also served the organizational interests of the Elmira Reformatory. Critics might, indeed, question the effectiveness of Brockway's traditional Elmira system, but challenging less ambitious aims of custody and control was far more difficult. How could incapacitating dangerous-pathological-chronic offenders not reduce the crime rate? How could Elmira's new emphasis on social defense not protect the public?

Finally, Elmira's new approach to crime control served broader societal interests. Eugenic prison science—echoing nativist, xenophobic, racist themes—conveniently deflected blame away from American economic, political, and

---

64. The notion of iatrogenesis—disease caused by medical professionals—is developed by Ivan Illich in *Medical Nemesis*. Cohen applies this concept to criminal justice in *Visions of Social Control*, 169–75.

social institutions. The research of Drs. Christian and Harding demonstrated that capitalism, democracy, class conflict, inequalities in wealth, and the exploitation of the working classes were not responsible for America's crime problem. Eugenical prison science reaffirmed existing class relations and legitimized the incarceration of the criminal lumpenproletariat.

Chapter Six

Triumphant Defeat: The Decline of Prison Science, 1900–1920

David J. Rothman's *Conscience and Convenience* is widely regarded as the most comprehensive and authoritative account of American penology during the Progressive Era. Rothman maintains that the first decades of the twentieth century witnessed the spread of new ideas toward the handling of criminals, delinquents, and the mentally ill. Progressive Era reformers, acting out of kind intentions or "conscience," introduced new programs to initiate reform: juvenile court, probation, parole, outpatient clinics, as well as new regimens in prisons, juvenile reformatories, and insane asylums. But conscience gave way to "convenience"—that is, personal and organizational needs. These "reforms" expanded the state's network of social control but did little to help or heal wards of the state.

Unfortunately, Rothman's analysis says little about the Elmira Reformatory, the adult reformatory movement, the discovery of the mentally defective offender, the introduction of eugenic prison science, or the racist and sexist dimensions of the new penology. This chapter addresses this gap in the literature by examining Elmira's nineteenth-century ideological rivals, the Michigan and Massachusetts reformatories, and the period's most "innovative" institution, the Indiana Reformatory. The promise and practice of the ten adult reformatories opened between 1889 and 1899, as well as eight new reformatory-prisons opened between 1901 and 1916, are assessed to outline the contours of the American adult reformatory movement. I close the chapter by examining the differential handling of minority offenders at the Minnesota, Iowa, Kentucky, and District of Columbia reformatories.

A complex portrait of America's third penal system emerges. Progressive Era adult reformatory keepers did not blindly follow Elmira's lead and introduce eugenic prison science. Institutions continued to exercise organizational autonomy and develop unique state-specific approaches to reform—so there were multiple "consciences"—which were aimed at a common end: disciplining criminal elements of the working class. These reforms, much like those examined by Rothman, were largely unsuccessful. By 1920, the keepers of America's third penal system lost their pre-eminent position in the field of criminal justice. Faith in the power of prison science and the rehabilitative ideal was in full-scale retreat.

Penal Pioneers Revisited: The Michigan and Massachusetts Reformatories

The keepers of the Michigan and Massachusetts reformatories, Elmira's nineteenth-century ideological and programmatic rivals, continued to exercise personal and organizational autonomy throughout the Progressive period. Otis Fuller, the iron-willed maverick warden of the Michigan Reformatory, belittled treatment and reform. Fuller used a regimen based on punishment and profit to civilize his charges. The Massachusetts Reformatory replaced its eclectic regimen with a more scientific psycho-biogenic approach. Under the direction of the institution's physician, Dr. Guy W. Fernald, the Massachusetts Reformatory, along with the Elmira and Indiana reformatories, emerged as the nation's foremost advocate of eugenic prison science.

Fuller, warden of the Michigan Reformatory until 1918, continued to rail against the Elmira system and the new penology. He mocked "collegiate reformatories" and their misguided "wooden gun parades, gymnasium exercises, course dinners, daily vaudeville shows and idleness." He charged that these institutions "aim to make prison life 'one glad, sweet song' for those who drift into prison." Furthermore, Elmira-type institutions cost two and one-half to fifteen times as much as his institution without more beneficial results. "And the taxpayer is the patient and long-suffering goat for the political prison reformer."[1]

---

1. Michigan Reformatory, *Sixteenth BR, 1910–1912* (1912), 10.

The aims and programs of the Michigan Reformatory remained remarkably stable throughout the Progressive Era, although the name did change from the Michigan House of Correction and Reformatory to the Michigan Reformatory in 1901.[2] The institution continued to accept a wide range of felons, misdemeanants, and recidivists; there were no age restrictions; programs associated with the new penology were ignored. Fuller supported laws introducing parole (1895) and indeterminate sentencing (1903) but not in the spirit of benevolent reform. Indeterminate sentences extended punishment and served as a deterrent:

A good indeterminate sentence law, wisely administered, will keep in prison, for long terms of years, the horde of parasites upon society who drift from state to state and live by picking pockets, lifting diamonds, blowing safes, forging bank checks, swindling hotels and burglarizing homes."

Similarly, parole extended social control into the community: "The average term of imprisonment under the present indeterminate sentence law are considerably longer than under the old law, when it was not unusual for a professional crook to get off with six months to a year."[3]

Fuller continued to advocate the "somewhat old fashioned but now unpopular" approach:

The fact remains that the reformation of convicts without steady labor of some kind is an idle dream. Most young men who get into prison have been truants at school and idlers in their work. If they are not taught in prison that an honest and faithful day's work is not a great hardship, they will become idlers upon their discharge, and worthless and dangerous members of society, as idleness generally leads to crime. If they are taught habits of industry in prison and are taught to do a full day's work and do it well, they can secure plenty of work upon their discharge.[4]

The Protestant ethic, tempered with punishment and deterrence, was his prescription for shaping law-abiding citizens.

Progressive Era penologists at the Massachusetts Reformatory were optimistic about their approach to saving youthful offenders. Superintendent Joseph Scott reported that Massachusetts's eclectic regimen fulfilled the promise of the Declaration of Principles. "It persuades the willing, compels the willful, and punishes the obdurate." Scott concluded: "We believe that the reformatory principle is scientific, economical, and ethical."[5]

2. Michigan State House of Correction and Reformatory, *Eleventh BR, 1900–1902* (1903), 7. "An Act Providing for Changing the Name."

3. Michigan Reformatory, *Thirteenth BR, 1904-1906* (1906), 14.

4. Ibid., 9.

5. Scott, "Massachusetts Reformatory," 81, 90.

Scott and his successor, Charles Hart (1903–1906), made few changes. Most of their efforts aimed at "perfecting" Massachusetts's eclectic approach. Scott viewed the slow pace of change as beneficial: "The progress of the reformatory from year to year may not be marked, but, viewing it from the beginning, considerable advancement has been made, not only in the material arrangements but in the development of the system."[6]

The appointment of Alvah S. Baker as superintendent in 1906 set the stage for a new approach to human engineering. One seemingly innocuous decision by Baker had an enormous impact on the institution's future; Baker hired a full-time physician and introduced a "physical culture class." The appointment of Dr. Guy G. Fernald in November 1908 was a pivotal event in the history of the Massachusetts Reformatory. Fernald upgraded the quality of health care and started the physical culture class. Following after the system introduced at Elmira, inmates participated in daily calisthenics and drills. The results, according to Fernald, were "educative and uplifting." More important, Fernald introduced "personal interviews." These "sought to reach the motives and ideals of the subject, to arrive at an estimate of his intellectual and moral capacity, and to advise him in forming and following well-chosen plans for his future."[7]

The medical department gradually expanded over the next several years. Fernald started a venereal disease clinic in 1910; more important, he began to dabble in psychological testing. Baker was pleased with these efforts. Fernald was given a room—designated the "pathological workroom"—to continue his research into the biological and psychological roots of crime. One hundred forty psychological examinations took place in 1911. Selected inmates received an ethical discrimination test and an achievement capacity test in 1912, but psychological testing was still a "spare time" activity.[8]

By 1913, Fernald was confident that psychological testing had gone beyond the experimental stage. With Baker's blessing, he opened the Massachusetts Reformatory Psychopathic Laboratory, using the "psychiatrist's method" and "clinical approach" to diagnose each incoming inmate. Fernald's aim was clear:

The criminologist's problem is to ascertain the capacity and handicaps of his subject, and to utilize and stimulate the good qualities and suppress the inimical traits and habits,

6. Massachusetts Prison Commissioners, *First AR* (1902), 87.

7. Massachusetts Prison Commissioners, *Ninth AR* (1910), 43–44.

8. Massachusetts Prison Commissioners, *Tenth AR* (1911), 42–44; *Eleventh AR* (1912), 43–45; *Twelfth AR* (1913), 40–42.

so as to rouse into healthful, well-directed action the moral and intellectual mechanisms of the man."[9]

However, the findings of the new Psychopathic Laboratory were not hopeful. Only forty-two percent of the inmates admitted between 1914 and 1915 could be classified as "adult" (i.e. normal). The remaining fifty-eight percent were mentally defective offenders who fell into a variety of categories: sex pervert, psychopath, moron, feeble-minded, imbecile, congenital syphilitic, epileptic, alcoholic degenerate, and drug addict (mostly heroin, morphine, cocaine).[10] Later tests confirmed these findings: forty percent of the inmates committed between 1914 and 1920 were "adult"; forty-three percent were "subnormal"; seventeen percent were "segregable." Fernald's conclusion was clear: the Massachusetts Reformatory, like the Elmira Reformatory, was filled with a wide range of mental defectives and social misfits who were drawn from the "less cultured classes."[11]

Fernald's prognosis was decidedly pessimistic. Some mentally deficient inmates would respond to treatment, but others were beyond salvation.[12] Like his counterparts at Elmira (Drs. Christian and Harding), Fernald recommended prison colonies, special custodial institutions, and sterilizations for hopeless cases.

The value of the eugenic proposal that the feeble-minded be prevented from propagation — lies in its promise of ultimate relief from the "burden of feeble-mindedness" [concluded Fernald]. Their segregation for training to self-support would prevent their propagation and eliminate one very perplexing factor in our sociologic and economic problem.[13]

The keepers of the Massachusetts Reformatory, like those at Elmira, were now ardent proponents of eugenic prison science. Custody, control, incapacitation, and social defense became the new aims of the Massachusetts Reformatory.[14]

9. Massachusetts Prison Commissioners, *Thirteenth AR* (1914), 45.

10. Fernald, "Mental Examination," 396.

11. Massachusetts Commissioner of Correction, *AR, 1920* [1921], 62; Fernald, "Current Misconceptions."

12. Fernald, "Mental Examination," 393; idem, "Reformatory Prisoner," 128–29.

13. Fernald, "Segregation of the Unfit," 606.

14. Fernald maintained that pathological laboratories were good public relations tools. "There is thereby added in their minds [of inmates and the public] a sense of completeness of equipment which inspires confidence." Psychological tests and scientific methods "tend to diminish the stigma of a reformatory sentence, and to increase respect for the purpose for which reformatories exist" ("Laboratory," 100–101).

Social Darwinism in "Progressive" Indiana

America's most "innovative" treatment strategy came from an unlikely source: the Indiana Reformatory. Under the direction of Superintendents Alvin T. Hert (1897–1902), Joseph Byers (1902–1903), W. H. Whittaker (1903–1909), and David Peyton (1909–1918), the Indiana Reformatory introduced a number of modifications in prison science and the medical model which placed it at the forefront of the Progressive Era reform debate.

Administrators at the Indiana Reformatory confronted enormous problems when the institution went from a prison to an adult reformatory in 1897. However, they made rapid progress between 1897 and 1900 to correct these deficiencies: an ancient cellblock, built in 1822, was replaced; abominable health conditions improved; hardened criminals on fixed sentences left over from the old prison were removed; to some extent, overcrowding abated; academic classes, industrial education, military drill, and parole were introduced. The Indiana Reformatory rapidly took on the form of an Elmira-type institution.[15]

The keepers of the Indiana Reformatory did not, however, blindly copy Brockway's Elmira system. Despite the institution's recent opening and extensive internal problems, Indiana's penologists assumed a leading role in the eugenics movement and redirected the debate in Progressive Era penology by introducing sterilization into American corrections.

The institution's physician, Dr. Harry Sharp, was the catalyst for Indiana's experiment in eugenic prison science. Dr. Sharp stumbled onto the idea of sterilizing inmates during an examination in October 1899. Sharp's nineteen-year-old patient was an inveterate masturbator, indulging in the practice four to ten times each day. Although Sharp had only experimented on animals, he felt that surgery was the last hope for a cure. Sharp characterized the vasectomy, which was performed without anesthesia, as a "brilliant success":

The boy ceased to practice masturbation; notwithstanding the fact that desire still existed, he had mustered enough will power to desist. His mental habitude and physical condition greatly improved. He gained twenty-two pounds in sixty days, and the superintendent of our schools assured me that the boy was quite studious and was making rapid advancement in his studies. There was no cystic degeneration or atrophy, no development of nervous symptoms.[16]

Sharp reported that his patient was delighted with the outcome and recommended it to his fellow inmates. More important, sterilization protected society

---

15. Ellison, "Indiana Prison System," 183–213.
16. Sharp, "Rendering Sterile," 178.

from future generations of defectives: "It renders them powerless to reproduce their kind and it is an undoubted fact that the progeny of degenerates becomes a charge upon the state."[17]

Sharp performed twenty-four operations between 1899 and 1900. One hundred seventy-six inmates were sterilized by 1904; 206 inmates received the procedure between 1904 and 1906, bringing the total to 382.[18] The managers enthusiastically endorsed Sharp's efforts. Superintendent Whittaker concluded in 1907 that fifty percent of the inmates were "not subject to reformation."[19] Sterilizations or lifetime custodial care on penal farms were the ideal solution. Sharp called for a mandatory sterilization law for Indiana's degenerate class: "I therefore suggest that you endeavor to secure such legislation as will make it mandatory that this operation be performed on all convicted degenerates."[20]

Sharp's work impressed Governor Hanly and the members of the legislature. In 1907 Indiana passed the nation's first sterilization law in the spirit, as Sharp put it, of "race purity and civic righteousness."[21] The law authorized the institution to hire two full-time physicians to assist Sharp. Inmates who exhibited "no probability of improvement" were candidates for sterilization. Sharp was delighted. "Is there any brutality in this? Is it cruel and inhuman?" Reabsorption of the "Elixir of Life" improved the inmate-patient's physical and mental well-being:

When it is reabsorbed (just as any fluid injected hypodermically is absorbed) and appropriated by the system, it acts a wonderful nerve and muscular tonic, and it has been conclusively proven that this secretion, when thus reabsorbed, has a remarkable influence upon the nervous system, mental and physical vigor.[22]

"Thank God," concluded Sharp, "Indiana has harkened."[23]

Indiana's experiment in eugenic prison science attracted widespread national attention. Increasing concern with the quality of America's new wave of immigrants (especially "inferior" southern Europeans), the findings of cacogenic family studies, and general concerns about increasing crime and social disorder

17. Indiana Reformatory, *Fourth BR* (1904), 52.

18. Indiana Reformatory, *Second BR* [1900], 33; *Fourth BR* (1904), 53; *Fifth BR* (1906), 65, 68.

19. Indiana Reformatory, *AR, 1906–1907* (1907), 9. Whittaker held monthly meetings with his staff to discuss the programs and problems. Staff members even wrote papers, which are published in Indiana Reformatory, *Ideas on Reformation.*

20. Indiana Reformatory, *Fourth BR* (1904), 52.

21. Sharp, "Rendering Sterile," 179.

22. Sharp, "Indiana Plan," 37.

23. Sharp, "Rendering Sterile," 180.

strengthened support for the eugenics movement. Conservative crusaders called for immigration restriction, marriage laws, and sterilizations.[24] Sterilization laws were passed in Washington State, California and Connecticut in 1909; by 1917, thirteen states followed suit.[25] The Indiana Reformatory was at the forefront of one the Progressive Era's most controversial "reforms."

The diffusion of sterilization laws did not go unchallenged. The discussion of Sharp's practices at the 1909 American Prison Association meeting reveals that many penologists did not share his views. F. H. Mills, a delegate from New York, opened the salvo against Sharp. "In the first place this association never intended to assume the function of the Almighty God. You haven't any right to cut a man's arm off and you haven't any right to interfere with his physical makeup." F. O. Hellstrom, warden of the North Dakota State Prison, was equally opposed.

In 99 cases out of 100 the man who has committed an overt act and become a criminal has become criminal largely from force of circumstances and through environment. If you want to suppress crime you should educate, and not only educate but see that justice is done to man.

Hellstrom placed sterilizations in a personal context: "I should like to ask you who are advocates of this doctrine, will you submit yourselves to the operation?" He concluded: "I say the doctrine is damnable. It is dangerous. It is inhuman and it is unchristian."[26]

Other critics raised moral, medical, legal, and religious objections. Hastings H. Hart charged that Sharp's methods were ill conceived, ineffective, and "monstrous and so abhorrent." Charles Boston, an attorney, mocked the Indiana law.

We find the legislative wiseacres of Indiana, declaring that two skilled surgeons and a chief physician, after forming a $3.00 opinion, may, upon the recommendation of the board of lay managers, sterilize a human being. ... I defy anyone to prove the fact that a man has committed rape, is any indication that there will be transmitted to his offspring any undesirable hereditary trait.

---

24. Richard Dugdale's 1877 study of *"The Jukes"*, an allegedly criminally inclined and degenerate New York family, provided a major impetus for late nineteenth-century social Darwinists. Dugdale did not demonstrate that the Jukes were a crime wave, but this is how the study was widely interpreted. Subsequent cacogenic studies lent further support to nativist fears that America was being inundated with degenerate families who were passing criminal genes on to their progeny. For an excellent review and analysis of these studies, see Rafter, "Introduction"; and on social and "reform" Darwinism, Bannister, *Social Darwinism*.

25. Laughlin, *Historical, Legal and Statistical Review*; Haller, *Eugenics*, 130–41.

26. "Discussion," 1909, 40–42.

Boston concluded that sterilization laws "authorize probably ignorant boards of managers, probably ignorant, if not to say malicious, wardens and superintendents, and possibly, if not probably, ignorant institutional physicians to select individual victims for the sacrifice." Raymond Pearl, a geneticist, warned that the Indiana plan would not work: "But it is clear that unless a sterilization programme is thoroughly comprehensive in its scope and carried out rigorously and unremittingly for a period of probably at least a hundred years, no significant, eugenic results will come from it."[27]

These criticisms did not go unheeded in Indiana. Although Dr. Sharp and Superintendents Whittaker and Peyton continued to support sterilization, Governor Thomas Marshall and a number of legislators became increasingly skeptical. Ironically, sterilizations declined in Indiana at the same time they increased in other states: one inmate was sterilized in 1909, none in 1910 or 1911, four in 1912.[28] Sharp submitted his resignation as physician in 1908 to become a member of the board of trustees. His resignation as president of the board in 1911 effectively ended Indiana's experiment in eugenics and social Darwinism.

The void left by the precipitous decline of the sterilization program was filled by the opening of a psychopathic clinic, the Department of Research, in 1911. As in New York and Massachusetts, physicians provided the impetus for the new department. In 1909, Dr. David C. Peyton became superintendent. Dr. Peyton had complete faith in his colleagues.

The medical profession has ever been the champion of humanity. ... That profession has always had more wisdom than it could get permission to employ; and in this very age if the world would turn over its greatest human problems to the medical guild, and give it free rein, civilization and progress will go forward with accentuated speed."[29]

Peyton planned to build a model correctional hospital: "I am getting within the Indiana Reformatory as many physicians in one way or another, except as prisoners, as I possibly can."[30] By 1910, the Indiana Reformatory had five "correctional psychiatrists": Drs. Sharp and Peyton, as well as the institution's physician, Dr. H. H. Smith, and his two full-time assistants.

27. Hart, "Extinction of the Defective Delinquent," 224; Boston, "A Protest against Laws," 327–28, 330; Pearl, "Sterilization of Degenerates," 5.
28. Hart, "Extinction of the Defective Delinquent," 222; Indiana Reformatory, *AR, 1911–1912* (1912), 39.
29. Peyton, *Crime as an Expression of Feeble-mindedness*, 1.
30. "Discussion," 1914, 145.

The Department of Research, under the direction of Rufus von Kleinsmid, employed the latest developments from the fields of medicine, psychology, sociology, and social welfare.[31] However, the findings of this department were not positive. Indiana's inmates, like their counterparts in New York and Massachusetts, were mentally defective. "Our investigations," announced Director von Kleinsmid, "have gone to show that at least half of the population of the institution are sub-normal."[32] Superintendent Peyton characterized Indiana's youthful offenders as "mental dwarfs."[33] The daily regimen changed to meet the needs of the new breed of inmate: academic education received less emphasis; more difficult industrial education classes were scaled back; military drill expanded; farming and general labor were extended.

Indiana penologists were, however, far more optimistic than their colleagues in New York and Massachusetts. Amos Butler, secretary of the Indiana State Board of Charities, concluded that at least seventy-five percent of these offenders were reformed.[34] In 1917, Assistant Superintendent James Walker concluded:

From every standpoint we believe the institution is in the best condition it has ever attained—the high water mark of its history—and nothing untoward happening the next year will be a banner one, but in human affairs calamity is usually invited by great success.[35]

Walker's words were prophetic. The fortunes of the Indiana Reformatory dramatically reversed when a fire of unknown origin struck on 5 February 1918. A committee appointed by the governor concluded that the damage was beyond repair.[36] The skeleton of the Indiana Reformatory remained open until a new structure was completed at Pendelton in 1923. With the fall of the Indiana Reformatory, the Elmira and Massachusetts institutions emerged as the primary defenders of eugenic prison science and the nation's most innovative adult reformatories.

31. Descriptions of the Department of Research are in Indiana Reformatory, *AR, 1913* [1913], 7–12; *AR, 1913–1914* [1914], 5–8; *AR, 1914–1915* (1915), 10–12; *AR, 1915–1916* (1916), 9–11; *AR, 1916–1917* [1917], 12–13.

32. Indiana Reformatory, *AR, 1913* [1913], 8.

33. Peyton, *Differential Diagnosis of Crime*, 7.

34. Butler, "Statistics"; idem, "Operation of the Indeterminate Sentence," 182.

35. Indiana Reformatory, *AR, 1916-1917* [1917], 10.

36. Miller et al., *Report of the Commission.*

Triumphant Defeat: The Fall of America's Third Penal System

Otis Fuller and the managers of the Michigan Reformatory stubbornly pursued their punishment and profit approach throughout the Progressive Era. Penologists at the Elmira, Massachusetts, and Indiana reformatories advocated eugenic prison science. But what course did other reformatory-prisons follow during this pivotal period in American correctional history? Did the institutions which opened between 1889 and 1899 adopt eugenic prison science? What path did new adult reformatories opened between 1901 and 1916 follow in their attempt to socialize the dangerous classes?

The Pennsylvania, Minnesota, Colorado, Illinois, Kansas, Ohio, and Wisconsin reformatories maintained an unwavering approach between 1900 and 1920: they shunned both the punishment and profit approach and eugenic prison science and supported Brockway's traditional Elmira system. The keepers of these institutions did not dispute the importance of fiscal concerns or research findings on mentally defective offenders. In fact, studies at several reformatories (e.g. Minnesota, Kansas, Illinois) concluded that many inmates were, indeed, idiots, morons, dullards, or feeble-minded. However, the custodians of these institutions were confident that Brockway's Elmira system saved normal and mentally defective offenders. The superintendent of the Pennsylvania Industrial Reformatory announced that sixty percent of his charges went on to "live honest lives." The superintendent of the Ohio Reformatory reported that at least seventy-five percent of his inmates became "re-established in good citizenship."[37] Given this presumed level of success, why change the Elmira system? Why disrupt a regimen of reform which, in theory, reduced recidivism and contributed to America's search for social order?

Several southern, western, and less innovative northeastern states opened reformatory-prisons during the Progressive Era. However, each institution's approach to human engineering varied and reflected state-specific social, political, and economic contexts, as well as criminal justice system traditions, needs, and interests. Reformatories that opened in New Jersey, Iowa, Washington State, and Connecticut copied Brockway's Elmira system. The Kentucky and Oklahoma reformatories adopted Michigan's punishment and profit approach. The Missouri and District of Columbia institutions were, to put it generously, aborted reform efforts.

37. Pennsylvania Industrial Reformatory, *Ninth BR, 1905–1906* [1907], 8; Ohio State Reformatory, *Twenty-third AR* (1907), 7. Other superintendents were equally optimistic: Scott, "American Reformatories"; Leonard, "Reformatory Methods."

The New Jersey State Reformatory, opened in Rahway on 6 August 1901, emulated Elmira. Commitments were restricted to male, first-time offenders between the ages of sixteen and thirty. The reformatory copied key components of the Elmira system: indeterminate sentencing, mark and classification system, industrial and academic education, labor, military drill, and parole.[38] Implementing these programs was not, however, an easy task. Superintendents James Heg (1901–1902) and Joseph Martin (1902–1908) had the arduous task of completing the institution's buildings. Crowding was a serious problem: 250 inmates slept on cots in the halls in 1906. Security was a constant concern. The institution's wall was a "an old dilapidated tumbling down and unsafe board fence." A permanent wall was not completed until 1912. A 1908 legislative investigation was highly critical: inmates suffered "cruel treatment" (they were whipped and locked in "underground dungeons"); hardened convicts were admitted; the trade school was ineffective. The report concluded that the notorious Trenton State Prison was more humane than the new adult reformatory.[39]

Frank Moore's appointment as superintendent in 1909 marked the onset of a brighter period in the institution's history. Under Moore, the New Jersey State Reformatory developed a reputation for strong vocational and academic education, including a college correspondence course introduced in 1914. Psychological testing in 1910 revealed that an alarming number of inmates were "feebleminded" (yearly estimates ranged from one third to one half of the population). These findings concerned Moore. Defective offenders would, in his judgment, be better off in penal colonies or special institutions. However, he remained optimistic and did not implement eugenic prison science. "The word HOPE in big letters has been written over the doors of our reformatory institutions, and so it ought to be." Moore maintained that seventy-five percent of his charges were saved, even though many came from the "junk heap" of humanity.[40]

The Iowa State Reformatory opened in 1907. Although this institution was modeled on Elmira, its history, character, and problems were unique. In April 1907, legislators passed a bill transforming the Iowa State Penitentiary at An-

38. "An Act Relating to a State Reformatory"; "New Jersey's New Reformatory," *New York Times*, 20 October 1895, 25; Barnes, *History of the Penal, Reformatory and Correctional Institutions*, 283–99.

39. Hahn, Sullivan, Van Blarcom, and Jess, *Report to the General Assembly*.

40. New Jersey Reformatory, *Thirteenth AR, 1913* [1914], 14. The results of psychological testing are in *Tenth AR, 1910* [1911], 15–16, and in the *Supplement to the Twelfth AR* {1913], 2–4. The treatment of defectives and the institution's aims and regimen are discussed in Moore, "Education and Work"; idem, "Address"; idem, "Classification."

amosa into an adult reformatory. Male first-time offenders between the ages of sixteen and thirty were to be accepted. Reformatory inmates were committed on indeterminate sentences, exposed to programs designed to foster reform, and released on parole. "We are doing all we can with the means we have to carry out the spirit of the law," said Warden Marquis Barr in 1908, "our aim being to make the Institution in fact what is in name—a Reformatory."[41]

Warden Barr and his successors, Charles McClaughry and J. N. Baumel, had a number of serious problems. Most important, the 1907 legislation ordered them to receive Iowa's female offenders, as well as the state's criminally insane. Three institutions operated under one roof: an adult reformatory for males, a female reformatory-prison, and a hospital-prison for the criminally insane. Warden McClaughry vigorously campaigned for the removal of female and insane offenders. "The insane criminals should not be, of course, included with the reformable subjects which this institution, as a reformatory only, should properly handle." The inclusion of females was "hurtful in the extreme."[42] Warden Baumel was pleased when women were transferred away in 1918.

Legislation founding the Washington State Reformatory, which opened in Monroe on 1 August 1909, was also modeled on New York's, with several differences. Commitments were restricted to male offenders between sixteen and thirty, guilty of crimes other than first or second degree murder. Legislators wisely recognized the folly of attempting to impose the "first offender" clause. Recidivists with one or two prior commitments were admitted. Offenders were committed under indeterminate sentences and released on parole, with the governor making release decisions. The aims of the institution became clear: "His instruction and training in the reformatory have two ends in view—to teach him how to live with other men and earn an honest living."[43]

The keepers of the Washington State Reformatory faced numerous problems in attempting to achieve this end. The first superintendent, Cleon Roe (1909–1913), shouldered the responsibility of completing the first cell house and basic structures. In 1916 the managers declared that these buildings were "in a most flattering condition," but the "temporary wood" wall continued to pose a security risk.[44] Roe and his successor, Donald Olson (1914–1920), ini-

---

41. Iowa Reformatory, *Eighteenth BR, 1906–1908* [1909], 7; "An Act to Revise the Law"; Remley, "History of the Anamosa Penitentiary," 61–69.

42. Iowa Reformatory, *Twentieth BR, 1910–1912* [1913], 4–5.

43. Washington State Reformatory, *Third BR, 1910–1912* (1912), 6; "An Act Creating the Washington State Reformatory."

44. Washington State Board of Control, *Eighth BR, 1914–1916* (1916), 259.

tiated many innovations. They made efforts to raise the quality of the staff. An "Officers' Study Club" started in 1912. Administrators, guards, and treatment staff met to discuss the nature and causes of crime, the purposes of treatment, and even the Declaration of Principles. Roe allowed inmates out on "temporary leave" (now called a furlough). Olson started an inmate self-government system, including an honors tier and community court. The "Greeters Committee" met new arrivals. The managers became confident that seventy-eight percent of their parolees were "making good."[45]

The Oklahoma State Reformatory opened in Granite on 10 April 1910. Kate Barnard, Commissioner of Charities and Corrections, was the driving force behind the institution. Barnard envisioned an institution modeled after the "great Elmira New York Reformatory." However, Barnard's bill met stiff resistance when placed before the 1909 Oklahoma legislature. Conservatives rejected the notion of reform and pushed for another adult prison. A political compromise was struck; the institution would be called an adult reformatory. Offenders between sixteen and twenty-five who committed an offense with a five-year maximum could, at the judge's discretion, be sent to Granite. But there were no provisions for indeterminate sentencing, parole, or any programs which were hallmarks of the new penology. The Oklahoma State Reformatory was designed as a prison for youthful felons.[46]

Commissioner Barnard was disappointed. In 1911 she declared that Oklahoma's "methods of dealing with the crime problem and the criminal still smack of the dark ages."[47] Although she managed to get the legislature to pass a "good time" bill, she was still not pleased with the reformatory. "There is no attempt to teach trades nor anything useful. The old idea of punishment is followed."[48] The institution made little progress over the next several years. In 1912 Warden Reed reported that construction was "progressing very slowly." The buildings, which were still temporary, were "unfit," "unsanitary," and "unsafe." In 1914 an inmate arsonist destroyed much of the structure. Warden George Waters provided a concise assessment of the reformatory's first de-

45. Washington State Board of Control, *Seventh BR, 1912–1914* (1917), 173. The institution was investigated in 1911 but escaped serious criticism: Goldsmith, Reed, and Reed, *Report of Conditions*.

46. "Penal Institutions"; Oklahoma Commissioners of Charities and Corrections, *Second AR, 1909–1910* [1911], 31–34. The spirit of the Oklahoma Reformatory was similar to that of a prison. Five inmates were stabbed and seven were shot by guards (one fatally) in 1912 (Oklahoma State Reformatory, *First BR, 1910–1912* [1913], 24).

47. Oklahoma Commissioners of Charities and Corrections, *Third AR, 1910–1911* [1912], 7.

48. Oklahoma Commissioners of Charities and Corrections, *Fourth AR, 1911–1912* [1913], 15.

cade: "The Oklahoma State Reformatory was operated as a Penitentiary, on par with the McAlester prison, until July 1, 1920, when it was changed by Executive Order to a Reformatory in fact as well as in name."[49]

The Kentucky State Reformatory followed a similar path. In 1910 the legislature transformed the state prison at Frankfort into an adult reformatory. Offenders under the age of thirty (no minimum was specified) who had not committed "atrocious crimes" and were not "habitual criminals" were eligible for admission. Inmates were to receive a common school education as well as industrial training so that they could become "self reliant and self supporting."[50] The institution was, in fact, a prison. The inmates were not youthful offenders. One thousand three hundred eighty-six inmates were committed between 1917 and 1919: ages ranged from fifteen to eighty-five; 361 (26.0%) were guilty of murder or manslaughter; 206 (14.8%) received life sentences; 385 (27.7%) were serving a five-year minimum. The schools were, in the chaplain's estimation, "simply makeshift." The contract system was a "handicap" and the buildings were "archaic, relics of barbarism."[51]

A 1920 inspection by the State Board of Charities confirmed the chaplain's negative assessment. Joseph Byers, Commissioner of Public Institutions, found the reformatory (which had opened in 1797 and still occupied the original facilities) in abysmal condition. "It is obsolete, unsanitary, and entirely unsuited for Reformatory purposes." It bore little resemblance to a treatment-oriented institution: "inhumane punishments" were still used; escapes and inmate violence became constant threats; a generally "hostile atmosphere" prevailed; the guard staff was untrained; the superintendent (a political appointment) was incompetent; the parole system was totally ineffective. The commissioners concluded that there was little hope for the Kentucky State Reformatory. They called for a new treatment-oriented reformatory to replace the ancient structure.[52]

The Connecticut Reformatory opened in Cheshire on 24 June 1913. It removed youthful offenders from prisons, where they "touch elbows with hardened and professional criminals," and from jails, which make "no systematic effort to straighten the crooked and tangled habits of their inmates."[53] Male first-time offenders between sixteen and twenty-five were committed under a

49. Oklahoma State Reformatory, *AR, 1921* [1922], unnumbered p. 3.
50. "An Act to Amend an Act"; "An Act to Repeal an Act."
51. Kentucky State Reformatory, *BR, 1917–1919* [1920], 255, 244, 256, 216.
52. Kentucky State Board of Charities and Correction, *BR, 1919–1921* [1922], 6–7, 24–25, 76.
53. *Report of the Reformatory Commission of Connecticut*, 3.

complex sentencing system which prescribed indeterminate sentences for some inmates and fixed sentences for others, in accordance with the offender's age and offense. Between 1913 and 1920 the Connecticut Reformatory introduced an Elmira-type regimen. Buildings were completed. Academic and vocational education, military drill, and recreation tried to instill inmates with "respect for law and authority, the necessity and value of industry … the upbuilding of Christian manhood." In 1920 the directors announced that sixty to sixty-five percent of the "graduates" of the Connecticut Reformatory "take their places among the industrious law-abiding people who make up the community."[54]

The Missouri and District of Columbia reformatories were token institutions. Missouri legislators passed a bill in 1915 changing the name of the Missouri Training School for Boys at Boonville to the Missouri Reformatory. The new Missouri Reformatory was to receive juveniles as well as offenders between sixteen and thirty. What might have been an interesting experiment (the Missouri Reformatory was a cottage institution, without walls) never came into being. A fiscal crisis caused the governor to veto the appropriation. The institution's name changed, but young adults were not admitted.[55]

The District of Columbia Reformatory at Lorton, Virginia, opened on 13 November 1916. It was, by design, a "workhouse site." Sixty inmates were transferred from the Leavenworth Penitentiary and fifty from the Federal prison at Atlanta to serve as laborers and erect buildings. In 1916 Superintendent W. H. Whittaker estimated that the construction would take ten years to complete. His assessment was accurate. In 1918 the inmates were still working on "temporary buildings"; in 1920 only four of twenty-nine planned structures had even been started.[56]

At face value, proponents of the adult reformatory movement had much to be pleased about in 1920. Eighteen states and the Federal government had passed laws establishing reformatory-prisons. Thousands of offenders were incarcerated in these institutions at the close of World War I; tens of thousands had been incarcerated since Elmira received its first offender in 1876. However, America's third penal system was badly splintered and on the verge of collapse. Reformatory keepers in Pennsylvania, Minnesota, Colorado, Illinois,

54. Connecticut Reformatory, *BR, 1912–1914* (1914), 30; *BR, 1918–1920* (1920), 7; "An Act Establishing the Connecticut Reformatory"; "An Act Amending an Act"; Erskine, "Industrial Instruction"; *Rules and Regulations*; Connecticut Reformatory, *Inmate Case Histories*.

55. "An Act to Change the Name"; Missouri Reformatory, *Fourteenth BR, 1915–1916* [1916], 17; Pettijohn, "Need of a Reformatory," 16–20.

56. District of Columbia Reformatory, *AR, 1916* (1916), 3–4, 11; *AR, 1918* (1918), 3–5, 11; *AR, 1919* (1919), 3–4; *AR, 1920* (1920), 3; Hart, "Prison Dormitory System."

Kansas, Ohio, Wisconsin, New Jersey, Iowa, Washington, and Connecticut continued to embrace multifactor positivism, advocate reform, and support Brockway's traditional Elmira system. The keepers of the Elmira, Massachusetts, and Indiana reformatories advocated psycho-biogenic theories, believing that custody, control, and eugenic prison science were needed to deal with mentally defective offenders. Penologists in Michigan, Oklahoma, and Kentucky based their "reform" efforts on punishment, deterrence, and profit. The Eastern New York Reformatory was still Elmira's custodial dumping ground.

By the close of the Progressive Era the seeds of triumphant defeat had taken root: the adult reformatory movement had, indeed, triggered a paradigmatic revolution which transformed the American criminal justice system. However, the myriad approaches to reform which developed between 1900 and 1920 left the movement without a common identity and prescription for America's ongoing crisis in crime and social disorder.[57] By 1920, the adult reformatory movement self-destructed; with it went America's faith in the rehabilitative ideal.

Forgotten Offenders: Race, Gender, and the New Penology

The American criminal justice system has a long and well-documented history of racism, sexism, and discrimination. Adult reformatories also subjected minority offenders to inferior care, which reflected their position in the American social, economic, and political order. However, historical data sources suggest that the form of racist and sexist care was dynamic and varied by institution. All adult reformatories for males opened between 1876 and 1920 received black males, but only three accepted females: the Minnesota, Iowa, and Kentucky reformatories. An examination of the records of these institutions, along with the District of Columbia Reformatory, exposes the racist and sexist dimensions of the new penology.[58]

57. Penologists' declining faith in the reformatory prison movement was reflected in Nalder, "The American State Reformatory." Nalder, who was the director of education at the Washington State Reformatory, visited Elmira as well as adult reformatories in Pennsylvania, Colorado, Kansas, Ohio, Indiana, and New Jersey in 1914 and 1915. He offered a wide range of insightful criticisms: superintendents were unqualified; guards were incompetent; treatment programs were ineffective; guard and inmate subcultures undermined efforts at reform; institutional staff focused their attention on troublesome inmates and on "routinism" and "restraint" (i.e. custody and control). Nalder concluded, "There is reason to doubt whether much that is popularly regarded and sometimes exploited as reformation deserves the name" (p. 291).

58. On the treatment of minorities, see Sellin, *Slavery and the Penal System*; Rafter, *Partial Justice*; idem, "Gender, Prisons, and Prison History"; idem, "Prisons for Women"; idem, "Chastising the Unchaste"; idem, "Hard Times"; Hahn, "Female State Prisoners"; idem, "Too Dumb to

The Minnesota Reformatory (1889) was widely regarded as an enlightened reformatory—an example of the benevolent spirit of America's new penology. Under the direction of Superintendent Frank Randall (1900–1914), one of the nation's most respected penologists, the institution developed a national reputation as an Elmira-type reformatory. However, the presumed benefits of the Minnesota Reformatory were not intended for minority inmates. Randall's diagnostic notes in the Inmate History and Record (case histories) reveal that he viewed black, female, and Native American inmates as biologically, mentally, and morally inferior.

Randall's assessment of "colored boys"—much like Brockway's—reflected societal prejudices and stereotypes. Black inmates were untrustworthy, irresponsible, lazy, obtuse, immoral, and prone to vice. Randall's assessment of L. L., a twenty-one-year-old black male committed for second degree assault, reflected these views: "Enough white blood and brightness to spoil him as a negro, but far from being a Caucasian in any way. No morals. Easily provoked to laughter and anger." E. B., a twenty-one-year-old grand larcenist, was "a very fine specimen of his race, and his crime of the peculiar weakness of which the negro is heir. The result of his criminal act will likely deter him from a repetition if he refrains from drink." Twenty-year-old L. J. was "a dangerous young nigger because he gets drunk, and then ugly. ... Might not have been tough, if he had not taken to liquor, but I think he probably would have been."[59]

Females were viewed as the victims of bad luck, bad men, environmental circumstances, and inherent weaknesses of the fairer sex. Seventeen-year-old M. D., admitted for second degree grand larceny, was not responsible: "She is a girl of possibilities, being quick and apparently desirous of doing better. She has been brought up under circumstances quite disadvantageous. ... She needs a good woman friend." Randall's assessment of twenty-year-old E. S., another grand larcenist, was similar: "She has no equal for apparent candor and respectability among all women we have ever had. Seems sincere. I should judge that her husband is a rogue, and that he has blinded her to his faults, without corrupting her." Twenty-one-year-old S. M. was also the victim of a bad man:

Know Better"; Freedman, *Their Sisters' Keepers*; idem, "Their Sisters' Keepers"; Brenzel, *Daughters of the State*; idem, "Lancaster Industrial School"; idem, "Domestication as Reform"; Pisciotta, "Race, Sex and Rehabilitation." On the treatment of women under the Irish system, see B. Smith, "Female Prisoner in Ireland."

59. Records of the St. Cloud State Reformatory, *Inmate History and Record*, vol. 4, 1902–1904, Case History #1511; vol. 9, 1912–1913, Case History #3041; vol. 6, 1906–1908, Case History #2030. Randall's predecessors, Superintendents William E. Lee and W. H. Houlton, expressed similar views about black inmates in *Record of Interviews with Inmates and Contacts with References, 1893–1896* (see, e.g., pp. 157, 160, 173).

Infatuated with a criminal who used her as he has used other girls, to pass forged checks. She has not yet recovered from it. What seems to be the only trouble. ... she wanted to get a man. I doubt her story of a mock marriage & I think she simply went away with him. He should have been arrested at La Crosse with her."[60]

Randall's views on Indian inmates also reflected societal stereotypes. They were simple, childish, and prone to vice, particularly "firewater." But on a positive note, they seemed to be ideal inmates. H. V., a forger, was "a young man with the usual characteristics of an Indian. I regard him favorably and wish that the white inmates were as truthful as he seems to be." Nineteen-year-old L. D., an arsonist, "did what almost any Indian can be gotten to do when drunk. A heavy, slow and strong young buck. Needs education and training and needs it badly." Eighteen-year-old C. P. was

an Indian who is very ignorant, but think he may do very well here if he is like all other Indians that we have had, but I do not have confidence enough in him to be trusted on the outside of the stockade as I hardly think he knows right from wrong.

M. W. was "a simple son of the forest, but not as simple as he would be if he were a full-blood. His white blood, and associations with a white man, have done him no good."[61]

However, Randall did not isolate black, female, and Indian inmates in separate departments. Chronic overcrowding, limited staffing, and the small number of minority inmates (usually four or fewer females and between five and thirty "colored" and "red" inmates each year) made segregation organizationally inexpedient.[62] Black and Indian males were mixed in with their white counterparts. Randall viewed female inmates as a chronic nuisance. They boarded in local jails whenever possible; as an alternative, they worked at the superintendent's house and were released as soon as they had served their minimum sentence. Randall urged legislators to correct this "intolerable situation" and build an institution for women. "It is my judgement that young men and women should not be kept in confinement at or near the same place, but if it is to be done, the necessary equipment should be furnished."[63]

60. *Inmate History and Record,* vol. 6, 1906–1908, Case History #2222 and #2252; vol. 7, 1908–1910, Case History #2307.

61. *Inmate History and Record,* vol. 4, 1902–1904, Case History #1424; vol. 5, 1904–1906, Case History #1763 and 1867; vol. 6, 1906–1908, Case History #2014.

62. The number of female, black, and Indian inmates is not specified in every annual report. In 1910 the institution held 147 inmates, including four females, two black, and two Indian inmates. In 1915 it held 625 inmates, including nineteen blacks and six Indians. The number of females was not reported (Minnesota State Reformatory, *BR, 1908–1910* [1911], 62; *BR, 1915–1916* [1917], 8).

63. Minnesota State Reformatory, *BR, 1908–1910* [1911], 1–2.

The Iowa State Reformatory (1907) handled minority inmates, particularly females, differently. Warden Marquis Barr, unlike Randall, welcomed women and fully supported the aims and programs of the "Female Department." Under the direction of Matron Anna Treman, Iowa's fallen females underwent a regimen designed to prepare them to assume their proper roles as wives, mothers, and domestics. "The greatest need is firm, yet kindly, discipline and, next to that, systematic training of the hand and brain," explained the matron.[64]

Iowa's female offenders were rigidly isolated from their male counterparts. The rules in the female and male divisions were the same, but their daily regimens differed. Academic education received less emphasis in the female department. The girls learned how to make fruit baskets, table mats, and sandwich bags as part of their "academic training." Women also had extra doses of religious instruction. Visits from philanthropic ladies supplemented lectures on proper womanly behavior. The matron explained the focus of her department: "The work now, as heretofore, consists of cooking, baking, laundry and general cleaning, also the sewing for the department, and fancy needlework; many of our women being very proficient in the latter."[65] Each female offender was, as Sheila Rothman aptly put it, prepared to assume her place as a "Protestant Nun."[66] Warden Barr was pleased with the "commendable work" being done in the Female Department.

The resignation of Warden Barr in 1912 and the appointment of Charles McClaughry as his successor set the stage for the demise of the Female Department. McClaughry shared Barr's views on the nature of fallen women and supported Matron Treman's efforts to transform the "girls" into Protestant Nuns. But there was no room, in McClaughry's view, for a female division at the Iowa State Reformatory.

I consider the incorporation of the female department as a part of this reformatory to be hurtful in the extreme [said the new warden]. It has had a demoralizing influence upon both departments of the institution if stories related and what I have observed since coming here are to be taken as evidence, and has largely nullified reformatory work.[67]

McClaughry's campaign to remove females eventually paid off. In 1915 the legislature authorized the construction of a reformatory-prison for female offenders. Iowa's fallen females transferred to the Industrial Reformatory for Women at Rockwell City in 1918.[68]

64. Iowa Reformatory, *Eighteenth BR, 1906–1908* [1909], 47.
65. Ibid., 48.
66. S. Rothman, *Woman's Proper Place*, 63–93.
67. Iowa Reformatory, *Twentieth BR, 1910–1912* [1913], 5.
68. "An Act to Establish an Industrial Reformatory."

Female and black inmates were exposed to sexist and racist care at the Kentucky State Reformatory. Women lived in isolation in the Female Department. Black and white males were also rigidly segregated. White males lived in the "white cell house"; black males, in the "colored cell house." These inmates attended separate religious services and separate schools; even the hospital wards were segregated.

However, racial social control took on a special form and significance at the Kentucky State Reformatory. Christopher Adamson has demonstrated that the number of blacks incarcerated in southern prisons precipitously increased after the Civil War as southerners looked for methods of social control to replace slavery.[69] The population and aims of the Kentucky State Reformatory reflected this trend. In 1917, 1,352 men were incarcerated: 748 (55.3%) were "colored" and 604 (44.7%) were white. Thirty-four females were incarcerated: 23 (67.6%) were "colored" and 11 (32.4%) were white.[70] The Kentucky State Reformatory was technically classified as a rehabilitation-oriented adult reformatory. In practice, it was a punitive-custodial prison which reflected Kentucky apartheid and was committed to taming and training the state's dangerous classes: "colored criminals" and "poor white trash."

The District of Columbia Reformatory, opened in 1916, was also designed with race, sex, and class control in mind. A report submitted to President Roosevelt in 1908 on Washington, D.C. was alarming: crime was reaching epidemic proportions and the District's penal system was overburdened and ineffective. "The property class, and they comprise the vast majority of our population, live in a state of siege." The commissioners concluded that "colored people" were responsible for much of the city's crime, deviance, and disorder. Although they comprised only one third of the city's population, they committed five sixths of the assaults, three fourths of petty larcenies, over half of the murders, and seven eighths of the "fornication offenses." The report concluded that "the criminal instincts of the colored people are such as belong to the childhood of a race rather than such as require planning and deliberation."[71]

The report called for the opening of an adult reformatory to deal with the "colored problem": "It is highly probable that a large majority of those who would be candidates for a reformatory in this District would belong to the colored race." This institution would instill "colored criminals" with respect for

69. Adamson, "Punishment After Slavery."

70. Kentucky State Reformatory, *BR, 1917–1919* [1920], 254.

71. Quoted in District of Columbia Reformatory, *First AR, 1915* (1915), 4, 8.

law and order, preparing them to assume their "proper place" in society: "Shift-less and awkward specimens of these people are transformed by the discipline and training to competent and often highly efficient workmen" (but mostly, into common laborers). The commissioners recommended that the new reformatory receive female offenders. "They could be employed in kitchen and laundry work and should be trained to useful service in various lines."[72]

The handling of minority offenders at the Minnesota, Iowa, Kentucky, and District of Columbia reformatories exposes four approaches to building docile bodies: white males (except those labeled mentally defective) were trained as craftsmen and prepared to assume their place as honest, obedient, lower-class workers; white females were trained as domestic servants and prepared to assume positions as wives and mothers; black males were channeled into the most menial laboring positions; black females, the victims of race and gender discrimination, had the lowest position in the hierarchy of "reform": menial servants and the mothers of the next generation of social outcasts.[73] The new penology and promise of benevolent treatment served a common end: legitimizing racism, sexism, and the repression of America's dangerous classes.

Conclusion

Elmira experienced tumultuous changes during the Progressive Era; however, the pace of change at other adult reformatories was institution-specific. At one extreme, the Michigan Reformatory maintained its unwavering commitment to punishment and profit. In contrast, the Indiana Reformatory introduced sterilizations and eugenic prison science. The cost of organizational independence was high. By 1920, the adult reformatory movement was a loose collection of highly diverse institutions parading under a common banner. Their "triumphant defeat" laid the foundation for the demise of the rehabilitative ideal.

These findings provide guarded support for David Rothman's interpretation of Progressive Era reforms. Reformers did, indeed, act out of "conscience" and yield to "convenience," but the dynamics of the process were far more complex than he suggests. Rothman's social context perspective minimizes the importance of economic considerations and class conflict; it fails to recognize that there were multiple consciences and social contracts between citizens and states. The notion of "convenience" is also simplistic. An organizational-and-

72. Ibid., 9, 6.
73. The racist and sexist dimensions of "treatment" in juvenile institutions is analyzed in Pisciotta, "Race, Sex, and Rehabilitation."

social-systems-theory approach would have revealed that the failures of Progressive Era "reforms" were, in large part, due to the inherent defects of total institutions and the medical model—their failure to build docile bodies was, then, normal and expected.

The presumed benefits of the new penology were not, however, intended to extend to America's forgotten offenders: blacks, females, and other dangerous classes (e.g. Minnesota's "red men"). Nicole Hahn Rafter's penetrating study of the incarceration of women in nineteenth- and twentieth-century American prisons and adult reformatories concludes that they were the victims of "partial justice"; that is, "conditions that were simultaneously milder and harsher than those of men in state prisons."[74] This theme can be extended to describe the experience of minorities in other correctional facilities. Inmates incarcerated at the Minnesota, Iowa, Kentucky, and District of Columbia reformatories were subjected to paternalistic coercion which reflected racism, sexism, and nativism in the broader social structure. Their treatment was, at times, less harsh, as in the early release of females because they were a "nuisance" or the exclusion of women from hard labor; at times, more harsh, as in the substandard housing afforded black and female inmates or separate sexist and racist regimens of reform. To be sure, prison science and the new penology were more stigmatizing, humiliating, and painful for minorities.

74. Rafter, *Partial Justice*, xxx.

Conclusion

The standards of a nation's civilization can be judged by opening the doors of its prisons.— F. M. Dostoevsky, *The House of the Dead*

Adult reformatories are no longer a central component of the American correctional system; in fact, they are a peripheral concern. The Elmira Reformatory (Elmira Correctional Facility) is now a maximum security prison for felons, irrespective of age. The Massachusetts Reformatory (Massachusetts Correctional Institution at Concord) is a medium security prison for adult offenders serving sentences of at least two and one half years. The Michigan Reformatory receives seventeen-to-twenty-six-year-old "incorrigible offenders" and is classified as a "close security facility with a maximum security component." Most of the other institutions which constituted the adult reformatory movement have become adult prisons, juvenile reformatories, or simply closed—an ignominious ending for the movement which introduced the new penology and dominated American and international corrections for nearly a half-century.

However, a closer look reveals that the legacy of Zebulon Brockway, the Elmira Reformatory, the adult reformatory movement, and the new penology is far-reaching and long-lasting. We cannot understand the history of American penology, the nature of contemporary corrections, or the future of punishment

150

and social control without considering the contributions of America's third penal system.

On Contemporary Corrections

Michel Foucault's history of penology led him to conclude that, "word for word, from one century to the other, the same fundamental propositions are repeated."[1] This observation is simplistic. Modern correctional institutions do not blindly mirror the past; the keepers of late twentieth-century prisons and reformatories are not reincarnations of Zebulon Brockway. However, a comparison of past and present penal systems reveals many common aims, programs, problems, and practices—disturbing similarities which suggest that current approaches to crime, punishment, and social control are products of our barbaric past.

Adult prisons, juvenile reformatories, and the few remaining reformatory-prisons continue to incarcerate America's dangerous classes. The grist of late nineteenth- and early twentieth-century institutions—impoverished Irish, Italian, German, and "Hebrew" immigrants and their children—has been replaced with poor, uneducated, unskilled, city-raised blacks, Hispanics, and "white trash."[2] Penal institutions (including Elmira) continue to serve as storage dumps for capitalism's unwanted human refuse, a mixture of alienated "social junk" and "social dynamite."[3]

The aims of contemporary prisons and reformatories are essentially unchanged. On a positive note, the more blatant forms of institutional racism, sexism, and nativism have been eliminated. However, the keepers of contemporary institutions—just like Zebulon Brockway, Otis Fuller, and Gardiner Tufts—still attempt to build docile bodies by instilling their charges with the habits of order, discipline, self-control, and respect for God, law, and country. Black, Hispanic, and lower-class white offenders who follow the path of

---

1. Foucault, *Discipline and Punish*, 270.
2. A profile of prisoners in state prisons in 1986 exposes America's new dangerous class: 63.9% were less than thirty years old and 36.1% were thirty years and older; 95.6% were males, 4.4% females; 49.7% were white, 46.9% were black, 3.4% were "other"; 87.4% were non-Hispanic and 12.6% were Hispanic; 61.6% had less than a twelfth-grade education, 38.4% had twelve or more years of study; 69.0% were employed when they were arrested and 31.0% were unemployed; however, of the employed inmates, 60.0% earned less than $10,000 in the year prior to their arrest (Maguire and Flanagan, *Sourcebook:* the age statistics are for admissions in thirty-six states in 1985, p. 612; other statistics are for 1986, p. 614).
3. These terms are from Spitzer, "Toward a Marxian Theory of Deviance."

"primary adjustment" and act contrite, participate in treatment programs, and appear to internalize the Protestant ethic are paroled. Inmates who follow the course of "secondary adjustment" and fight the system, fail to act like Christian gentlemen, or reject their "proper place" in the social and economic order can count on extended doses of "treatment and reform" in our modern "punitive-plague cities."

A variety of innovative and exotic treatment programs have been introduced over the last several decades: individual counseling, group counseling, individual psychotherapy, group psychotherapy, reality therapy, behavior modification, therapeutic communities, Transactional Analysis, Transcendental Meditation, relaxation therapy, family therapy, wilderness programs, work release, study release, furloughs, plastic surgery, drug therapy, and even color therapy. However, the core programs of contemporary institutions—academic and vocational education, labor, religion, recreation, mark and classification systems, along with the nation's latest reform panacea (military drill and boot camps)—are firmly rooted in Brockway's Elmira system.[4] These traditional programs and more recent innovations share a common end: transforming America's new dangerous classes into law-abiding and socially and economically productive working-class citizens.

Indeterminate sentencing and parole are still integral components of the American criminal justice system. In the mid to late 1970s, punishment-oriented theorists launched a counterrevolution which challenged the rehabilitative ideal.[5] Conservative legislators—not wanting to appear "soft on crime" (especially drug offenses and chronic offenders)—passed new laws which reintroduced fixed sentencing and limited, or even abolished, parole.[6] But this trend has been reversed. In 1990, three percent of American adult males were under the supervision of probation or parole officers.[7] However, community correc-

4. Elmira is still employing Brockway's multifactor positivist approach: "Medical, dental, and psychiatric evaluations identify the resident's needs and enable individualized program planning. Although residents project many common traits, each is an individual whose behavior and needs must be approached on an individual basis" (Beltzer and Spear, *Elmira*, 31).

5. Wilson, *Thinking about Crime*; van den Haag, *Punishing Criminals*; Fogel, *"...We are the Living Proof..."*; and von Hirsch, *Doing Justice*, were the leading voices calling for a return to punishment during this period. Early defenders of rehabilitation included Palmer, *Correctional Intervention*, and Cullen and Gilbert, *Reaffirming Rehabilitation*. Currie, *Confronting Crime*, provides a penetrating critique of the ensuing punishment versus rehabilitation debate.

6. The arguments of Wilson, van den Haag, and other conservatives regarding indeterminate sentencing and parole are simplistic and historically incorrect. These innovations were not introduced as "soft" and "liberal" reforms. They were grounded on the notion of social defense and were intended to lengthen—not shorten—terms of incarceration.

7. U.S. Department of Justice, Bureau of Justice Statistics, *Probation and Parole 1990*, 1. In 1990, state and Federal institutions reported that 531,407 adult offenders were on parole and 2,670,234 were on probation. The national incarceration rate per 100,000 adult residents increased

tions continues to focus on America's "dangerous classes." In some urban areas—including our nation's capital—over 30 percent of African American males are now on probation or parole.[8]

The decarceration movement has, as Andrew Scull observed, served to "expand the reach of social control agencies and expose new populations to their (generally unwelcome) attentions." Stanley Cohen's analysis of master patterns of punishment demonstrates that the return of the community-based corrections movement—including parole—has resulted in a wider, deeper, stronger, and more sophisticated network of social control. "The most fundamental fact about what is going on in the new agencies is that it is much the same as what went on and is still going on in the old system," concludes Cohen. "The same old experts have moved office to the community and are doing the same old things they have always done."[9] Modern parole officers, much like their late nineteenth- and early twentieth-century counterparts, extend the power, authority, and "surveillance space" of the state into the community—but often with limited results.

Contemporary correctional institutions continue to experience many of the same problems which undermined late nineteenth- and early twentieth-century social control efforts. Many institutions are still overcrowded, underfunded, and in poor structural condition (witness the continued use of the Auburn and Sing Sing Prisons). Correctional facilities are still plagued by the defects of total institutions, the limitations of the medical model ("tinkering science"), and the problem of prisoner resistance (violence, gangs, riots, drugs, theft, smuggling, arson, predatory sex, suicide).[10] Have we solved the riddle of human behavior? Are contemporary prison and reformatory keepers capable of

from 138/100,000 in 1980 to 271/100,000 in 1989. The rate for parole increased from 136/100,000 in 1980 to 248/100,000 in 1989. The rate for probation was 1,369/100,000 in 1989 (rate statistics for 1980 were not included) (Maguire and Flanagan, *Sourcebook*, 564, 604, 666).

8. Two studies by Miller are revealing. Thirty percent of the African-American males ages 18–35 who were living in Baltimore, Maryland, in 1991 were on probation or parole. Twenty-one percent of the African-American males in Washington, D.C., were under the supervision of probation or parole officers. Miller also discovered that fifty-six percent of the black males in Baltimore and forty-two percent in Washington were either in jail or prison, on probation or parole, out on bail, or wanted by the police. He concludes that African-American males are now regarded as "the enemy" by the American criminal justice system, which is, as he puts it, "in a disastrous feeding frenzy" (*Hobbling a Generation: Baltimore*, 2–3. *Hobbling a Generation: Washington, D.C.*, 3.

9. Scull, *Decarceration*, 179–80. Cohen, *Visions of Social Control*, 75.

10. On prisoner resistance by inmates in state and Federal correctional facilities in 1989: 113 committed suicide; 66 were murdered by other inmates; 8,717 escaped [1988] from minimum, medium, and maximum security state and Federal facilities; 122,156 sentenced prisoners were admitted to state and Federal institutions for violating the conditions of parole. These numbers do not reflect failed attempts at suicide, attacks which did not result in death, attempted escapes, or parole violations which went undetected. In short, these numbers reflect a small percentage of inmate secondary adjustments (Maguire and Flanagan, *Sourcebook*, 661, 667, 673).

diagnosing the root causes of crime and applying prison science and the medical model? Custody, control, and maintenance of order are still the primary aims of modern penal institutions. Balancing the conflicting aims of benevolent reform and benevolent repression and taming and training America's new "human variety" remains a difficult if not impossible task.

On Doing Correctional History

To be sure, criminal justice historians have made significant progress in analyzing the history of crime, punishment, and social control. The works of Foucault, Garland, Rusche and Kirchheimer, and David Rothman, to name a few, present penetrating interpretations of the adult prison and juvenile reformatory movements. However, these studies are all historically incomplete on one crucial point: they totally overlook the contributions of Elmira and America's third penal system.

This book addresses this gaping void in the literature but is not intended to stand as the definitive or final history of the American adult reformatory movement. My purpose has been to call attention to the new penology, outline the general contours of the reformatory-prison movement, and expose some of American penology's grandest myths—most notably, the tale of benevolent reform at Elmira that has been perpetrated by march-of-progress historians. The lack of prior research on this movement has led me to employ an institutional focus—history from the inside out. Social historians, intellectual historians, legal historians, criminal justice historians, and cliometricians will, no doubt, find missed opportunities for historical inquiry and speculation, as well as simplistic interpretations. This study may raise more questions than it answers; hopefully, it will lay the foundation for more penetrating and sweeping analyses in the future.

Much work remains to be done. More case histories of specific reformatories and prisons are needed to understand how institutions were similar and different, and how they reflected state-specific social, economic, political, cultural, and demographic contexts. Historians will then be in a position to attempt more ambitious studies which explore the linkages between adult prisons, juvenile reformatories, reformatory-prisons for adults—including institutions for females—and neglected penal facilities, such as jails and county penitentiaries. Researchers should employ organizational theory and social systems theory. Future studies should link penal institutions with law enforcement agencies and the courts, as well as other forms of socialization and social control, ranging from the family, church, and school to social welfare agencies.

Comparative international studies will allow us to understand more fully the roots and diffusion of American strategies of social control. How did other countries—especially monarchies which were not capitalist or democratic—adapt the new penology to build docile bodies and tame and train their dangerous classes? Future studies should, as Garland has argued, apply and test some of the grand theories of punishment and society: those of Karl Marx, Max Weber, Emile Durkheim, Norbert Elias, Georg Rusche and Otto Kirchheimer, and Michel Foucault.[11] Cliometric studies are needed to measure changes in the size, scope, focus, and impact of the American social control networks, including the diffusion of parole and community-based corrections. In short, criminal justice historians should attempt to develop a Millsian sociological imagination—that is, the ability to find the intersection of history, biography, and social structure in cross-cultural and comparative settings.[12]

On the Future

Historians rightly take exception to George Santayana's often cited observation that "those who cannot remember the past are condemned to repeat it." However, the similarities between past and present penal systems are, indeed, unsettling and do not bode well for the future.

Our failure to learn from the past is largely due to ignorance and indifference. Contemporary criminal justice administrators, legislators, and even many academics view the study of history, to put it bluntly, as a waste of time. The pressing problems of crime, corrections, and social control require, in the judgment of many policymakers, immediate action. "History, then, is something of a luxury if not a distraction," note David J. Rothman and Stanton Wheeler in *Social History and Social Policy*. "It may offer some interesting background information. But when it comes down to the core of issues, to the hard process of reaching a decision, the historian has no central role to play."[13]

The failure of contemporary criminal justice policymakers to consult historians is unfortunate. The study of the past will not provide contemporary correctional administrators and policymakers with a roadmap to reform. The study of the past may, however, provide a heightened sensitivity to the complexities of the crime problem and the timeless roadblocks to human and social engi-

---

11. Garland's *Punishment and Modern Society* comprises an extensive discussion of the needs and limitations of criminal justice historiography.

12. Mills, *The Sociological Imagination*, chapter 8, offers suggestions on the development of interdisciplinary approaches to doing history.

13. P. 1.

neering. Historian Ysabel Rennie's concluding comments in *The Search for Criminal Man* provide food for thought:

In the mental storehouse where penologists keep their theories, there should be a sign clearly posted above each storage bin. It should read: WARNING: THIS IDEA WAS TRIED IN THE __TH, __TH, AND __TH CENTURIES, AND DID NOT WORK. Perhaps this would not discourage anyone for long, but it would at least put the burden of proof on the advocates to show that their ideas would work better this time.[14]

14. P. 274.

Declaration of Principles Adopted and Promulgated by the Congress

(Wines, *Transactions of the National Congress*, 541–47)

I. Crime is an intentional violation of duties imposed by law, which inflicts an injury upon others. Criminals are persons convicted of crime by competent courts. Punishment is suffering inflicted on the criminal for the wrong done by him, with a special view to secure his reformation.

II. The treatment of criminals by society is for the protection of society. But since such treatment is directed to the criminal rather than to the crime, its great object should be his moral regeneration. Hence the supreme aim of prison discipline is the reformation of criminals, not the infliction of vindictive suffering.

III. The progressive classification of prisoners, based on character and worked on some well-adjusted mark system, should be established in all prisons above the common jail.

IV. Since hope is a more potent agent than fear, it should be made an ever-present force in the minds of prisoners, by a well-devised and skilfully-applied system of rewards for good conduct, industry and attention to learning. Rewards, more than punishments, are essential to every good prison system.

V. The prisoner's destiny should be placed, measurably, in his own hands; he must be put into circumstances where he will be able, through his own exertions, to continually better his own condition. A regulated self-interest must be brought into play, and made constantly operative.

VI. The two master forces opposed to the reform of the prison systems of our several states are political appointments, and a consequent instability of administration. Until both are eliminated, the needed reforms are impossible.

VII. Special training, as well as high qualities of head and heart, is required to make a good prison or reformatory officer. Then only will the administration of public punish-

157

ment become scientific, uniform and successful, when it is raised to the dignity of a profession, and men are specially trained for it, as they are for other pursuits.

VIII. Peremptory sentences ought to be replaced by those of indeterminate length. Sentences limited only by satisfactory proof of reformation should be substituted for those measured by mere lapse of time.

IX. Of all reformatory agencies, religion is first in importance, because most potent in its action upon the human heart and life.

X. Education is a vital force in the reformation of fallen men and women. Its tendency is to quicken the intellect, inspire self-respect, excite to higher aims, and afford a healthful substitute for low and vicious amusements. Education is, therefore, a matter of primary importance in prisons, and should be carried to the utmost extent consistent with the other purposes of such institutions.

XI. In order to [achieve] the reformation of imprisoned criminals, there must be not only a sincere desire and intention to that end, but a serious conviction, in the minds of the prison officers, that they are capable of being reformed, since no man can heartily maintain a discipline at war with his inward beliefs; no man can earnestly strive to accomplish what in his heart he despairs of accomplishing.

XII. A system of prison discipline, to be truly reformatory, must gain the will of the convict. He is to be amended; but how is this possible with his mind in a state of hostility? No system can hope to succeed, which does not secure this harmony of wills, so that the prisoner shall choose for himself what his officer chooses for him. But, to this end, the officer must really choose the good of the prisoner, and the prisoner must remain in his choice long enough for virtue to become a habit. This consent of wills is an essential condition of reformation.

XIII. The interest of society and the interest of the convicted criminal are really identical, and they should be made practically so. At present there is a combat between crime and laws. Each sets the other at defiance, and, as a rule, there is little kindly feeling, and few friendly acts, on either side. It would be otherwise if criminals, on conviction, instead of being cast off, were rather made the objects of a generous parental care; that is, if they were trained to virtue and not merely sentenced to suffering.

XIV. The prisoner's self-respect should be cultivated to the utmost, and every effort made to give back to him his manhood. There is no greater mistake in the whole compass of penal discipline, than its studied imposition of degradation as a part of punishment. Such imposition destroys every better impulse and aspiration. It crushes the weak, irritates the strong, and indisposes all to submission and reform. It is trampling where we ought to raise, and is therefore as unchristian in principle as it is unwise in policy.

XV. In prison administration, moral forces should be relied upon, with as little admixture of physical force as possible, and organized persuasion be made to take the place of coercive restraint, the object being to make upright and industrious freemen, rather than orderly and obedient prisoners. Brute force may make good prisoners; moral training alone will make good citizens. To the latter of these ends, the living soul must be won; to the former, only the inert and obedient body.

XVI. Industrial training should have both a higher development and a greater breadth than has heretofore been, or is now, commonly given to it in our prisons. Work is no less an auxiliary to virtue, than it is a means of support. Steady, active, honorable labor is the basis of all reformatory discipline. It not only aids reformation, but is essential to it. It was a maxim with Howard, "make men diligent, and they will be honest"—a maxim which this congress regards as eminently sound and practical.

XVII. While industrial labor in prisons is of the highest importance and utility to the convict, and by no means injurious to the laborer outside, we regard the contract system of prison labor, as now commonly practised in our country, as prejudicial alike to discipline, finance and the reformation of the prisoner, and sometimes injurious to the interest of the free laborer.

XVIII. The most valuable parts of the Irish prison system—the more strictly penal stage of separate imprisonment, the reformatory stage of progressive classification, and the probationary stage of natural training—are believed to be as applicable to one country as another—to the United States as to Ireland.

XIX. Prisons, as well as prisoners, should be classified or graded so that there shall be prisons for the untried, for the incorrigible and for other degrees of depraved character, as well as separate establishments for women, and for criminals of the younger class.

XX. It is the judgment of this congress, that repeated short sentences for minor criminals are worse than useless; that, in fact, they rather stimulate than repress transgression. Reformation is a work of time; and a benevolent regard to the good of the criminal himself, as well as to the protection of society, requires that his sentence be long enough for reformatory processes to take effect.

XXI. Preventive institutions, such as truant homes, industrial schools, etc., for the reception and treatment of children not yet criminal, but in danger of becoming so, constitute the true field of promise, in which to labor for the repression of crime.

XXII. More systematic and comprehensive methods should be adopted to save discharged prisoners, by providing them with work and encouraging them to redeem their character and regain their lost position in society. The state has not discharged its whole duty to the criminal when it has punished him, nor even when it has reformed him. Having raised him up, it has the further duty to aid in holding him up. And to this end it is desirable that state societies be formed, which shall co-operate with each other in this work.

XXIII. The successful prosecution of crime requires the combined action of capital and labor, just as other crafts do. There are two well defined classes engaged in criminal operations, who may be called the capitalists and the operatives. It is worthy of inquiry, whether a more effective warfare may not be carried on against crime, by striking at the capitalists as a class, than at the operatives one by one. Certainly, this double warfare should be vigorously pushed, since from it the best results, as regards repressive justice, may be reasonably hoped for.

XXIV. Since personal liberty is the rightful inheritance of every human being, it is the sentiment of this congress that the state which has deprived an innocent citizen of this right, and subjected him to penal restraint, should, on unquestionable proof of its mistake, make reasonable indemnification for such wrongful imprisonment.

XXV. Criminal lunacy is a question of vital interest to society; and facts show that our laws regarding insanity, in its relation to crime, need revision, in order to bring them to a more complete conformity to the demands of reason, justice and humanity; so that, when insanity is pleaded in bar of conviction, the investigation may be conducted with greater knowledge, dignity and fairness; criminal responsibility be more satisfactorily determined; the punishment of the sane criminal be made more sure, and the restraint of the insane be rendered at once more certain and more humane.

XXVI. While this congress would not shield the convicted criminal from the just responsibility of his misdeeds, it arraigns society itself as in no slight degree accountable for the invasion of its rights and the warfare upon its interests, practised by the criminal classes. Does society take all the steps which it easily might, to change, or at least to improve, the circumstances in our social state that lead to crime; or, when crime has been committed, to cure the proclivity to it, generated by these circumstances? It cannot be pretended. Let society, then, lay the case earnestly to its conscience, and strive to mend in both particulars. Offences, we are told by a high authority, must come; but a special woe is denounced against those through whom they come. Let us take heed that that woe fall not upon our head.

XXVII. The exercise of executive clemency in the pardon of criminals is a practical question of grave importance, and of great delicacy and difficulty. It is believed that the annual average of executive pardons from the prisons of the whole county reaches ten per cent of their population. The effect of the too free use of the pardoning power is to detract from the *certainty* of punishment for crimes, and to divert the mind of prisoners from the means supplied for their improvement. Pardons should issue for one or more of the following reasons, viz.: to release the innocent, to correct mistakes made in imposing the sentence, to relieve such suffering from ill-health as requires release from imprisonment, and to facilitate or reward the real reformation of the prisoner. The exercise of this power should be by the executive, and should be guarded by careful examination as to the character of the prisoner and his conduct in prison. Furthermore, it is the opinion of this congress that governors of states should give to their respective legislatures the reasons, in each case, for their exercise of the pardoning power.

XXVIII. The proper duration of imprisonment for a violation of the laws of society is one of the most perplexing questions in criminal jurisprudence. The present extraordinary inequality of sentences for the same or similar crimes is a source of constant irritation among prisoners, and the discipline of our prisons suffers in consequence. The evil is one for which some remedy should be devised.

XXIX. Prison statistics, gathered from a wide field and skillfully digested, are essential to an exhibition of the true character and working of our prison systems. The collection, collation and reduction to tabulated forms of such statistics can best be effected through a national prison discipline society, with competent working committees in every state, or by the establishment of a national prison bureau, similar to the recently instituted national bureau of education.

XXX. Prison architecture is a matter of grave importance. Prisons of every class should be substantial structures, affording gratification by their design and material to a pure taste, but not costly or highly ornate. We are of the opinion that those of moderate size are best, as regards both industrial and reformatory ends.

XXXI. The construction, organization, and management of all prisons should be by the state, and they should form a graduated series of reformatory establishments, being arranged with a view to the industrial employment, intellectual education and moral training of the inmates.

XXXII. As a general rule, the maintenance of penal institutions, above the county jail, should be from the earnings of their inmates, and without cost to the state; nevertheless, the true standard of merit in their management is the rapidity and thoroughness of reformatory effect accomplished thereby.

XXXIII. A right application of the principles of sanitary science in the construction and arrangements of prisons is a point of vital importance. The apparatus for heating and ventilation should be the best that is known; sunlight, air and water should be afforded according to the abundance with which nature has provided them; the rations and clothing should be plain but wholesome, comfortable, and in sufficient but not extravagant quantity; the bedsteads, bed and bedding, including sheets and pillow cases, not costly but decent, and kept clean, well aired and free from vermin; the hospital accommodations, medical stores and surgical instruments should be all that humanity requires and science can supply; and all needed means for personal cleanliness should be without stint.

XXXIV. The principle of the responsibility of parents for the full or partial support of their criminal children in reformatory institutions has been extensively applied in Europe, and its practical working has been attended with the best results. It is worthy of inquiry whether this principle may not be advantageously introduced into the management of our American reformatory institutions.

XXXV. It is our conviction that one of the most effective agencies in the repression of crime would be the enactment of laws by which the education of all the children of the state should be made obligatory. Better to force education upon the people than to force them into prison to suffer for crimes, of which the neglect of education and consequent ignorance have been the occasion, if not the cause.

XXXVI. As a principle that crowns all, and is essential to all, it is our conviction that no prison system can be perfect, or even successful to the most desirable degree, without some central authority to sit at the helm, guiding, controlling, unifying and vitalizing the whole. We ardently hope yet to see all the departments of our preventive, reformatory and penal institutions in each state moulded into one harmonious and effective system; its parts mutually answering to and supporting each other; and the whole animated by the same spirit, aiming at the same objects, and subject to the same control; yet without loss of the advantages of voluntary aid and effort, wherever they are attainable.

XXXVII. This congress is of the opinion that, both in the official administration of such a system, and in the voluntary co-operation of citizens therein, the agency of women may be employed with excellent effect.

Bibliography

Articles, Books, Dissertations

(arranged by author)

Adamson, Christopher R. "Hard Labor and Solitary Confinement: Effects of the Business Cycle and Labor Supply on Prison Discipline in the United States, 1790–1835." *Research in Law, Deviance and Social Control* 6 (1984): 19–56.
————. "Punishment after Slavery: Southern State Penal Systems, 1865–1890." *Social Problems* 30 (June 1983): 555–69.
————. "Toward a Marxian Penology: Captive Criminal Populations as Economic Threats and Resources." *Social Problems* 31 (April 1984): 435–58.
Allen, Fred C., comp. *Handbook of the New York State Reformatory at Elmira.* Elmira, N.Y.: The Summary Press, 1916.
Altgeld, John Peter. *Our Penal Machinery and its Victims.* Chicago: A. C. McClurg and Company, 1886.
American Correctional Association. *The American Prison: From the Beginning ... A Pictorial History.* n.p.: author, 1983.
Asbury, Herbert. *The Gangs of New York: An Informal History of the Underworld.* New York: Alfred A. Knopf, 1928.

Bannister, Robert C. *Social Darwinism: Science and Myth in Anglo-American Social Thought.* Philadelphia: Temple University Press, 1979.
Baran, Paul A., and Paul M. Sweezy. *Monopoly Capital: An Essay on the American Economic and Social Order.* New York: Monthly Review Press, 1966.
Barnes, Harry Elmer. *The Evolution of Penology in Pennsylvania: A Study in American Social History.* Indianapolis: The Bobbs-Merrill Company, 1927.

163

————. *A History of the Penal, Reformatory and Correctional Institutions of the State of New Jersey: Analytical and Documentary.* Trenton: MacCrellish and Quigley, 1918.

————. *The Story of Punishment: A Record of Man's Inhumanity to Man.* 2d ed., rev. 1930. Reprint. Montclair, N.J.: Patterson Smith, 1972.

Barnes, Harry Elmer, and Negley K. Teeters. *New Horizons in Criminology: The American Crime Problem.* New York: Prentice-Hall, 1945.

Barrows, Samuel J. "Introduction: The Reformatory System in the United States." In *The Reformatory System in the United States,* 7–15.

————. "Safeguarding the Indeterminate Sentence." In Prison Association of New York, *Sixty-first Annual Report, 1905–1906,* 110–15. Albany, N.Y.: Brandow Printing, 1906.

Beccaria, Cesare. *On Crimes and Punishments* (1764), translated by Henry Paolucci. Indianapolis: Bobbs-Merrill Company, 1963.

Beirne, Piers. "Inventing Criminology: The 'Science of Man' in Cesare Beccaria's *Dei Delitti E Delle Pene* (1764)." *Criminology: An Interdisciplinary Journal* 29 (November 1991): 777–820.

Bellingham, Bruce. "Institution and Family: An Alternative View of Nineteenth-Century Child Saving." *Social Problems* 33 (October/December 1986): 33–57.

Beltzer, Warren, and Elaine Spear, eds. *Elmira: 1876–1976 Centennial Acknowledgement of Its History, Programs and Purpose.* Published by the New York State Department of Correctional Services, Office of Public Relations, n.p., [1976].

Bernstein, Iver. *The New York City Draft Riots: Their Significance for American Society and Politics in the Age of the Civil War.* New York: Oxford University Press, 1990.

A Biographical Record of Chemung County, New York. New York: S. J. Clarke Publishing Company, 1902.

Boies, Henry M. *The Science of Penology: The Defence of Society Against Crime.* New York: G.P. Putnam, 1901.

Bookstaver, William, George Blair, and Enos W. Barnes. *Report of the Prison Labor Reform Commission of the State of New York.* Albany, N.Y.: The Argus Company, 1887.

Boston, Charles A. "A Protest against Laws Authorizing the Sterilization of Criminals and Imbeciles." *Journal of the American Institute of Criminal Law and Criminology* 4 (September 1913): 326–58.

Boyer, Paul S. *Urban Masses and Moral Order in America, 1820–1920.* Cambridge, Mass.: Harvard University Press, 1978.

Brace, Charles Loring. *The Dangerous Classes of New York and Twenty Years Work among Them.* New York: Wynkoop and Hallenbeck, 1872.

Braverman, Harry. *Labor and Monopoly Capital: The Degradation of Work in the Twentieth Century.* New York: Monthly Review Press, 1974.

Brenzel, Barbara M. *Daughters of the State: A Social Portrait of the First Reform School for Girls in North America, 1856–1905.* Cambridge, Mass.: MIT Press, 1983.

———. "Domestication as Reform: The Socialization of Wayward Girls, 1856–1905." *Harvard Educational Review* 50 (May 1980): 196–213.

———. "Lancaster Industrial School for Girls: A Social Portrait of a Nineteenth-Century Reform School for Girls." *Feminist Studies* 3 (Fall 1975): 40–53.

Briggs, Franklin H. *Industrial Training in Reformatory Institutions.* 2d ed. Syracuse, N.Y.: C. W. Bardeen, 1898.

Brinkerhoff, Roeliff. "The Reformation of Criminals: Ohio Methods—Progressive Steps in Legislation and Administration." In *The Reformatory System in the United States,* 171–82.

Brockway, Zebulon R. "An Absolute Indeterminate Sentence." In Prison Association of New York, *Sixty-second Annual Report, 1907,* 71–77. Albany, N.Y.: J. B. Lyon, 1907.

———. "Abstract of Paper by Hon. Z. R. Brockway." In *Report and Proceedings of the Seventh International Prison Congress, 1905,* 64–72. Washington: Government Printing Office, 1907.

———. "Address by Hon. Z. B. [sic] Brockway." In American Prison Association, *Proceedings, 1910,* 162–69.

———. "The American Reformatory Prison System." *The American Journal of Sociology* 15 (January 1910): 454–77.

———. "Crime." In *Papers in Penology,* 4th series, 71–97. Elmira, N.Y.: Reformatory Print Press, 1899.

———. *Fifty Years of Prison Service: An Autobiography.* 1912. Reprint. Montclair, N.J.: Patterson Smith, 1969.

———. "The Ideal of a True Prison System for a State." In *Transactions of the National Congress on Penitentiary and Reformatory Discipline,* edited by Enoch C. Wines, 38–65. Albany, N.Y.: Weed, Parsons and Company, 1871.

———. "Prisoners and Their Reformation." In *Transactions of the International Penitentiary Congress Held in London, 1872.* edited by Edwin Pears, 612–23. London: Longmans, Green, and Company, 1872.

———. "Reformatory Prison Discipline." In *Transactions of the Third National Prison Reform Congress,* edited by E. C. Wines, 205–16. New York: Office of the Association, 1874.

———. "The Reformatory System." In *The Reformatory System in the United States,* 17–27.

Brown, JoAnne. "Professional Language: Words That Succeed." *Radical History Review* 34 (1986): 33–51.

Butler, Amos. "Introduction to an Address by Z. B. [sic] Brockway." In American Prison Association, *Proceedings, 1910,* 162.

———. "The Operation of the Indeterminate Sentence and Parole Law in Indiana." *The Institutional Quarterly* 8 (March 1917): 179–85.

———. "Statistics." *Journal of the American Institute of Criminal Law and Criminology* 5 (July 1914): 302.

Byrne, Thomas E. *Chemung County, 1890–1975.* Elmira, N.Y.: Chemung County Historical Society, n.d.

Byrnes, Thomas F. *Professional Criminals of America.* New York: Cassell and Company, 1886.

Call, Arthur. "Education versus Crime: A Study of the State Reformatory at Elmira, N.Y." *Education* 22 (June 1902): 587–603.

Cavallo, Dominick. *Muscles and Morals: Organized Playgrounds and Urban Reform, 1880–1920.* Philadelphia: University of Pennsylvania Press, 1981.

Christian, Frank L. *A Group of Youthful Robbers.* Elmira, N.Y.: New York State Reformatory, n.d.

———. *How We Obtain Detailed Information Concerning Our Inmates and Their Environment.* Elmira: New York State Reformatory, 1919.

———. *The Management of Penal Institutions.* Elmira, N.Y.: The New York State Reformatory, n.d..

———. *Statistics and Comments.* Elmira, N.Y.: The New York State Reformatory, [1921].

———. *A Study of Five Hundred Parole Violators.* Elmira, N.Y.: New York Reformatory, [1918].

Cohen, Stanley. *Visions of Social Control: Crime, Punishment and Classification.* Cambridge, England: Polity Press, 1985.

Cohen, Stanley, and Andrew Scull, eds. *Social Control and the State: Historical and Comparative Essays.* New York: St. Martin's Press, 1985.

Comfort, James. "The Return of Escaped Prisoners and Parole Violators." In National Prison Association, *Proceedings, 1905,* 149–62.

Conley, John. "Criminal Justice History as a Field of Research: A Review of the Literature, 1960–1975." *Journal of Criminal Justice* 5 (Spring 1977): 13–28.

———. "Economics and the Social Reality of Prisons." *Journal of Criminal Justice* 10 (1982): 25–35.

———. "Prisons, Production and Profit: Reconsidering the Importance of Prison Industries." *Journal of Social History* 14 (Winter 1980): 257–75.

———. "Revising Conceptions about the Origin of Prisons: The Importance of Economic Considerations. *Social Science Quarterly* 62 (June 1981): 247–58.

Convict #6627. "Sentence as a Motive." In *Papers in Penology,* 3rd series, 71–73. Elmira, N.Y.: Reformatory Print Press, 1898.

Crapsey, Edward. *The Nether Side of New York; or, the Vice, Crime and Poverty of the Great Metropolis.* 1872. Reprint. Montclair, N.J.: Patterson Smith, 1969.

Cullen, Francis T., and Karen E. Gilbert. *Reaffirming Rehabilitation.* Cincinnati, Ohio: Anderson Publishing Company, 1982.

Currie, Elliot. *Confronting Crime: An American Challenge.* New York: Pantheon Books, 1985.

———. "Managing the Minds of Men: The Reformatory Movement, 1865–1920." Ph.D. diss., University of California, Berkeley, 1973.

"Discussion." In American Prison Association, *Proceedings, 1909,* 40–48.
"Discussion." In American Prison Association, *Proceedings, 1914,* 143–47.

Doerner, Klaus. *Madmen and the Bourgeoisie: A Social History of Insanity and Psychiatry*, translated by Joachim Neugroschel and Jean Steinberg. Oxford: Basil Blackwell, 1981.

Dorado, P. "The Elmira Reformatory as Viewed through Spanish Eyes." In *Papers in Penology*, 3rd series, 9–60. Elmira, N.Y.: Reformatory Print Press, 1898.

Dowd, Douglas. *The Twisted Dream: Capitalist Development in the United States Since 1776*. 2d ed. Cambridge, Mass.: Winthrop Publishers, 1977.

Dugdale, Richard L. *"The Jukes": A Study in Crime, Pauperism, Disease and Heredity; also, Further Studies of Criminals*. New York: Putnam's, 1877.

Dumm, Thomas L. *Democracy and Punishment: Disciplinary Origins of the United States*. Madison: The University of Wisconsin Press, 1987.

Dwyer, Ellen. *Homes for the Mad: Life inside Two Nineteenth-Century Asylums*. New Brunswick, N.J.: Rutgers University Press, 1987.

Ellis, David M., James A. Frost, Harold C. Syrett, and Harry J. Carman. *A History of New York State*. Ithaca, N.Y.: Cornell University Press, 1967.

Ellison, T. E. "The Indiana Prison System." In *The Reformatory System in the United States*, 183–213.

"An English Opinion of Elmira." *The International Record of Charities and Correction*, edited by Frederick Howard Wines. 1 (March 1886): 3.

Eriksson, Torsten. *The Reformers: An Historical Survey of Pioneer Experiments in the Treatment of Criminals*. New York: Elsevier, 1976.

Erskine, George C. "Industrial Instruction for Reformatory Inmates." In American Prison Association, *Proceedings, 1922*, 259–66.

Fallows, Samuel. "The Illinois State Reformatory." In *The Reformatory System in the United States*, 141–58.

Ferdinand, Theodore. "The Criminal Patterns of Boston since 1849." *The American Journal of Sociology* 73 (July 1967): 84–99.

———. "Criminality, the Courts, and the Constabulary in Boston, 1702–1967." *Journal of Research in Crime and Delinquency* 17 (July 1980): 190–208.

Fernald, Guy G. "Current Misconceptions Regarding Reformation." *Mental Hygiene* 3 (October 1919): 646–49.

———. "The Laboratory and the Men's Reformatory." In American Prison Association, *Proceedings, 1920*, 99–102.

———. "The Mental Examination of Reformatory Prisoners." *Journal of the American Institute of Criminal Law and Criminology* 7 (September 1916): 393–404.

———. "The Reformatory Prisoner: His Needs." In American Prison Association, *Proceedings, 1916*, 126–36.

———. "Segregation of the Unfit in Reformatories." *Mental Hygiene* 1 (October 1917): 602–6.

Flint, Austin, and Israel Deyo. "The Report of the Majority." In *Nineteenth Year Book of the N.Y.S. Reformatory for the Fiscal Year Ending September 30, 1894*, 14–46. Elmira, N.Y.: n.p., 1895.

Flower, Roswell P. "In the Matter of the Charges Preferred against the Managers of the New York State Reformatory at Elmira—Opinion." In *Public Papers of Roswell P. Flower, Governor, 1894*, 424–46. Albany, N.Y.: Argus, 1895.

Fogel, David. *"... We are the Living Proof ...": The Justice Model for Corrections.* Cincinnati: Anderson Publishing, 1975.

Fogelson, Robert M. *Big-City Police.* Cambridge, Mass.: Harvard University Press, 1977.

Ford, Tirey L., Charles Sonntag, C. E. Clinch, Robert Devlin, and W. R. Porter. *Report of the State Board of Prison Directors of the State of California upon a Proposed Reformatory for Young Offenders.* Sacramento: W. W. Shannon, 1910.

Foucault, Michel. *Discipline and Punish: The Birth of the Prison* (1975), translated by Alan Sheridan. New York: Vintage Books, 1977.

Freedman, Estelle B. "'Their Sisters' Keepers: An Historical Perspective on Female Correctional Institutions in the United States, 1870–1900." *Feminist Studies* 2 (1974): 77–95.

————. *Their Sisters' Keepers: Women's Prison Reform in America, 1830–1930.* Ann Arbor: The University of Michigan Press, 1981.

Friedman, Lawrence M. "Plea Bargaining in Historical Perspective." *Law and Society Review* 13 (Winter 1979): 247–60.

Gardner, Gil. "The Emergence of the New York State Prison System: A Critique of the Rusche-Kirchheimer Model." *Crime and Social Justice* 29 (1987): 88–109.

Garland, David. *Punishment and Modern Society: A Study in Social Theory.* Chicago: University of Chicago Press, 1990.

————. *Punishment and Welfare: A History of Penal Strategies.* Brookfield, Vt.: Gower Publishing Company, 1985.

Gehring, Thom. "Zebulon Brockway of Elmira: 19th Century Correctional Education Hero." *Journal of Correctional Education* 33 (1982): 4–7.

Gill, Howard. "State Prisons in America, 1787–1937." In *Penology: The Evolution of Corrections in America*, edited by George G. Killinger, Paul F. Cromwell and Jerry M. Wood, 60–86. 2d ed. St. Paul, Minn.: West Publishing Company, 1979.

Gillin, John. *Criminology and Penology.* New York: The Century Company, 1926.

Glenn, Myra C. *Campaigns against Corporal Punishment: Prisoners, Sailors, Women, and Children in Antebellum America.* Albany: State University of New York Press, 1984.

Glueck, Sheldon, and Eleanor T. Glueck. *Five Hundred Criminal Careers.* New York: A. A. Knopf, 1930.

Goddard, Henry H. *Feeble-mindedness: Its Causes and Consequences.* New York: The Macmillan Company, 1914.

————. *The Kallikak Family: A Study in the Heredity of Feeble-mindedness.* New York: The Macmillan Company, 1912.

Goffman, Erving. *Asylums: Essays on the Social Situation of Mental Patients and Other Inmates.* Garden City, N.Y.: Anchor Books, 1961.

Goldsmith, May B., Anna Y. Reed, and J. A. Reed. *Report of Conditions at the State Training School and the State Reformatory Together with Recommendations for*

Needed Changes in Administration and Legislation. Olympia, Wash.: E. L. Board-man, 1911.

Gould, Stephen Jay. *The Mismeasure of Man.* New York: W. W. Norton, 1981.

Grob, Gerald N. *Mental Illness and American Society, 1875–1940.* Princeton, N.J.: Princeton University Press, 1983.

———. *Mental Institutions in America: Social Policy to 1875.* New York: The Free Press, 1973.

Guillaume, Dr. "Address by Dr. Guillaume, Secretary, International Prison Congress." In American Prison Association, *Proceedings, 1910,* 179–82.

Hahn, Nicolas Fischer [Nicole Hahn Rafter]. "The Defective Delinquent Movement: A History of the Born Criminal in New York State, 1850–1966." Ph.D. diss., State University of New York, Albany, 1978.

———. "Female State Prisoners in Tennessee: 1831–1879." *Tennessee Historical Quarterly* 39 (Winter 1980): 485–97.

———. "Too Dumb to Know Better: Cacogenic Family Studies and the Criminology of Women." *Criminology: An Interdisciplinary Journal* 18 (May 1980): 3–25.

Hahn, Simon, Mark A. Sullivan, John D. Van Blarcom, and Frank B. Jess. *Report to the General Assembly of the State of New Jersey for the Year 1908, by the Committee Appointed under Resolution Passed June 20th, 1907, to Investigate the Subject of State Expenditures.* Trenton: MacCrellish and Quigley, 1908.

Hall, Richard H. *Organizations: Structure and Process.* 2d ed. Englewood Cliffs, N.J.: Prentice-Hall, 1977.

Haller, Mark H. *Eugenics: Hereditarian Attitudes in American Thought.* New Brunswick, N.J.: Rutgers University Press, 1984.

———. "Plea Bargaining: The Nineteenth Century Context." *Law and Society Review* 13 (Winter 1979): 273–79.

Harding, John R. "One Thousand Reformatory Prisoners as Seen in Perspective." In American Prison Association, *Proceedings, 1919,* 425–33.

Hart, Hastings H. "The Extinction of the Defective Delinquent: A Working Program." In American Prison Association, *Proceedings, 1912,* 205–25.

———. "The Prison Dormitory System at the District of Columbia Reformatory, Lorton, Virginia, Part I." *The American Architect* 124 (no. 2430) (10 October 1923): 289–92.

Hawes, Joseph M. *Children in Urban Society: Juvenile Delinquency in Nineteenth-Century America.* New York: Oxford University Press, 1971.

Hayakawa, S. I., and Alan R. Hayakawa. *Language in Thought and Action.* 5th ed. San Diego, Calif.: Harcourt Brace Jovanovich, 1990.

Healy, William. *The Individual Delinquent: A Text-Book of Diagnosis and Prognosis for All Concerned in Understanding Offenders.* Boston: Little, Brown, and Company, 1915.

Healy, William, and Benedict S. Alper. *Criminal Youth and the Borstal System.* New York: The Commonwealth Fund, 1941.

Henderson, Charles R., ed. *Correction and Prevention.* 4 vols. New York: Charities Publication Committee, 1910.

Hindus, Michael S. "The History of Crime: Not Robbed of Its Potential, But Still on Probation." In *Criminology Review Yearbook*, edited by Sheldon L. Messinger and Egon Bittner, 1:217–41. Beverly Hills, Calif.: Sage Publications, 1979.

———. *Prison and Plantation: Crime, Justice, and Authority in Massachusetts and South Carolina, 1767–1878.* Chapel Hill: The University of North Carolina Press, 1980.

Hirsch, Adam J. *The Rise of the Penitentiary: Prisons and Punishment in Early America.* New Haven: Yale University Press, 1992.

History and Development of the Pennsylvania State Institution, Huntingdon, Pennsylvania, 1878–1952. n.p., n.d.

Holl, Jack M. *Juvenile Reform in the Progressive Era: William R. George and the Junior Republic Movement.* Ithaca, N.Y.: Cornell University Press, 1971.

Ignatieff, Michael. "State, Civil Society, and Total Institutions: A Critique of Recent Social Histories of Punishment." In *Crime and Justice: An Annual Review of Research*, edited by Michael Tonry and Norval Morris, 3:153–92. Chicago: University of Chicago Press, 1981.

Illich, Ivan. *Medical Nemesis: The Expropriation of Health.* New York: Pantheon Books, 1976.

Indiana Reformatory. *Ideas on Reformation.* Jeffersonville: Reformatory Printing Trade School, 1907.

Infantry Tactics in Use at the N.Y.S. Reformatory Adapted from Upton. Elmira, N.Y.: Reformatory Press, 1889.

"The Institutional Experiences of Peter Luckey." In Allen, comp., *Handbook of the New York State Reformatory at Elmira*, 71–110.

Jacobs, James B. *Stateville: The Penitentiary in Mass Society.* Chicago: The University of Chicago Press, 1977.

Jenkins, Philip. "The Radicals and the Rehabilitative Ideal, 1890–1930." *Criminology: An Interdisciplinary Journal* 20 (November 1982): 347–72.

———. "Temperance and the Origins of the New Penology." *Journal of Criminal Justice* 12 (1984): 551–65.

Johnson, David R. *Policing the Urban Underworld: The Impact of Crime on the Development of Urban Police, 1800–1887.* Philadelphia: Temple University Press, 1979.

Johnson, Herbert A. *History of Criminal Justice.* Cincinnati, Ohio: Anderson Publishing Company, 1988.

Joselit, Jenna Weissman. *Our Gang: Jewish Crime and the New York Jewish Community, 1900–1940.* Bloomington: Indiana University Press, 1983.

Klein, Philip. *Prison Methods in New York State: A Contribution to the Study of the Theory and Practice of Correctional Institutions in New York State.* New York: Columbia University Press, 1920.

Kuhlman, F. "The Mental Examination of Reformatory Cases." In American Prison Association, *Proceedings, 1914*, 132–43.

Lane, Roger. "Crime and Criminal Statistics in Nineteenth Century Massachusetts." *Journal of Social History* 2 (Winter 1968): 156–63.

Langbein, John H. "Understanding the Short History of Plea Bargaining." *Law and Society Review* 13 (Winter 1979): 261–72.

Langmuir, J. W., chairman. *Report of the Commissioners Appointed to Enquire into the Prison and Reformatory System of the Province of Ontario.* Toronto: Warwick and Sons, 1891.

Laughlin, Harry H. *Historical, Legal, and Statistical Review of Eugenical Sterilization in the United States.* New Haven: The American Eugenics Society, [1925].

Leonard, James A. "Reformatory Methods and Results." In *Penal and Reformatory Institutions,* edited by Charles R. Henderson, 121–28. Philadelphia: William F. Fell, 1910.

Lewis, Charlton T. "The Indeterminate Sentence." In *The Reformatory System in the United States,* 59–70.

Lewis, Orlando F. *The Development of American Prisons and Prison Customs, 1776–1845, with Special Reference to Early Institutions in the State of New York.* [Albany?]: Prison Association of New York, [1922].

Lewis, W. David. *From Newgate to Dannemora: The Rise of the Penitentiary in New York, 1796–1848.* Ithaca, N.Y.: Cornell University Press, 1965.

———. "The Reformer as Conservative: Protestant Counter-Subversion in the Early Republic." In *The Development of an American Culture,* edited by Stanley Coben and Lorman Ratner, 64–91. Englewood Cliffs, N.J.: Prentice-Hall, 1970.

Lincoln, Charles Z. *State of New York Messages from the Governors,* vol. 5, *1857–1868;* vol. 6, *1869–1876;* vol. 7, *1877–1884.* Albany: James B. Lyon, 1909.

Lindsey, Edward. "Historical Sketch of the Indeterminate Sentence and Parole System." *Journal of the American Institute of Criminal Law and Criminology* 16 (May 1925): 9–126.

Link, Arthur S., and Richard L. McCormick. *Progressivism.* Arlington Heights, Ill.: Harlan Davidson, 1983.

Lombroso, Cesare. *L'uomo delinquente.* Milan: Hoepli, 1876.

Lombroso-Ferreo, Gina. *Criminal Man, According to the Classification of Cesare Lombroso.* New York: G.P. Putnam's Sons, 1911.

Lovelock, Christopher H., and Charles B. Weinberg. *Marketing for Public and Nonprofit Managers.* New York: John Wiley and Sons, 1984.

Maguire, Kathleen, and Timothy J. Flangan, eds. U.S. Department of Justice, Bureau of Justice Statistics, *Sourcebook of Criminal Justice Statistics 1990.* Washington: Government Printing Office, 1991.

Masten, V. M. *Military Training at the New York State Reformatory.* Elmira, N.Y.: New York State Reformatory, 1920.

McClaughry, R. W. "Address by Major R. W. M'Claughry." In American Prison Association, *Proceedings, 1910,* 169–71.

McKelvey, Blake. *American Prisons: A History of Good Intentions.* Montclair, N.J.: Patterson Smith, 1977.

Melossi, Dario, and Massimo Pavarini. *The Prison and the Factory: Origins of the Penitentiary System*, translated by Glynis Cousin. Totowa, N.J.: Barnes and Noble Books, 1981.

Mennel, Robert M. "Attitudes and Policies toward Juvenile Delinquency in the United States: A Historiographical Review." In *Crime and Justice: An Annual Review of Research*, edited by Michael Tonry and Norval Morris, 4:191–224. Editors. Chicago: University of Chicago Press, 1983.

———. "'The Family System of Common Farmers': The Early Years of Ohio's Reform Farm, 1858–1884." *Ohio History* 89 (Summer 1980): 279–322.

———. "'The Family System of Common Farmers': The Origins of Ohio's Reform Farm, 1840–1858." *Ohio History* 89 (Spring 1980): 125–56.

———. *Thorns and Thistles: Juvenile Delinquents in the United States, 1825–1940.* Hanover, N.H.: The University Press of New England, 1973.

Miller, Jerome G. *Hobbling a Generation: Young African American Males in the Criminal Justice System of America's Cities: Baltimore, Maryland.* Alexandria, Va.: National Center on Institutions and Alternatives, 1992.

———. *Hobbling a Generation: Young African American Males in Washington D.C.'s Criminal Justice System.* Alexandria, Va.: National Center on Institutions and Alternatives, 1992.

Miller, Martin B. "At Hard Labor: Rediscovering the 19th Century Prison." *Issues in Criminology* 9 (Spring 1974): 91–114.

———. "Sinking Gradually into the Proletariat: The Emergence of the Penitentiary in the United States." *Crime and Social Justice* 14 (Winter 1980): 37–43.

Miller, Wilbur R. *Cops and Bobbies: Police Authority in New York and London, 1830–1970.* Chicago: University of Chicago Press, 1977.

Miller, Winfield, Robert Bracken, George A. H. Shideler, S. E. Smith, and Amos Butler. *Report of the Commission Appointed by Governor James P. Goodrich to Investigate the Advisability of Relocating the Indiana Reformatory.* Indianapolis: William B. Burford, [1918?].

Mills, C. Wright. *The Sociological Imagination.* New York: Oxford University Press, 1959.

Monkkonen, Eric. *The Dangerous Class: Crime and Poverty in Columbus, Ohio, 1860–1885.* Cambridge, Mass.: Harvard University Press, 1975.

Montanye, W. J. "The State Reformatory at Elmira." In *Papers in Penology*, 4th series, 1–13. Elmira, N.Y.: Elmira Reformatory Press, 1899.

Moore, Frank. "Address." In American Prison Association, *Proceedings, 1916*, 39–44.

———. "Classification, What Has It Accomplished?" In American Prison Association, *Proceedings, 1922*, 51–60.

———. "Education and Work in a Reformatory." *The Survey* 30 (21 June 1913): 391–92.

Nalder, Frank Fielding. "The American State Reformatory with Special Reference to Its Educational Aspects." Ph.D. diss., University of California, Berkeley, 1916.

Oliver, Robert T. *History of Public Speaking in America.* Boston: Allyn and Bacon, 1965.

Osborough, Nial. *Borstal in Ireland: Custodial Provision for the Young Adult Offender, 1906–1974.* Dublin: Institute of Public Administration, 1975.

Palmer, Ted. *Correctional Intervention and Research: Current Issues and Future Prospects.* Lexington, Mass: Lexington Books, 1978.

Pearl, Raymond. "Sterilization of Degenerates and Criminals Considered from the Standpoint of Genetics." *The Eugenics Review* 11 (April 1919): 1–6.

Pearson, Geoffrey. *Hooligan: A History of Respectable Fears.* New York: Schocken Books, 1983.

Peirce, Bradford K. *A Half Century with Juvenile Delinquents: The New York House of Refuge and Its Times.* New York: D. Appleton and Company, 1869.

Perrow, Charles. *Complex Organizations: A Critical Essay.* 2d ed. Glenview, Ill: Scott, Foresman and Company, 1979.

Petchesky, Rosalind P. "At Hard Labor: Penal Confinement and Production in Nineteenth-Century America." In *Crime and Capitalism: Readings in Marxist Criminology,* edited by David F. Greenberg, 341–57. Palo Alto, Calif..: Mayfield Publishing, 1981.

Pettijohn, A. C. "Need of a Reformatory in Missouri for Adults." In Missouri Conference of Charities and Corrections, *Third Annual Meeting Proceedings,* 16–20. Kansas City: Frank T. Riley, n.d.

Peyton, David C. *Crime as an Expression of Feeble-mindedness.* Jeffersonville: Indiana Reformatory, 1913.

———. *The Differential Diagnosis of Crime.* Jeffersonville: Indiana Reformatory, 1912.

Pickett, Robert S. *House of Refuge: Origins of Juvenile Reform in New York State, 1815–1857.* Syracuse, N.Y.: Syracuse University Press, 1969.

Pisciotta, Alexander W. "Child Saving or Child Brokerage?: The Theory and Practice of Indenture and Parole at the New York House of Refuge, 1825–1935." In *The History of Juvenile Delinquency: A Collection of Essays,* edited by Albert Hess and Priscilla Clement, vol. 2, pp. 533–55. Aalen, Germany: Scientia Publishers, 1993.

———. "Corrections, Society and Social Control: A Metahistorical Review of the Literature." In *Criminal Justice History: An International Annual,* edited by Henry Cohen, 2:109–30. New York: John Jay Press, 1981.

———. "A House Divided: Penal Reform at the Illinois State Reformatory, 1891–1915." *Crime and Delinquency* 37 (April 1991): 165–85.

———. "*Parens Patriae,* Treatment and Reform: The Case of the Western House of Refuge, 1849–1907." *New England Journal on Criminal and Civil Confinement* 10 (Winter 1984): 65–86.

———. "Race, Sex and Rehabilitation: A Study of Differential Treatment in the Juvenile Reformatory, 1825–1920." *Crime and Delinquency* 29 (April 1983): 254–69.

———. "Saving the Children: The Promise and Practice of *Parens Patriae,* 1838–1898." *Crime and Delinquency* 28 (July 1982): 410–25.

————. "Scientific Reform: The 'New Penology' at Elmira, 1876–1900." *Crime and Delinquency* 29 (October 1983): 613–30.

————. "Theoretical Perspectives for Historical Analyses: A Selective Review of the Juvenile Justice Literature." *Criminology: An Interdisciplinary Journal* 19 (May 1981): 115–29.

————. "Treatment on Trial: The Rhetoric and Reality of the New York House of Refuge, 1857–1935." *American Journal of Legal History* 29 (April 1985): 151–81.

————. "Zebulon Reed Brockway." In *Biographical Dictionary of Social Welfare in America*, edited by Walter I. Trattner, 134–37. Westport, Conn.: Greenwood Press, 1986.

Platt, Anthony M. *The Child Savers: The Invention of Delinquency.* 2d ed. Chicago: The University of Chicago Press, 1977.

————. "The Rise of the Child-Saving Movement: A Study in Social Policy and Correctional Reform." *Annals of the American Academy of Political and Social Sciences* 381 (January 1969): 21–38.

————. "The Triumph of Benevolence: The Origins of the Juvenile Justice System in the United States." In *Criminal Justice in America: A Critical Understanding*, edited by Richard Quinney, 356–89. Boston: Little, Brown, 1974.

Putney, Snell, and Gladys J. Putney. "Origins of the Reformatory." *Journal of Criminal Law, Criminology and Police Science* 53 (December 1962): 437–45.

Rafter, Nicole Hahn. "Chastising the Unchaste: Social Control Functions of a Woman's Reformatory, 1894–1931." In *Social Control and the State: Historical and Comparative Essays*, edited by Stanley Cohen and Andrew Scull, 288–311. New York: St. Martin's Press, 1983.

————. "Gender, Prisons, and Prison History." *Social Science History* 9 (Summer 1985): 233–47.

————. "Hard Times: Custodial Prisons for Women and the Example of the New York State Prison for Women at Auburn, 1893–1933." In *Judge, Lawyer, Victim, Thief: Women, Gender Roles, and Criminal Justice*, edited by Nicole Hahn Rafter and Elizabeth Stanko, 237–60. Boston: Northeastern University Press, 1982.

————. "Introduction." In *White Trash: The Eugenic Family Studies, 1877–1919*, edited by N. H. Rafter, 1–31. Boston: Northeastern University Press, 1988.

————. *Partial Justice: Women, Prisons, and Social Control.* 2d ed. New Brunswick, N.J.: Transaction Publishers, 1990.

————. "Prisons for Women, 1790–1980." In *Crime and Justice: An Annual Review of Research*, edited by Michael Tonry and Norval Morris, 5:129–81. Chicago: The University of Chicago Press, 1983.

The Reformatory System in the United States: Reports Prepared for the International Prison Commission, Samuel J. Barrows, Commissioner. Washington: Government Printing Office, 1900.

Remick, Cecile. "The House of Refuge of Philadelphia." Ed.D. diss., University of Pennsylvania, 1975.

Remley, H. M. "History of the Anamosa Penitentiary." *Bulletin of Iowa Institutions* 3 (January 1901): 61–69.

Rennie, Ysabel. *The Search for Criminal Man: A Conceptual History of the Dangerous Offender.* Lexington, Mass.: Lexington Books, 1978.

Reppetto, Thomas A. *The Blue Parade.* New York: The Free Press, 1978.

Resch, John Phillips. "Ohio Adult Penal System, 1850–1900: A Study in the Failure of Institutional Reform." *Ohio History* 81 (Autumn 1972): 236–62.

Richards, C. R. "Manual Training—Where Is Its Benefit?" *Papers in Penology,* 3d series, 74–78. Elmira, N.Y.: Reformatory Print Press, 1898.

Richardson, James F. *The New York Police, Colonial Times to 1901.* New York: Oxford University Press, 1970.

Riis, Jacob A. *The Battle with the Slum.* New York: The Macmillan Company, 1902.

———. *The Children of the Poor.* 1892. Reprint. New York: Arno Press, 1971.

———. *How the Other Half Lives: Studies among the Tenements of New York.* New York: C. Scribner's Sons, 1890.

Robinson, Louis N. *Penology in the United States.* Philadelphia: The John C. Winston Company, 1921.

Rogers, Everett M. *Diffusion of Innovations.* New York: Free Press of Glencoe, 1962.

Rogers, Everett M., with F. Floyd Shoemaker. *Communication of Innovations: A Cross-Cultural Approach.* 2d ed. New York: The Free Press, 1971.

Rothman, David J. *Conscience and Convenience: The Asylum and Its Alternatives in Progressive America.* Boston: Little, Brown, 1980.

———. *The Discovery of the Asylum: Social Order and Disorder in the New Republic.* Boston: Little, Brown, 1971.

Rothman, David J., and Stanton Wheeler, eds. *Social History and Social Policy.* New York: Academic Press, 1981.

Rothman, Sheila. *Woman's Proper Place: A History of Changing Ideals and Practices, 1870 to the Present.* New York: Basic Books, 1978.

Rusche, Georg, and Otto Kirchheimer. *Punishment and Social Structure.* New York: Columbia University Press, 1939.

Sanborn, Franklin B. "The Development of Reformatory Discipline." In *Papers in Penology,* 5th series, 1–23. Elmira, N.Y.: Reformatory Press, 1900.

———. "The Elmira Reformatory." In *The Reformatory System in the United States,* 28–47.

Sanborn, Joseph. "A Historical Sketch of Plea Bargaining." *Justice Quarterly* 3 (June 1986): 111–38.

Schlossman, Steven L. "Juvenile Justice in the Age of Jackson." *Teachers College Record* 76 (September 1974): 119–33.

———. *Love and the American Delinquent: The Theory and Practice of "Progressive" Juvenile Justice, 1825–1920.* Chicago: The University of Chicago Press, 1977.

Schlossman, Steven L., and Alexander W. Pisciotta. "Identifying and Treating Serious Juvenile Offenders: The View from California and New York in the 1920s." In *Intervention Strategies for Chronic Juvenile Offenders: Some New Perspectives,* edited by Peter Greenwood, 7–38. Westport, Conn.: Greenwood Press, 1986.

Schneider, John C. *Detroit and the Problem of Order, 1830–1880: A Geography of Crime, Riot and Policing*. Lincoln: University of Nebraska Press, 1980.

Scott, Joseph F. "American Reformatories for Male Adults." In *Penal and Reformatory Institutions*, edited by Charles R. Henderson, 89–120. Philadelphia: William F. Fell Company, 1910.

———. "The Massachusetts Reformatory." In *The Reformatory System in the United States*, 80–100.

Scull, Andrew T. *Decarceration: Community Treatment and the Deviant—A Radical View*. 2d ed. New Brunswick, N.J.: Rutgers University Press, 1984.

———. *Museums of Madness: The Social Organization of Insanity in Nineteenth-Century England*. New York: St. Martin's Press, 1979.

Sellin, J. Thorsten. *Slavery and the Penal System*. New York: Elsevier, 1976.

———. "Zebulon Reed Brockway." *The National Cyclopaedia of American Biography*, 19:160–61. New York: James T. White, 1926.

Sharp, Harry C. "The Indiana Plan." In American Prison Association, *Proceedings, 1909*, 36–40.

———. "Rendering Sterile of Confirmed Criminals and Mental Defectives." In National Prison Association, *Proceedings, 1907*, 177–81.

Shelden, Randall. "Convict Leasing: An Application of the Rusche-Kirchheimer Thesis to Penal Changes in Tennessee, 1830–1915." In *Crime and Capitalism: Readings in Marxist Criminology*, edited by David F. Greenberg, 358–66. Palo Alto, Calif.: Mayfield Publishing Company, 1981.

Smith, Beverly A. "Female Admissions and Paroles of the Western House of Refuge in the 1880s: An Historical Example of Community Corrections." *Journal of Research in Crime and Delinquency* 26 (February 1989): 36–66.

———. "The Female Prisoner in Ireland, 1855–1878." *Federal Probation* 54 (December 1990): 69–81.

———. "The Irish General Prisons Board, 1877–1885: Efficient Deterrence or Bureaucratic Ineptitude?" *The Irish Jurist* 15 (Summer 1980): 122–36.

———. "The Irish Prison System, 1885–1914: Land War to World War." *The Irish Jurist* 16 (Winter 1981): 316–49.

———. "Military Training at New York's Elmira Reformatory, 1888–1920." *Federal Probation* 52 (March 1988): 33–40.

Smith, Eugene. "The Indeterminate Sentence for Crime: Its Use and Abuse." In Prison Association of New York, *Sixty-second Annual Report, 1907*, 64–71. Albany: J. B. Lyon Company, 1907.

Smith, Joan, and William Fried. *The Uses of American Prison: Political Theory and Penal Practice*. Lexington, Mass.: Lexington Books, 1974.

Smith, Steven. "Methods of Discipline in Reformatories." *The Independent* 51 (no. 2651) (21 September 1899): 2561–63.

Spitzer, Steven. "Toward a Marxian Theory of Deviance." *Social Problems* 22 (June 1975): 638–51.

Starr, Paul. *The Social Transformation of American Medicine*. New York: Basic Books, 1982.

Steinberg, Allen. "From Private Prosecution to Plea Bargaining: Criminal Prosecution, the District Attorney, and American Legal History." *Crime and Delinquency* 30 (October 1984): 568–92.

Stephens, Mitchell. *A History of News: From the Drum to the Satellite.* New York: Viking, 1988.

Strong, W. F., and John A. Cook. *Persuasion: A Practical Guide to Effective Persuasive Speech.* Dubuque, Iowa: Kendall/Hunt, 1987.

Sullivan, James, ed. *History of New York State, 1523–1927*, vol. 7. New York: Lewis Historical Publishing Company, n.d.

Sutton, John R. *Stubborn Children: Controlling Delinquency in the United States, 1640–1981.* Berkeley and Los Angeles: University of California Press, 1988.

Sykes, Gresham. *The Society of Captives: A Study of a Maximum Security Prison.* Princeton: Princeton University Press, 1958.

Takagi, Paul. "Revising Liberal Conceptions of Penal Reform: A Bibliographic Overview." *Crime and Social Justice* 5 (Spring–Summer 1976): 60–64.

———. "The Walnut Street Jail: A Penal Reform to Centralize the Powers of the State." *Federal Probation* 39 (December 1975): 18–26.

Teeters, Negley K. *The Cradle of the Penitentiary: The Walnut Street Jail at Philadelphia, 1773–1835.* [Philadelphia: Pennsylvania Prison Society, 1955.]

———. "The Early Days of the Philadelphia House of Refuge." *Pennsylvania History* 27 (April 1960): 165–87.

Teeters, Negley K., and John Shearer. *The Prison at Philadelphia, Cherry Hill: The Separate System of Prison Discipline, 1829–1913.* New York: Columbia University Press, 1957.

Thompson, E. P. *The Making of the English Working Class.* New York: Vintage Books, 1963.

Towner, Ausburn. *Our County and Its People: A History of the Valley and County of Chemung from the Closing Years of the Eighteenth Century.* Syracuse: D. Mason and Company, 1902.

U.S. Department of Justice, Bureau of Justice Statistics. *Probation and Parole 1990.* Washington: Government Printing Office, 1991.

Vambery, Rusztem. "The Indeterminate Sentence." *The Medico-Legal Journal* 2 (September 1910): 112–13.

van den Haag, Ernest. *Punishing Criminals: Concerning a Very Old and Painful Question.* New York: Basic Books, 1975.

von Hirsch, Andrew. *Doing Justice: The Choice of Punishments.* New York: Hill and Wang, 1976.

Waite, Robert G. "From Penitentiary to Reformatory: Alexander Machonochie, Walter Crofton, Zebulon Brockway, and the Road to Prison Reform—New South Wales, Ireland, and Elmira, New York, 1840–70." In *Criminal Justice History: An Interna-*

tional Annual, edited by Louis A. Knafla, 85–105. Westport, Conn.: Greenwood Press, 1993.

Walker, Charles I., Henry W. Lord, Z. R. Brockway, and Uzziel Putnam. *Special Report of the Board of State Commissioners for the General Supervision of Charitable, Penal, Pauper, and Reformatory Institutions.* Lansing, Mich.: W. S. George and Company, 1875.

Walker, Samuel. *A Critical History of Police Reform.* Lexington, Mass: Lexington Books, 1977.

———. *Popular Justice: A History of American Criminal Justice.* New York: Oxford University Press, 1980.

Warner, Charles Dudley. "Education as a Factor in Prison Reform." *Harper New Monthly Magazine* 72 (December 1885–May 1886): 444–48.

———. "A Study of Prison Management." *North American Review* 140 (341) (April 1885): 291–308.

———. "What Shall Be Done with the Criminal Class?" In *The Reformatory System in the United States*, 71–79.

Weber, Max. *The Protestant Ethic and the Spirit of Capitalism*, translated by Talcott Parsons. New York: Charles Scribner's Sons, 1958.

Weiss, Robert. "Humanitarianism, Labour Exploitation, or Social Control? A Critical Survey of Theory and Research on the Origin and Development of Prisons." *Social History* 12 (October 1987): 331–50.

Wiebe, Robert H. *The Search for Order, 1877–1920.* New York: Hill and Wang, 1967.

Williams, William Appleman. *The Contours of American History.* Cleveland: World Publishing, 1961.

Wilson, James Q. *Thinking about Crime.* New York: Basic Books, 1975.

Wines, Enoch C. *The State of Prisons and of Child-Saving Institutions in the Civilized World.* Cambridge, Mass.: J. Wilson and Son, 1880.

———, ed. *Transactions of the National Congress on Penitentiary and Reformatory Discipline.* Albany, N.Y.: Weed, Parsons and Company, 1871.

Wines, Enoch C., and Theodore W. Dwight. *Report on the Prisons and Reformatories of the United States and Canada.* 1867. Reprint. Albany, N.Y.: AMS Press, 1973.

Wines, Frederick H. *Punishment and Reformation: A Study of the Penal System.* New York: T. Y. Crowell and Company, 1910.

Winter, Alexander. *The New York State Reformatory in Elmira.* London: Swan Sonnenschein and Company, 1891.

Wistar, Isaac J. "The Pennsylvania Industrial Reformatory." In *The Reformatory System in the United States*, 134–40.

Wolfer, Henry. "The Reformatory System in Minnesota." In *The Reformatory System in the United States*, 214–22.

Legislation, Archival Materials, Reports

(arranged by state)

COLORADO

"An Act to Establish the Colorado State Reformatory in the County of Chafee; To Provide for the Selection of a Site and the Erection of Buildings; For the Purchase of Machinery Therefor, and to Provide for its Government, Management and Maintenance, and to Make Appropriations Therefor." 1889 *Colo. Sess. Laws*, 418–33.

Colorado State Board of Charities. *Report on the Investigation of the State Reformatory.* Denver: Smith-Brooks Printing Company, 1895.
Colorado State Reformatory (Buena Vista). *Reports*, 1892, 1894–1896, 1898–1900.

CONNECTICUT

"An Act Establishing the Connecticut Reformatory." 1909 *Conn. Pub. Acts*, chap. 162.
"An Act Amending an Act Concerning the Connecticut Reformatory." 1915 *Conn. Pub. Acts*, chap. 186.

Connecticut Reformatory [Office of the Superintendent, Connecticut Reformatory, Cheshire, Connecticut]
    Inmate Case Histories

Connecticut Reformatory (Cheshire). *Reports*, 1912–1914, 1918–1920.
Report of the Reformatory Commission of Connecticut to the General Assembly, January Session, 1905. Hartford: Daniels, 1905.
Rules and Regulations Governing Officers of the Connecticut Reformatory. Cheshire: [Reformatory Press], 1920.

DISTRICT OF COLUMBIA

District of Columbia Reformatory (Lorton, Virginia). *Reports*, 1916–1920.

ILLINOIS

"An Act to Establish the Illinois State Reformatory, and Making an Appropriation Therefor." 1891 *Ill. Laws*, 52–59.
"An Act to Amend an Act Entitled 'An Act to Establish the Illinois State Reformatory, and Making an Appropriation Therefor,' Approved June 18, 1891." 1893 *Ill. Laws*, 168–71.

Illinois State Reformatory [Department of Corrections, Pontiac Correctional Center, Illinois State Archives, Springfield, Illinois]

Parole and Pardon Index
Register of Prisoners

Illinois State Reformatory (Pontiac). *Reports*, 1892–1894, 1896–1898.

INDIANA

"An Act to Establish the Indiana Reformatory et seq." 1897 *Ind. Acts*, chap. 53.
"An Act Concerning the Manner of Procedure in the Trial of Certain Felonies, and Pre-
scribing Punishment Therefor, and Appointing a Commission on Parole, and Authorizing it to Make Rules for the Government Thereof." 1897 *Ind. Acts*, chap. 143.

Indiana Reformatory (Jeffersonville). *Reports*, 1896–1900, 1902–1907, 1911–1917.

IOWA

"An Act to Revise the Law Relating to the Sentence and Commitment of Persons Con-
victed of Crime, and Providing for a System of Reform and Parole and to Create the
Necessary Officers Therefor, Defining their Powers and Duties, and to Fix Their
Compensation, and Appropriating the Money Necessary to Carry the Same into
Effect, and to Repeal all Acts and Parts of Acts in Conflict Therewith." 1907 *Iowa
Acts*, chap. 192.
"An Act to Establish an Industrial Reformatory for Women et seq." 1915 *Iowa Acts*,
chap. 216.

Iowa Reformatory (Anamosa). *Reports*, 1906–1908, 1910–1912.

KANSAS

"An Act Establishing a Reformatory and Making Provisions for Governing and Controlling the Same, and Repealing All Acts or Parts of Acts in Conflict with the Provisions of this Act." 1895 *Kan. Sess. Laws*, chap. 200.

Kansas State Industrial Reformatory. *Escaped Men and Parole Violators*. Topeka: State
Printing Office, [1911].
Kansas State Industrial Reformatory (Hutchinson). *Reports*, 1895–1900.
Kansas State Industrial Reformatory. *Rules and Regulations for the Discipline and
Government of the Kansas State Industrial Reformatory at Hutchinson*. Topeka:
State Printing Office, 1909.

KENTUCKY

"An Act to Amend an Act Entitled, 'An Act to Create a Board of Penitentiary Commissioners and Regulate the Penal Institutions of this Commonwealth' which Became a
Law March 5, 1898." 1910 *Ky. Acts*, chap. 15.

"An Act to Repeal an Act Entitled, 'An Act Concerning the Parole of Convicts, Approved March 21, 1900 et seq." 1910 *Ky. Acts,* chap. 16.

Kentucky State Board of Charities and Correction. *Reports,* 1919–1921.
Kentucky State Reformatory (Frankfort). *Reports,* 1917–1919.

MASSACHUSETTS

"An Act to Establish a Reformatory for Male Prisoners." 1884 *Mass. Acts*, chap. 255.

Massachusetts State Reformatory [Records of the Massachusetts Reformatory, Massachusetts State Archives, Boston, Massachusetts]
  Case Histories

Massachusetts Commissioner of Correction. *Report,* 1920.
Massachusetts Prison Commissioners. *Reports,* 1901–1902, 1909–1914.
Massachusetts State Reformatory (Concord). *Reports,* 1884–1892, 1899.

MICHIGAN

"An Act to Establish a State House of Correction, and Make Appropriation Therefor." 1873 *Mich. Pub. Acts*, Number 170.
"An Act to Regulate and Govern the State House of Correction and Reformatory at Ionia." 1877 *Mich. Pub. Acts*, Number 176.
"An Act Providing for Changing the Name of the State House of Correction and Reformatory at Ionia." 1901 *Mich. Pub. Acts*, Number 75.

Michigan Reformatory [Records of the Michigan Reformatory, Michigan State Archives, Lansing, Michigan]
  Register of Residents

Michigan State House of Correction and Reformatory [Michigan Reformatory after 1901] (Ionia). *Reports,* 1877–1880, 1882–1884, 1892–1894, 1900–1908, 1910–1912.

MINNESOTA

Minnesota State Reformatory [Records of the Saint Cloud State Reformatory, State Archives, Minnesota Historical Society, St. Paul, Minnesota]
  Board of Control: The Agent's Correspondence, 1909–1910
  Board of Parole Correspondence
  Conduct Ledgers, 1889–1891
  Escapee Record, 1913
  Inmate History and Record
  Misconduct Record, 1889–1897

Record of Interviews with Inmates and Contact with References, 1893–1896
Record of Special Punishment, 1889–1897
Solitary Register, 1907–1912
Superintendent's Correspondence Regarding Fugitives, 1900–1910

Minnesota State Reformatory. *Laws, By-Laws, Rules and Regulations for the Government and Discipline of the Minnesota State Reformatory.* St. Cloud: Minnesota State Reformatory, 1898.
Minnesota State Reformatory (St. Cloud). *Reports*, 1889–1900, 1908–1910, 1915–1916.

MISSOURI

"An Act to Change the Name of 'the Missouri Training School for Boys' to 'the Missouri Reformatory' et seq." 1915 *Mo. Laws*, 209–16.

Missouri Reformatory (Boonville). *Reports*, 1915–1916.

NEW JERSEY

"An Act Relating to a State Reformatory." 1895 *N.J. Laws*, chap. 357.

New Jersey Reformatory (Rahway). *Reports*, 1910, 1912 (Supplement), 1913.

NEW YORK

"An Act Authorizing the Appointment of Commissioners to Locate a State Penitentiary or Industrial Reformatory." 1869 *N.Y. Laws*, chap. 408.
"An Act in Relation to the State Reformatory." 1870 *N.Y. Laws*, chap. 427.
"An Act Relating to the Building Commissioners for the Erection of the State Reformatory at Elmira, Chemung County." 1873 *N.Y. Laws*, chap. 600.
"An Act to Provide a Government for the New York State Reformatory at Elmira, and to Provide for the Completion of the Same, and to Make an Appropriation Therefor." 1876 *N.Y. Laws*, chap. 207.
"An Act in Relation to the Imprisonment of Convicts in the New York State Reformatory at Elmira, and the Government and Release of Such Convicts by the Managers." 1877 *N.Y. Laws*, chap. 173.
"An Act to Establish the Eastern New York Reformatory and for the Appointment of Commissioners to Secure a Site Therefor." 1892 *N.Y. Laws*, chap. 336.
"An Act to Provide for the Better Security of the Freedom of Religious Worship in Certain Institutions." 1892 *N.Y. Laws*, chap. 396.
"An Act to Provide for the Construction of the Eastern New York Reformatory, and Making an Appropriation Therefor." 1894 *N.Y. Laws*, chap. 299.

"An Act to Provide for the Organization, Management and Construction of the Eastern New York Reformatory, an Making an Appropriation Therefor." 1900 *N.Y. Laws*, chap. 348.

"An Act to Revise, Consolidate and Amend the Several Acts Relating to the New York State Reformatory at Elmira." 1900 *N.Y. Laws*, chap. 378.

"An Act Amending Section Sixteen of chap. Three Hundred and Seventy-Eight of the Laws of Nineteen Hundred Relative to the Transfers of Prisoners from the New York State Reformatory at Elmira to Eastern New York Reformatory at Napanoch and to State Prisons." 1903 *N.Y. Laws*, chap. 138.

"An Act to Provide for a State Board of Managers of Reformatories, and to Vest in Said Board the Management of the State Reformatory at Elmira and the State Reformatory at Napanoch, and to Provide for their Management and the Transfer of Inmates." 1906 *N.Y. Laws*, chap. 684.

"An Act to Amend the Prison Law and the Mental Deficiency Law, in Relation to Converting the Eastern New York Reformatory into a State Institution for Mental Defectives." 1921 *N.Y. Laws*, chap. 483.

Eastern New York Reformatory at Napanoch [Records of the Eastern New York Reformatory, New York State Archives, Albany, New York]
    Discharge Register
    Receiving (Admission) Register, 1900–1908
    Record of Returned Men, 1916–1920
Eastern New York Reformatory (Napanoch). *Reports*, 1903–1907, 1909–1915, 1917.
New York State Agricultural and Industrial School (Western House of Refuge) [Records of the New York State Agricultural and Industrial School, New York State Archives, Albany, New York]
    Chaplain and Parole Officer Correspondence
New York State Reformatory [Records of the Elmira Reformatory, New York State Archives, Albany, New York]
    Biographical Register of Returned Men
    Conduct Ledgers
    Examining Physician's Memoranda File, 1918–1928
    Inmate Biographical Ledgers
    Inmate Consecutive Registers
    Register of Italian Inmates, 1915–1930
    Summary Register of Men Returned for Violation of Parole, 1907–1948

New York House of Refuge (Randall's Island). *Report*, 1910.
New York State. *Assembly Documents*, 1877, 1889, 1891, 1893–1894, 1896, 1900–1903, 1906, 1908, 1910–1911.
New York State. Legislative Assembly Documents, vol. 5, no. 116 (1882). Committee on State Prisons, *Report of the Committee on State Prisons Concerning the Treatment of Persons Committed to the State Reformatory at Elmira.*

New York State. Legislative Assembly Documents, vol. 8, no. 98 (1881). *Report of the Joint Committee of the Senate and Assembly Appointed to Investigate the Affairs of the New York State Reformatory.*

New York State. *Senate Documents*, 1881–1885, 1887, 1903, 1912–1916, 1918.

New York State Board of Charities. *Report*, 1894.

New York State Board of Charities. *Report and Proceedings of the State Board of Charities Relative to the Management of the State Reformatory at Elmira.* Albany, N.Y.: James B. Lyon, 1894.

New York State Commission of Prisons, *Reports*, 1903–1907, 1909, 1917.

New York State Reformatory (Elmira). *Reports*, 1876, 1880–1884, 1886, 1888, 1890, 1892–1893, 1895, 1899–1902, 1905, 1907, 1909–1915, 1917..

Prison Association of New York. *Thirty-ninth Annual Report.* Albany, N.Y.: Weed, Parsons, and Company, 1884.

Prison Association of New York. "The Indeterminate Sentence and Parole." *Seventy-third Annual Report, 1917,* 49–55. Albany: J. B. Lyon Company, 1918.

Prison Association of New York. "The Parole System of State Prisons." *Seventy-third Annual Report, 1917,* 72–85. Albany: J. B. Lyon Company, 1918.

Superintendent of New York State Prisons, *Reports*, 1902–1903.

Оніо

"An Act to Change the Name of the Intermediate Penitentiary to that of the Ohio State Reformatory, and to Organize and Govern the Same, and to Repeal a Certain Act Therein Named." 1891 *Ohio Laws*, 382–88.

Ohio State Reformatory [Records of the Ohio State Reformatory, Series 819, The Ohio Historical Society, Columbus, Ohio]
    Historical Conduct Record, 1896–1901
    Weekly List of Prisoners Punished for Infractions of the Rules

Ohio State Reformatory (Mansfield). *Reports*, 1898, 1907.

OKLAHOMA

"Penal Institutions." 1909 *Okla. Sess. Laws*, chap. 31, 474–77.

Oklahoma Commissioners of Charities and Corrections. *Reports*, 1909–1912.

Oklahoma State Reformatory (Granite). *Reports*, 1910–1912, 1921.

PENNSYLVANIA

Pennsylvania Industrial Reformatory [Records of the Pennsylvania Industrial Reformatory, Pennsylvania Historical Society and Museum, Harrisburg, Pennsylvania]
    Biographical and Descriptive Register
    Conduct Ledgers

Investigation into the Fire—August 14, 1892
Investigation of Edward Wood's Death—May 10, 1894
Investigation of the Escape by Hutson, Roach and Walton—July 18, 1896
Journal of the General Superintendent, 1891–1906
Minutes of the Board of Managers and Board of Trustees
Record of Special Punishments
Scrapbook, 1889–1929
Transcript and Stenographic Notes of Testimony Taken During the Investigation of the Pennsylvania Industrial Reformatory at Huntingdon, Beginning Wednesday, March 22, 1892

Pennsylvania Industrial Reformatory (Huntingdon). *Reports*, 1889–1892, 1905–1906.
"Report of the Committee on the Investigation of the Pennsylvania Industrial Reformatory, Huntingdon." In Pennsylvania Board of Commissioners of Public Charities. *Twenty-third Annual Report*, (1893): 413–32. Harrisburg: Edwin K. Meyers, 1893.

WASHINGTON

"An Act Creating the Washington State Reformatory, Providing for the Erection and Management Thereof and Making an Appropriation Therefor." 1907 *Wash. Laws*, chap. 167.

Washington State Board of Control, *Reports*, 1912–1916.
Washington State Reformatory (Monroe). *Reports*, 1910–1912.

WISCONSIN

"An Act to Establish a Reformatory for the Custody and Training of Certain Offenders Whose Ages of Commitment are from Sixteen to Twenty-five Years." 1897 *Wis. Laws*, chap. 346.

Wisconsin State Reformatory (Green Bay). *Reports*, 1896–1900.

Index

Aaron, Moses, 40, 70–71, 76, 77, 78
Academic education for prisoners: in adult prisons and juvenile reformatories, 27; called for in Declaration of Principles, 13; called for in Wines–Dwight report, 11; at Colorado Reformatory, 95; at Connecticut Reformatory, 142; at Elmira Reformatory, 20, 23, 109, 115; at Illinois Reformatory, 89; at Indiana Reformatory, 132, 136; at Iowa Reformatory, 146; at Kentucky State Reformatory, 141; at Massachusetts Reformatory, 86; at Michigan Reformatory, 84; at Minnesota Reformatory, 88; in modern correctional institutions, 5, 152; at New Jersey Reformatory, 138; at Pennsylvania Industrial Reformatory, 87–88, 93. *See also* Reformatory-prison movement; Vocational education
Adamson, Christopher, 147
Adult reformatory movement. *See* Reformatory-prison movement
Alcohol and drug abuse by prisoners, 5, 100, 103, 131, 153. *See also* Prisoner resistance
American Association of Clinical Criminology, 117
Arnot, Matthias H., 55, 57 n. 78
Arson and fires in correctional institutions, 5, 100, 103, 153. *See also* Prisoner resistance
Asylums: Essays on the Social Situation of

Mental Patients and Other Inmates (Goffman), 60
Auburn Prison (Auburn, N.Y.): and congregate system of labor, 10, 10 n. 6; goal of, 22; inmates transferred from Elmira Reformatory to, 45; inmates transferred to Elmira Reformatory from, 13–15; opening of, 10; sentencing at, 18

Babcock, T. F., 35
Bagley, John, 83
Baker, Alvah, 130
Barnard, Kate, 140
Barr, Marquis, 139, 146
Barrows, Samuel J., 105
Baumel, J. N., 139
Beach, Joseph, 50
Beccaria, Cesare, 18, 18 n. 28, 84
Beckwirth, E. F., 99
Beecher, Thomas, 56
Berry, Silas, 111
Binet–Simon Intelligence Test, 104, 116
Bloomer, J. J., 38, 47
Boston, Charles, 134–35
Brace, Charles Loring, 9
Brockway, Caroline, 28
Brockway, Hugh, 48, 66–67

187

Made in the USA
San Bernardino, CA
24 August 2014